LUCKY

A Portrait of a Legendary
Squash Champion

ANIL NAYAR'S STORY

Jean Nayar

FIVE RIVERS PRESS

An Affiliate of Sach Sports

Copyright © 2020 Jean Nayar

All rights reserved. No portion of this book may reproduced, stored in a retrieval system, or transmitted in any form or by any means—electronic, mechanical, photocopy, recording, scanning, or other—without the prior written permission of the author.

Published in the United States by Five Rivers Press.

Library of Congress Cataloging-in-Publication Data
Name: Nayar, Jean, author
Title: Lucky—Anil Nayar's story: a portrait of a legendary squash champion
Description: First Edition | New York: Five Rivers Press, May 2020

ISBN 978-1-7347973-0-5 (Softcover Book)
ISBN 978-1-7347973-1-2 (ebook)
Library of Congress Control Number: 2020906290

For information on special rates for bulk purchasing for educational, business, or fundraising use, please email info@fiveriverspress.net.

Printed in the United States of America

For our families and friends

Contents

Foreword vii
Introduction x
Prologue: Three-Wall Nick 1

Part One: Into the Dawn

Chapter One: Unlikely Sportsman 9
Chapter Two: Coach Yusuf Khan 25
Chapter Three: Mother, Father, Sister, Brothers 32

Part Two: Metamorphosis

Chapter Four: Bombay, Its Clubs, and Its Sportsmen 47
Chapter Five: The Golden Age of Indian Squash 60
Chapter Six: England and the Drysdale Cup 68

Part Three: American Dream

Chapter Seven: Harvard 81
Chapter Eight: Jack Barnaby—A New Mentor and Coach 97
Chapter Nine: Lessons Learned 106
Chapter Ten: American Counterculture 113
Chapter Eleven: Civil Rights and Unrest 129
Chapter Twelve: Winning, Losing, and Sportsmanship 140
Chapter Thirteen: Turning Point 164

Part Four: Return to India

Chapter Fourteen: East and West 171

Chapter Fifteen: Family Affairs 180

Chapter Sixteen: Homegrown Champ 188

Chapter Seventeen: Ennui 199

Chapter Eighteen: Crossroads 210

Part Five: The Unmaking of a Champion

Chapter Nineteen: America, Again 217

Chapter Twenty: Front Right Nick 227

Chapter Twenty One: Weekend Warrior 247

Part Six: Full Circle

Chapter Twenty Two: Fresh Start 255

Chapter Twenty Three: A Changed World 268

Chapter Twenty Four: Passages Through India 279

Chapter Twenty Five: Giving Back 292

Chapter Twenty Six: Loss 303

Chapter Twenty Seven: Reinvention 310

Chapter Twenty Eight: *Haardik Shukriya* 327

Acknowledgements 340

Foreword

As an unabashed admirer of Anil "Lucky" Nayar, I consider it a privilege to be asked by him and his wife, Jean, to introduce this unputdownable book, which is at once erudite and down to earth. A labour of love, it is a cerebral yet sensitive tour de force on the sports career of an exemplary human being and principled squash champion who played at two ends of the world—in India and the U.S.

As an also-ran squash player at the Cricket Club of India's squash courts, where Anil, when still just a teen, was lord and master of all he surveyed during my university days in Mumbai, I had only a nodding acquaintance with him before he left for the U.S. to pursue higher studies at Harvard University. It was a time just following the halcyon days of the Pakistani player Hashim Khan, some 30 years Anil's senior and eight-time winner of the British Open Squash Championship and patriarch of the Pashtun Khan clan, which ruled the game from the 1950s through the 1980s. This was a golden era when squash was called the Khan Game and the milieu in which Anil cut his milk teeth, in a manner of speaking, and went on to master his craft at the CCI courts under the solicitous tutelage of Yusuf Khan, progeny of the stock which produced the three greatest squash players the world has ever known, Hashim Khan, Jahangir Khan, and Jansher Khan.

Anil was off my radar for many years until I ran into him again in the last millennium at the squash courts at the CCI, during one of his then-infrequent yet regular visits to *urbs prima Indis*—the leading city of India. I asked him at that time when he would be putting pen to paper to enable his innumerable fans in the world's two largest democracies to get an insight into the attributes and circumstances responsible for his glittering exploits on the squash courts and, more importantly, for his development into an exemplary human being, one gifted with rare qualities of head and heart.

"Who will want to read about me?" Anil, self-effacing as ever, asked, beaming his broad smile modestly and adding, "Why don't *you* do it?" though he knew that all my energies were then fully committed to my publishing career. Nevertheless, I believe inspirational lives—and Anil Nayar's is certainly one of them—deserve to be recorded for posterity to inform, enlighten, and encourage future generations. And I never gave up on the idea that Anil's trailblazing story should be told in print. After all, no other Indian player has accomplished quite what he has in the sport of squash. His creative approach to the game, his discipline-induced fitness, his natural athleticism and mobility combined with his understanding of the alchemy of winning led to multiple champion titles in various parts of the globe as well as in India, where another player has yet to match his overall record. With so many international titles, it's hardly surprising that Anil would also be recognized with the highest accolades of the sport both in India and the U.S. And the naming of the CCI squash courts after Anil in 2001 was indubitably fitting and, in my opinion, akin to the naming of Mumbai's Wankhede Cricket Stadium East Stand after "Little Master" Sunil Gavaskar.

Fast forward to the new millennium and our next meeting, as it turned out, was along with his wife, Jean, in Mumbai. I asked the same question regarding his plans for writing an autobiography, or getting a biography done, to which the reply was the same as the last time. I summoned all my powers of persuasion and we parted, as before, full of good intent and resolve. Only, it was evident this time that my relentless exhortations were clearly heard by Jean, who concurred with the idea of getting the book done.

Though she had hoped to collaborate with a sportswriter in India to get a biography written, the project was put on pause for more than a decade and a half, thanks to her own busy career as the editor in chief of a group of magazines in the U.S. But after another fateful meeting in 2017, this time in Miami, we revived the idea and Jean finally opted to take on the storytelling herself in the form of a more personal biographical memoir.

Be that as it may, she has nonetheless thoughtfully researched her husband's career and interviewed dozens of fellow players with journalistic integrity, giving her subject the intellectual and historical weight it deserves. Notable for its flair and professional finesse, *Lucky*, the book, sheds light not only on Anil's razor-sharp squash acumen but also his intellect. It also captures the mood, spirit, and cultural background of a momentous period in both Indian and U.S. history.

This engrossing profile of a true champion, especially in the context of the burgeoning popularity of squash in India and the U.S., not only delineates candidly Anil Nayar's squash career and the importance of its place in the broader arena of the sport, but also his professional and personal life, replete with turmoil, vicissitudes, and all. Through his decades-long involvement with squash, Nayar's concern for the game's welfare internationally, especially in India and the U.S., is palpable. He speaks passionately from afar about the state of the game and its future in India and the world, with thoughts on positively propelling its continued evolution. And this account of his illustrious squash career should be required reading for young and old involved with the game of squash in both India and the U.S. as well as other parts of the globe.—*Khalid A. H. Ansari, founder of India's leading sports magazine* Sportsweek *and the Indian daily newspaper* MidDay

Introduction

By the time my husband, Anil Nayar, and I got married in 2001, I had become well versed in his extraordinary squash accomplishments—his multiple national titles in India, the U.S., Mexico, and Canada, his win in 1965 as the first Indian player of the coveted Drysdale Cup, his legacy as the number one player on Harvard University's squash team. But what I didn't realize until several months later, when we belatedly celebrated our marriage with our extended families, was how meaningful his accomplishments were to a broad swath of his own countrymen.

In November of that year, when we were enjoying a lovely reception with my family in St. Paul, Minnesota, Anil received a call from Raj Singh Dungarpur, then the president of the Cricket Club of India, informing him that the members of the CCI's executive committee had decided to hold a ceremony during which its squash courts would be dedicated in Anil's name. He was also advised that the chief minister of the state of Madhya Pradesh along with a group of other dignitaries would attend the proceedings and the committee members were requesting Anil's presence at the event, too. I knew then that notable people were committed to memorializing Anil's accomplishments in India and, despite his reluctance to accept this honor, I insisted that he should attend. Later, in the spring of 2002, we flew to Bombay to spend time in Anil's flat on Marine Drive with his family to quietly enjoy an Indian-style mini wedding and a belated celebration with an extended group of friends and relatives on the penthouse terrace adjoining our apartment. Of course, everyone spent a great deal of time reminding me of Anil's special achievements in the squash world. But one friend, Jao Mulchandani, saw Anil as much more than an international sports star. "Anil is a hero to many people in our country," he told me. "And India is sorely in need of heroes."

Seen from this light, it was no wonder everyone else seemed to be as enchanted with Anil as I was. As a journalist and author, it also occurred to me that someone needed to write a book about his career—and I was determined to figure out a way to get it done. Thankfully, Anil's friend Khalid Ansari, then the founder and publisher of India's leading sports magazine *Sportsweek* and daily newspaper *MidDay*, also believed a book on Anil's career needed to be written. Since this is a story that crosses cultures, spans decades, and is rooted in two countries, it was important to me to work with seasoned experts in India to aid in the reporting to properly tell it, especially given my lack of experience in sports writing. And several years later, after I decided to take on the storytelling myself, Khalid was instrumental in helping with this process by connecting Anil and me to established professionals in India's publishing community and laying the groundwork for various interviews with several of Anil's Indian squash contemporaries.

To bring more dimension to the story, I spent countless hours interviewing Anil and together we recorded volumes of his thoughts on a variety of themes, much of which adds extra depth and nuance to our telling of his story. I also spoke to dozens of American and Indian players, coaches, family members, and friends who know Anil and remember aspects of his squash career in detail or who are actively involved in the current squash scene in India and the U.S.—and their thoughts also augment this tale. Ultimately, Anil and I collaborated closely in crafting this memoir on his squash career, and much of it is dominated by quotes from Anil on very personal impressions of various stages of his life and the experiences that shaped his squash legacy and character. In the collected whole, we hope that you'll find, as we do, an inspiring tale of a memorable sports hero's exhilarating journey.—*Jean Nayar*

PROLOGUE

Three-Wall Nick

The score was 11-all in the fifth of the semi-final at Yale in the toughest national championship of Anil Nayar's life. Captain of his varsity team at Harvard, the stellar Indian squash player had captured the intercollegiate champion title for the past two years in a row and was gunning for a triple crown. Fresh off his first win of the U.S. men's national championship against the great Philadelphian player Sam Howe in February 1969, he started the match feeling as though he'd already had it in the bag. "I was relaxed, kind of cocky, and I thought this tournament would be a breeze," Anil said. "I was more focused on enjoyment and socializing than on squash and whom I was going to play."

But his opponent, Penn's number one player, Spencer Burke, turned out to be a more formidable foe than he had expected. "I lost the first game and I tried to regroup, but it didn't quite happen and I lost the second game as well," said Anil. "It took me until the third game to realize I needed to get tough and play the long points as Spencer was forcing me to do, rather than go for untimely winners." And with this strategy Anil was able to pull through to win the third and fourth games.

Having played Anil for the first time at Penn a month earlier, Burke recalled clearly the challenges he'd face if he were to meet

Anil again in New Haven. "Anil had completely annihilated me in a three-game match on my home turf, with all my fans, including some girlfriends, in the crowd of 300 spectators," Burke said. "He didn't even take his sweater off until halfway through the match. I wasn't doing anything to make him sweat, and I couldn't breathe after seven points. The speed of his balls were unlike anything I had ever experienced. I knew that Anil was good, but after that defeat, I realized that I was a piker compared to him." So following the match, the Penn player turned to his coach, Al Malloy, and asked him what he could do to step up his performance in future matches against Anil. And Malloy helped him to improve his fitness over the next few weeks and came up with a strategy to beat the Indian star.

"I worked on raising the ball higher than Anil's waist as opposed to hitting the low balls that he liked to take away his ability to hit as many winners," Burke said. "I had no misapprehensions on what the differences were between my game and Anil's and I was determined to work on a way to perform better the next time I played him." He also studied Anil's matches in Buffalo, New York, and Chicago. "Anil was so agile, so fleet of foot, he was like the Fred Astaire of the squash court—no one could move like him," said Burke. "He was unbelievably elegant, precise and executed his shots with flair."

Anil also recalled the distinct difference in Burke's level of play in this semi-final versus their prior match. "It was clear that Spencer had received some extra coaching," Anil said. "I realized this in the first game." He was sure that Malloy had advised Burke to slow things down, to keep the ball wide and deep at a medium pace, rather than engage in the rapid-fire exchanges that would have fed right into his quick racquet and speed. "Spencer kept the ball in play with far fewer errors than I did," Anil said. "As I was working hard at cranking up the pace, Spencer was eating me with patience and the medium-pace ball to extract errors from me."

Unlike Burke, Anil also admitted that he had not crafted a strategy for this match as he usually did. Part of his customary preparation in advance of an important match was to visualize his opponent making attacking shots from some of his favorite positions on the court. But he had not seen Burke play in this tournament and simply wasn't ready, so he struggled to find creative ways to stay in the match.

As the players neared the end of the fifth game, the pressure mounted as Burke increased his lead to 14-11. After two more long and grueling rallies, however, Anil put on a brilliant display of stunning shots and retrievals and managed to tighten the score to 13-14. But at the third match point, the Indian player hit a loose ball at the center front wall. When Anil moved to the left side of the court behind his opponent, Burke tapped a deceptive low roll corner off the left wall—wrong-footing Anil and making a shot that was impossible for him to retrieve. As the ball dropped to the floor, the crowd roared—wildly erupting into applause. *It's over—it's Spencer's match and all because of my over-confidence, carelessness, and lack of focus*, thought Anil as he reached out to shake the hand of his opponent and congratulate him on his hard-fought win. But Burke, who was the only one who saw the ball's trajectory, turned around, looked squarely at Anil, then at the judge and ref, and called out, "Not so fast, the ball nicked the tin." Utterly stunned, Anil and the crowd fell silent with the game now squared at 14-all. "It was the ultimate stroke of luck!" said Anil, as he reflected on one of the most meaningful matches of his career.

When the players and crowd regained their composure, Anil, having won the last point, was poised to serve, while Burke would choose how to finish out the match either by playing to 17 points or calling "no-set," which meant whoever won the next point would win the match. Betting his odds of beating Anil would be better in one point rather than three, the Penn player chose a one-point game. Anil then served hard to Burke's backhand and his opponent responded with a sharp cross-court shot, backing Anil into the forehand corner and leaving him with no choice but to go for a three-wall nick, an effective shot only with the American hardball. Luckily, he executed the shot perfectly and the ball caromed off the walls before dead rolling out of the front left corner. Again cheers bellowed from the gallery—but this time the ovations were for the Harvard man who had astonishingly and emphatically clinched the victory!

Curiously, both players left the court feeling at once elated and humbled. "My triumph was just being there," said Burke, even though he had lost the epic battle. "At the time, Anil was the greatest player in the country, perhaps the world, and it was one of the peak moments of my life to be playing with such a great champion." For Anil, on the other hand, the satisfaction of winning that match paled in comparison to his sense of appreciation and respect for Burke's integrity and high-minded spirit of fair play at such a critical moment. "Spencer was a sportsman in the truest sense," said Anil. "He judged himself out of the intercollegiate championship."

After the semi-final match ended with both players exhausted, Burke returned to the locker room to shower and change before joining coach Malloy on a road trip to the next stop on their journey. "I saw my coach sitting in his car, threw my gear in the back seat, then sat down in the front seat next to him," Burke said. "Al turned to me, looked me straight in the eye, paused for a second and said, 'That was the damnedest thing I've ever seen!' Then he put the car in gear, drove off, and never spoke about it again."

At the same time, Anil went on to play the finals against his fierce fellow player Larry Terrell, Harvard's number two man, and seized the national championship title in three games. The second player ever to win the intercollegiate national title three years in a row and the first collegiate athlete to win the U.S. men's national championship since Harvard's Germain Glidden took the title in 1936, Anil reached the climax of a perfect season and was described in a story in *The Harvard Crimson* as "the best individual performer in any sport Harvard has ever had." More than his own extraordinary accomplishments, however, it was the superb sportsmanship displayed by Burke in the semi-final that left the most indelible impression on the Indian player at the end of the season. "I have not been put to this extreme test," said Anil. "But I hope I would have called it the same way Spencer did."

Given his record as a top international player over the course of more than four decades, chances are Anil would likely have risen to the occasion as Burke did. For this championship event exemplified but one of the many matches that would shape the character, sports legacy, and life of Anil Nayar. At this point, while still just a college senior, he was only halfway toward reaching the apogee of an amateur athletic career that defined him not only as a sportsman, but also as a businessman, husband and father, role model, and transformative figure who revolutionized squash by pioneering a path toward democratizing this under-recognized sport, which had been created by the British more than a century earlier and was then played almost exclusively by the privileged elite in the private clubs and institutions of commonwealth countries. Yet Anil's lessons in sportsmanship—and athletic competition at the world-class level—didn't begin in the courts of the blue-blood clubs or Ivy League universities of New England. They had already been etched into his psyche in India, where his remarkable trailblazing journey began.

* * *

PART ONE

1946-1961: Into the Dawn

CHAPTER ONE

Unlikely Sportsman

In 1946, Jawaharlal Nehru told the journalist Jacques Marcuse that "when the British go, there will be no more communal trouble in India." In June of the following year, Lord Louis Mountbatten, India's last British Viceroy, announced that England's rule over India would formally come to an end and the country would be partitioned along religious lines with nebulous boundaries to form two independent nations, India and Pakistan. The ill-conceived plan was drafted with the involvement and support of Nehru, who was slated to become the first Prime Minister of India, and Mohammed Ali Jinnah, who would be named the first Governor-General of Pakistan. When Nehru made his 1946 prediction, the details of the plan were still in flux, and very likely neither he nor Jinnah foresaw the scale of the violence and devastation that would unfold as the British Raj came to a hasty and abrupt end a few months later. Mahatma Gandhi, who also participated in the planning of India's independence and had staunchly resisted cutting asunder the country, might have intuited the carnage that would take place after Britain's brisk and calamitous exit, having witnessed a prelude to the chaos during the sectarian riots that unfolded in 1946 in Calcutta, where 4,000 people were killed in the melee in India's northeastern state of Bengal. Part of this state would become the eastern bookend of the dual territories of Pakistan, which, after the partition, would eventually flank the northwestern and eastern sides of the roughly diamond-shaped country of India, with the still-disputed territory of Kashmir crowning India's northernmost peak in between.

Indeed, upon the stroke of midnight on August 15, 1947, when Nehru and Jinnah took over the reins of their respective nations, vast swaths of the two new countries quickly descended into chaos as the implications of dividing the empire along religious lines became clear to the millions of Hindus, Muslims, and Sikhs who happened to live on the wrong side of the borders. In the wake of the panic and brutal destruction that unfolded amidst the most devastating conflagration in the history of the subcontinent, as many as a million Indians were murdered, up to 15 million were uprooted or left homeless, and countless others were abducted, raped, or maimed. And the scars of the tumultuous transition continue to affect the people of both countries and others all around the world to this day as the reverberations of the seeds of identity politics that were planted then—and, indeed, throughout the duration of Britain's direct and indirect rule over the country for two centuries—play out on the global stage.

Over the more than 70 years since that cataclysmic event, historians have debated how to apportion the blame. Some see nothing inevitable in the complex tragedy and attempt to imagine how the devastation might have been averted. Others question how the country's fate may have unfolded differently if the expedited exit had taken place years earlier, or had been delayed for several months as originally envisioned, or even extended over a period of years, which had also been considered to enable a more orderly transition. But the reality of this aspect of history is clear: The birth of two nations and the unraveling of an empire occurred at midnight on August 15, 1947, when the British officially handed over what Winston Churchill, despite his hostile attitude towards Indians, had once described as "the jewel in the crown" of England's territories to its own people.

The events that followed would not only change the fate and trajectory of the world's largest democracy, they would also determine the destiny of my husband, Anil Nayar, who was born in this amazing country just a few months before the brutal split would occur. And the ripple effects of this momentous calamity would profoundly influence Anil's view of the world and, subsequently, how he chose to fashion his place in it. Just as it is tempting to speculate on how differently India's evolution as a democracy might have turned out had the bungled transfer of power been more thoughtfully handled, it's also intriguing to imagine how differently Anil's future might have unfolded, too. But then again, maybe it would have been quite similar after all. For shortly after Anil was born, his parents turned to the family *pandit* to work out his horoscope and were told that he was destined to bring fame and honor to the family. Quietly, yet unquestionably, he fulfilled this destiny in his own modest way—and he might have done so regardless of the broader circumstances surrounding his entree into the world.

And ultimately that is what this story is about: A world-class squash champion who broke barriers, blazed a trail to the highly competitive halls of redbrick Ivy League colleges in New England oceans away from his birthplace, traveled the world, and has been recognized for his athletic accomplishments as well as his sportsmanship not only by the uppermost echelons of the international squash community in Britain, America, Canada, Mexico, and India, but also by the government of India, where its president bestowed upon him the Arjuna award, India's top honor for a sportsman. His story is one of winning titles and trophies in India and on foreign shores, sometimes against significant odds, during an era when foreign travel out of India was bound down by extreme red tape and foreign currency—even for the wealthy—was strictly rationed. But it is also an extension of a broader narrative that traces the evolution of a rarefied sport across countries and cultures and was propelled forward in many ways with the pioneering accomplishments of this boy from Bombay.

Anil with arms akimbo as a toddler, c. 1948.

Anil's tale begins, though, in Chheharta, a rural town in the northwestern state of Punjab very close to the newly minted border between India and Pakistan, where he was born on October 13, 1946, just ten months before the partition of the country. As such, he was among a generation of Indians loosely associated with a group of people envisaged by the writer Salman Rushdie as Midnight's Children, who were characterized in his magical realist novel by the same name. In the allegorical tale, this imaginary group of Indians, who were born at the time of India's independence from Britain and imbued with supernatural powers, represent the hope of the nation. The idea is relevant to Anil and his story partly because the very impending trauma of the division of the vast country would not only directly impact the lives of his family, but also determine how his own life would ultimately take shape. For shortly after he was born, his family would be among those enmeshed in the panic, misery, distrust, violence, and displacement of vast communities that spiraled out of control after the map of India had been redrawn.

Before that time, the Nayars had been a comfortably settled land-owning family living in a compound far from the hodgepodge of shanties on the other side of the historical Grand Trunk Road where, after the rains, the dust turned to *kichad,* which, when mixed with cow dung, would morph into a pungent road surface. Yet, due to their home's proximity to the border, they were among the millions who would be displaced by what is commonly referred to in the subcontinent simply as "partition." And within a few months of the chaotic and deadly dawn of an independent India, Anil's parents set off by train with Anil, who then was just a 1-year-old baby, and his three elder siblings roughly 1,000 miles south for the more hospitable city of Bombay, where, thanks to the family's affluence, they were fortunate to be able to recreate a prosperous and urban life in the bustling western seaside metropolis.

The family settled in the spectacular and aristocratic part of the city known as South Bombay on the scenic Marine Drive. Shouting distance away from the enchanting Arabian Sea was their new home, which was situated next door to the iconic and beautifully appointed Cricket Club of India. Built by the British, the club was and still is home to a world-class cricket stadium named after Lord Brabourne, a former British governor of Bombay who laid the foundation stone for the facility in 1936. "Yes, it was a cricket club with the world-renowned Brabourne Stadium, but other sports thrived alongside, among them squash," said Anil. Within the context of this new setting, Anil and his older siblings, Asha, Vinod, and Vijay, grew up in a spacious and comfortable flat in a recently constructed residential building overlooking the sea and were exposed to a rather worldly and international life, much of

Marine Drive, c. 1945, photographed by Jean's father while on duty in India during WWII. St. James Court, Anil's family home, is the fourth building from the right.

which was experienced within the walls of the exclusive Cricket Club of India, known to locals as the CCI, where everyone enjoyed a convivial social atmosphere as well as the benefits of its sporting facilities.

Once ensconced in Bombay, life for Anil and his family fell into a pleasant pattern, which included regular visits to the hometowns of both of his parents in Punjab. "My parents and my three siblings would take the Frontier Mail, the train immortalized in the potboilers of John Masters, from Bombay Central Station to Amritsar once in summer and then again in winter, thus never losing touch with the heat and dust we had left behind after partition," Anil said. "In those days, there were individual first-class cabins, not the current corridor trains. And it was fun riding in them with the family, though the summers were scorching despite the enormous slabs of ice that were placed by the *coolies* on the cabin floor and covered in sawdust and salt. Above these floors our bedding rolls would be covered in a film of coal dust from the engine. In the days before air-conditioning, there was little choice!" Winter travel, on the other hand, was breezy and comfortably cool. As the train traveled north, though, the air often turned a tad too cold, so the family would close the windows to the chill and coal dust and enjoy what worked out to be regular seasonal family picnics aboard the train.

While Anil's immediate family had relocated to Bombay (now renamed Mumbai), some of his paternal uncles and aunts continued to live on the family estate in Chheharta, which is located about five miles from Amritsar, his father's birthplace and the train's last stop as it made its way north toward the famous Wagah-Attari India-Pakistan border. His paternal grandparents' family compound was an oasis of comfort when contrasted with the shanties on the GT Road. Composed of a quartet of bungalows with well-manicured gardens and sprawling lawns, the compound even housed a swimming pool and a cement badminton court!

Anil's sister, Asha, the eldest of his siblings, claimed the family owned just one pair of roller skates, however, and about eight children, including several cousins, took turns learning to use them on the badminton court—and without pads to protect them, they often wound up with plenty of bruises and open cuts. In a fenced-in pasture behind the swimming pool, his grandparents kept 35 cows. "The cowherd would take them for a walk twice a day through the main gate and they would leave droppings as they ambled along," Anil said. "These cows were the source of our morning and evening fresh milk, which was also delivered to the community nearby, courtesy of the Nayar family." Asha believed the family's strong bones could be attributed to the non-pasteurized, non-homogenized fresh milk the Nayars drank as children.

Batala, the village of Anil's maternal grandparents 25 miles north of Amritsar, presented an entirely different picture. It was dirty with open sewers and heaps of garbage, invariably covered with armies of flies, dumped outside the homes. Like other dwellings in the village, the home of Anil's maternal grandparents not

Portrait of Anil's paternal great-grandfather, Lala Tulsiram Nayar, c. 1930.

only lacked air conditioning, but also had no running water or flush system. And in contrast to the herd of livestock owned by his paternal grandparents, Anil's maternal grandparents owned just two cows to supply the family's milk. The temperature in both settings varied from as low as 40 degrees F in winter to 100 degrees F or more in summer, when the family slept on the terraces under the stars on *khatiyas*, wooden cots with mats made of woven jute, with each sibling taking turns to water the floor to keep the air as cool as possible. In winter, they slept indoors next to an *angeethi*, a coal-fueled heater, and relied on lots of blankets and *rajaaees* to stay warm.

Despite the challenging conditions in Batala, Anil had very happy memories of his maternal grandfather, Mulkh Raj Singh Bhalla. Known as Bauji to the grandchildren, he was a beloved local physician, who gained his medical degree from Khalsa College in Amristar before serving in the Indian army during WWI. He also remembered fondly his maternal grandmother, Channandevi, who surfaced at 5 o'clock every morning, reciting passages from the Guru Granth Sahib, the Sikh holy book, and often breaking into song. Young Anil would crawl into their beds, hide his head under the quilt and pretend to be asleep just to enjoy the moments he spent with them and make them linger.

The rural, yet indulgent experiences Anil encountered at the homes of his relatives in the north were pivotal in shaping his view of the world—and his character—as time went on. Here, he was mollycoddled and amply fed plenty of *sarson ka saag* and *makki ki roti* with *tarka dhal* and *gobi aloo* all cooked in ghee, which added the extra pounds to his small frame that would eventually serve as an impetus for his extreme success in squash. It was in Batala that he also developed a strong sense of compassion for the less-fortunate people around him, including Dunichand, who worked for his maternal grandfather as a compounder in his pharmacy.

"Dunichand had a walleye and lived in a *kholi* alongside the premises of my grandparents' home next to the stall where the cows were housed," said Anil. As Dunichand toiled in the dispensary of the hospital quarters, where Anil's grandfather treated his patients, Anil enjoyed spending time with him there pretending to help with the alchemy he used to make the prescriptions advised by his grandfather. The seeds of Anil's sense of generosity were sown here, too, as he witnessed his grandfather treating the poor at little or no cost and rewarding Dunichand for his loyalty and service by ultimately giving the compounder and his family the portion of the family property in which he lived and worked as a permanent dwelling.

Anil's paternal great-grandmother, Ratan Devi Nayar, c. 1930.

Back in Bombay in those days, Anil's paternal grandfather, Lachmandas Tulsiram Nayar, with his business acumen and foresight, was thriving. After settling there with Anil's paternal step-grandmother, Pushpa, his grandfather had purchased a considerable amount of commercial and residential properties and land in the 1940s, which, over time, would geometrically increase in value. (Anil's paternal grandmother, Ram Rakhi Devi Nayar, had died in 1943 at the age of 45 of high blood pressure, shortly after the birth of the last of her nine children, seven boys and two girls.) Following Anil's paternal grandfather to Bombay came the two eldest of his grown children, Anil's uncle Daulatram and his father, Kanhyalal, the first and second of the seven brothers, along with their families. His grandfather's multiple real estate holdings provided the platform for the well-to-do and comfortable life Anil's family enjoyed after moving to Bombay.

Of course, but for the forced displacement from Chheharta in the heartland of Punjab, the Nayars might never have moved south to Bombay. It was also coincidental that among the portfolio of real estate Anil's grandfather had opted to acquire before partition was a residential apartment building known as St. James Court, which was situated along the picturesque surroundings of Marine Drive and would become the setting of his family's new home. Also known as the Queen's Necklace and so called because the lights of the evenly spaced, uniformly elevated, and then recently built Art Deco buildings along the sweeping boulevard would sparkle like jewels at night under the moon and the stars, especially when the magnificent crescent was viewed from the heights of the Hanging Gardens to the north, Marine Drive possesses an irresistible charm—and its hold on the collective imagination has become the stuff of Bollywood legend. The shimmering swoop of the boulevard has appeared in scores of films and, aside from the Gateway of India and the Taj Mahal Hotel, is perhaps the city's most famous image with its open embrace of the sea appearing to welcome people and influences from the lands beyond.

Like much of Bombay, Marine Drive owes its existence to land reclamation and profiteering that began after its environs had been taken over and settled as a trading outpost of the British, who started to develop the city in the early 18th century by gradually joining together the seven islands that now comprise it and expanding it out into the water. Among the various reclamation projects that unfolded over time under the influence of the British was the Back Bay scheme, which was originally envisaged to extend all along the western side of the southern tip of the city and include a beautiful promenade with office buildings, public squares, and blocks of apartment buildings containing homes for the rich.

With financing by private investors, both European and Indian, work on the project began in 1919, when stone and mud quarried in the north in Kandivali were brought by train to the site and dumped into the sea. Though only a portion of the original plan was ultimately completed, the 16.6 acres now known as Marine Drive emerged from the sea in front of the imposing Gothic headquarters of the Western Railway and Churchgate station, which had until then had been the nearest buildings to the waterfront. As the reclamation project progressed, the glamorous Art Deco style that first appeared in France in the 1920s had spread to other parts of the globe and was beginning to influence the design of everything from apartment buildings, movie theaters, ocean liners, and trains to furniture, jewelry, and everyday objects like clocks, radios, and toasters—particularly in sea-facing resort cities like Los Angeles, Miami Beach, and Havana. In Bombay, the modern building style represented a breakaway from the grand Gothic and Indo-Sarcenic imperial structures that reflected the ethos of the Raj at the southern tip of the city, and the newly emerging Indian elite embraced it as an emblem of their aspirations. So along with British investors, many of the Indian merchants, financiers, and cinema tycoons who financed the string of apartment buildings that would spring up along Marine Drive in the 1930s constructed them in the streamlined Art Deco style that would give the crescent-shaped boulevard its distinctly modern and cosmopolitan character.

Most relevant to Anil in this serendipitous setting, though, was his home's proximity to the Cricket Club of India. And with the family apartment located so very close to the CCI, the club would become young Anil's second home by the time he was 10 years old. The geographical accident of the new family home next to the

Anil's paternal grandfather, far right, with English businessmen in Amritsar, c. 1942.

CCI might have ensured that Anil would start to play squash at its courts. But in the earliest days of his play, it was far from inevitable that he would excel at the sport. And when I met him more than two decades ago, even after he'd achieved his greatest victories, I was surprised to learn that he was a stellar sportsman. He was clearly healthy, physically disciplined and committed to staying fit and regularly training. But I didn't see in him that fiercely competitive streak, or "killer instinct," one generally expects to find in a top athlete. I wondered what it takes to become a world-class champion of any sport and I couldn't get my mind around the mental qualities that would enable him to get to the very top of his game on an international level. So when I met Anil's eldest brother, Vinod, for the first time a few months later, I asked him about Anil's early days as a squash player. He described to me with considerable pride Anil's budding squash skills as a boy. He was also quick to point out a few of Anil's weaknesses at the time. "He was so chubby when he was young that we called him Ladoo," said Vinod. Ladoo, I soon learned, was the Hindi word for an Indian sweet that's shaped like a little round ball. This new insight only contributed to the disconnect in my mind about who Anil appeared to be on the surface and the athletic prowess within him.

Anil readily admitted, then, that his initial motivation to play squash as a youngster was encouragement from his family to take up the game to shed some of his excess weight. His sister, Asha, Anil's eldest sibling, remembered another galvanizing remark from Anil's geography teacher, who had taught her years earlier as well. After spotting Anil sitting on the school quad following a round of sports at school, he told her, "I saw your fat brother melting in the sun." She shared the comment with Anil, whose self-esteem at the time was shaped to a large extent by wisecracks like these.

Anil, whose pet name then was Ladoo, getting a hug from an uncle at the family compound in Chheharta as a cousin looks on, c. 1956.

As a boy, Anil was teased regularly about his weight not just by family, but also by friends, who delighted in the parallel between his plump body and the sphere-shaped sweet and soon others began calling him Ladoo, too. As is the preoccupation of so many Indian families, Anil was also constantly warned that, as a chubby one, he would not have much of a say in the marriage market. In India, families usually want "fair and beautiful girls" and "tall and slim men" for arranged marriage. "My mother gave me mixed signals," said Anil. "On the one hand she fed me a farmer's diet high in fat and carbohydrates, and on the other hand she made a remark that my body type and physique would keep me from gaining a suitable alliance with the opposite sex. Fearing the latter, I decided to take up squash seriously and ran and ran to lose weight. I ran after every ball, successful or not. And that is how I got my speed and retrieving ability, which would serve me well in the years ahead."

Despite its uncertain start, squash became and remained a passion and an integral part of Anil's life. His determination to overcome the humiliations and taunts of his elders and peers, along with his talent and hard work, his capacity to learn and practice with Herculean application, and his ability to observe, assimilate, and adapt to changing patterns of the game grew with time and would be part of his armor in his wonderful journey. His first mentor was an outstanding professional by the name of Jamal Din, who, Anil believes, was not quite convinced that he would reach any level of proficiency let alone achieve champion status on an international level. Anil described his Pathan guiding light as "world class" and a spectacular player. "When he hit hard forehand and backhand shots with the old Silvertown ball, the noise could be heard across the CCI pool by the Patiala Pavilion a 100 yards away," he said. And his patient, if limited, guidance sufficed to get Anil off to a rolling start.

In the early days, though, it was pretty hard going for the preteenager to get courts to play on as club regulations determined that adult members would get court preference after 4:30 p.m., which most clubs in India observe to this day in all varieties of sports, including badminton, tennis, and table tennis. For juniors, this meant that, outside school holidays, they would be scrambling for playing space in the limited spans available to them after school and before the elders took over the courts and squeezing in whatever court time they could get.

* * *

CHAPTER TWO

Coach Yusuf Khan

A new era of squash was about to be launched in Anil's life with the arrival at the CCI of Yusuf Khan, who took over in the young squash player's life as mentor, guide, and hands-on coach. He came to Bombay in 1958 after Jamal had migrated to the U.K. Khan was a smart, canny player, according to Anil, who sees him as the finest coach India has ever had. Interestingly, a little known rumor about a pivotal player in the massive movie industry provided an amusing sidelight to Anil's relationship with his new mentor. Just as Anil's new coach was moving into the space vacated by Jamal Din, another Yusuf Khan was rising as the new superstar of the city's Bollywood circuit and, incredibly, would remain in the celluloid firmament for the next half century. But before lording it over the film scene of the rapidly expanding city, particularly in Bandra's Pali Hill, the movie mogul changed his name to Dilip Kumar, and some speculated he did so to eliminate any chance of being mistaken for the squash coach.

Bombay in the late 1950s was a city in transition. Some of the relaxed lifestyle, megabucks, thriving movie industry, and lazy outings on the beaches of the city would take on new dimension as thousands of families, like the Nayars, poured in from the border areas of northern India as well as from what was now the cross-border territory of Sind in Pakistan to settle here and make the western metropolis their home. In a 2003 essay on the spirit of the city at the time, Indian actor, author, and journalist Gerson da Cunha wrote:

> It was a welcoming, hopeful city in a newly free nation.... There was an amplitude about it, even in the *wadis* of Girgaum and neighbourhoods of Parel.... The economics of Bombay has a history and a strong hand in its distinctive make up.
>
> By the turn of the last century, Bombay was a world city by the sea to which international trade and commerce came.... People with the option to live and move elsewhere seemed to prefer Bombay just after the war.... The city attracted and held high quality people. Such talent can choose to go where it pleases. It chose Bombay substantially in the decade or so after independence. Its economics, quality of life and openness had much to do with the decisions....
>
> The kaleidoscope has many colours and shapes. But the details may fail to depict an essential and larger phenomenon going on in the city, the fusing of the city's disparate elements into its cosmopolitanism. High quality minds and spirits became greater because, like elements with unsatisfied valencies in an environment of constant collision, they combined to form valuable new compounds.... [Bombay was] a melting pot of communities....there was a consciousness of community. But the differences did not mean the separateness and threat that some elements pose to others today.

Within this robust and diverse context, it is hardly surprising that the youngsters who functioned under the wing of squash coach Yusuf Khan were a mixed bag. Anil's family, of course, hailed from Punjab, while many of his fellow players, like Fali Madon, Dinshaw Pandole, Pheroze Contractor, and Naval Pandole, all came from the minuscule Parsi community, an immensely talented group of people who shone as vastly successful legal brains, financial and industrial wizards, practitioners of the fine arts, theater and film personalities, and sportsmen. And the family of Anil Kapur, another of Anil's childhood friends and squash compatriots, came from Peshawar, the land of the legendary squash clan, the Khans.

"We were both chubby as children," said Kapur, who eventually moved to the U.S. to work for the World Bank and remains a friend to this day. "Our school mates teased both of us. So we went to play squash. I started when I was about 12 or 13 years old. Anil had already started at around 10 or 11." By the time Kapur started playing, Anil had already begun to shed some of his excess weight, thanks in large part to the discipline encouraged by coach Khan. "He was dedicated to running and trained like a dog," Kapur said. "He would knock at my window every morning and ask me to run with him. Most of the time, I said, 'I'm not going.' But he would run three to four miles almost every day."

Indeed, Khan was a hard taskmaster beginning with an early morning run in cricket's holy of holies, the Brabourne Stadium, and then out along the picturesque Marine Drive. He worked with his trainees in a car on occasion, driving in front with the whole pack of young players in hot pursuit. The runs stretched anywhere from three to ten miles, followed by court workouts for 45 minutes before the youngsters would head back to school and then return again to the courts at 4 p.m. ahead of the senior members. Khan's approach to coaching was classical—with directions on positioning with no open stance, drawing the racquet back early, and knowing when to drop, when to hit tight, speedy rails, and when to lob cross-court shots. This training would be supplemented by daily drills and actual play on courts, with Sunday a total day off. With persistence and under Khan's tutelage, Anil quite quickly became good enough to beat a large number of members and then, to no one's surprise, he was given the respect of court time as needed.

Today, participants and spectators alike talk a lot about fair play, especially as the notion of "winning at all costs" has become

View of Cricket Club of India and Brabourne Stadium with the Rajabai Clock Tower in the background at right.

something of a buzz phrase with the emergence of big money that now dominates all kinds of sports from chess and badminton to cricket and tennis. Throwing temper tantrums à la American tennis player John McEnroe or putting umpires under pressure, as tennis player Serena Williams did at the U.S. Open in 2018, are a few of the less-than-sportsmanlike tactics used to attempt to turn around a losing position to one's advantage. But in the charming 1950s, Khan was obsessed with the idea of playing fairly and with a high level of sportsmanship. Thus, gracious gestures, such as complimenting a good shot by one's opponent, were encouraged. Any question about whether a serve was over the top line was to be settled by being automatically called "out" by the server and any attempt to continue play after a second bounce was adamantly discouraged. While Khan's training sessions were always focused and strict, it's notable, however, that little attention was paid to managing diets or exercising for strength as would be priorities in any athlete's fitness program now. Instead, the emphasis, as Anil put it, was simply on "playing as much as you could like the Pathans did in Peshawar—play, play, play and perfect the strategy and shots." Although the Pathans, including all the renowned Pakistani Khans (to whom Yusuf was distantly related), always served as role models, Anil noted that he later observed that fair play was not always necessarily part of their practice. Nonetheless, Yusuf Khan operated with his singular approach. And while it may be true that the lure of money can sometimes clash with playing with integrity for sportspeople who play professionally, as an amateur, Anil was glad that he always chose the latter.

Along with his talent for coaching, Khan also possessed the famous Pathan temper. Anil recalled that sometimes his coach would carry his anger, perhaps just a bad mood, into the coaching arena and now and then railed at Anil and Fali Madon, the other star player among his peers who went on to win the western India regional tournaments in tournaments 1967 and 1968, for not showing up for practice, or for playing an inappropriate shot, or, sometimes, for no perceived reason at all.

It was also known that Khan had considerable interest in the trucking business. And the fact that he enjoyed a better lifestyle than others of his ilk meant it was probably quite lucrative. In addition to trucks, Khan was interested in cars. He drove big 1950s American cars—a Dodge, de Soto, or Buick. Hudsons and Packards were other popular vehicles then. This was also the era of Prohibition in Bombay imposed by Morarji Desai, an Indian independence activist who would later serve as prime minister of India. And a large number of *"bhais"*—those who ran contraband liquor—were Muslims, though Anil and his peers are certain that Khan was not among them.

Khan thus had two jobs. And he started his role as a squash instructor in an army cantonment in Deolali, where he was referred to as a marker, a term used in India to define the role of a person with a fair level of proficiency in squash or tennis who served as an official to aid the referee in matches or games. Markers were of a lower rank than professionals, who were expert players with coaching experience and were generally respected by the membership of the club or institution. In his capacity as a marker, Khan helped a Captain K.K. Hazare to win two national championships, which surely precipitated a step up for him in his later role at the CCI. If you were to ask Anil what qualities Khan had that made him an outstanding coach, he would tell you that key among his attributes was his understanding of the game—its angles and heights—but his finest quality was his capacity to effectively impart this knowledge. "He was especially good at offering ideas on how to regroup when the chips were down—such as slowing down the momentum with medium-paced deep parallels or deft cross-court lobs, which both throw off an opponent's stride and give you a chance to steady yourself," said Anil.

With Khan's committed interest and genuine support, Anil felt that his coach ultimately became like an elder brother, discarding the servility of the marker and freely offering his advice and direction. Khan also had a knack for creating nicknames for his wards. By this time, Anil's coach as well as his fellow squash players called him by his other more widely known nickname, Lucky, which many of his grammar schoolmates continue to call him to this day. Some conclude that the tag was the result of some fluke of fortune on the squash court, but his mother actually gave him the pet name on the day he was born. For after she had been fasting for *Karva Chauth*—a Hindu festival observed by married women to promote the longevity of their husbands—she endured a long and challenging labor before finally giving birth to Anil at home under a waning full moon in the wee hours of the morning, and the English doctor who delivered him declared that he was lucky to be born alive. All of Anil's squash buddies were called by familiar tags, too. Predictably, Fali Madon was called Bawa, an affectionate appellation for a member of the Parsi community. Anil Kapur's official alias was Billy. Another friend, Premal Shah, an occasional squash player and ex-champion pingpong player who later worked in the Kilachand construction business and moved to Dubai, was Tit. The pet name of Naval Pandole, a former vice president of the CCI, was Nolly. And Deepika Dalal, a savvy female player among the group who eventually won several championships, was simply called D.

Other friends at the CCI in Anil's group included Krishan Mittal, a tall, slender super-quad football and hockey player and classmate since kindergarten who was also known as Bulé Shah for reasons unknown; Mia Madraswalla, whom the boys imagined as their conduit to the underworld of Mohammed Ali Road; Hosi Vasunia, an actor who introduced the group to the world of cinema and theater; Yunus Varawalla, a fellow player whose shrill voice could be heard well beyond the courts when he was in trouble in a match; and "Shorty" Ootam, who later became a purser at Air India and provided access to hard-to-come-by foreign consumer goods. Another regular fixture at the courts was the patriarch of the Pandole family, Feroze Pandole, a boxer-turned-squash-player and a super athlete who required quiet and discipline in the court gallery, especially when it came to his sons, Dinshaw and Nolly, and later for his grandson, Darius.

On the court Khan was very much engaged in the sporting lives of his trainees, but off the court he maintained a delicate balance with Anil and his squash-playing friends about girlfriends—he wouldn't interfere nor would he comment about their dalliances. But there was no compromise on training. In any case, at this point in his life, Anil was focused far more on sport than he was on the opposite sex, so there should have been little concern to Khan that Anil's attention would stray far from the ball. But the lively goings-on among his older siblings at home were certainly beginning to open his eyes to the power and allure—and something of the pain—of romance.

* * *

CHAPTER THREE

Mother, Father, Sister, Brothers

In the life of a sportsman family influences are abiding, often lifelong, and can determine the direction of progress. They may act as inspiration, as challenges, or, sometimes, as obstacles. Anil grew up within the context of a variation of a traditional Indian joint family, the customary extended family arrangement prevalent in India in which the sons remain in their parents' home at marriage and bring their spouses to live with them. In the case of Anil's family, instead of everyone living under one roof, many of the family members eventually moved into their own flats in the same building, which in itself was a sign of the times. At the fountainhead were the grandparents—both paternal and maternal. The grand old patriarch, Lachmandas Nayar, Anil's father's father, was universally called Lalaji, and to the grandchildren Chachaji. As was, and indeed still is, the tradition in vast stretches of rural hinterland, one of his grandfather's life's tasks was to be particular in selecting suitable daughters-in-law for his sons and, as it relates to Anil, to determine who would marry the future squash champ's father.

When his grandfather identified Kailash Bhalla, a young 16-year-old from Batala, to be the appropriate mate, he knew there was the question of disparity in wealth between the two *sambandhi* families. This became more apparent when he visited the home of her parents to lay the groundwork to become the *sasural*—or in-law family—of Anil's father. Anil's grandfather, like other townspeople, had heard of Dr. Mulkh Raj Singh Bhalla, his mother's father, and his reputation as an honorable man. Dr. Bhalla, who was widely known as Bauji, had been a *mona* Sikh—someone who had discarded his trademark turban when entering the First World War—and had returned to his home, a congested village, to practice medicine, focusing on those who needed it most—the poor. But the primary focus for Lachmandas in this particular meeting was the good doctor's daughter, the beautiful young lady he had seen and admired who would go on to become Anil's mother.

Penned by great Indian novelists, many popular works of fiction at the time, such as Sarat Chandra Chatterjee's epic romantic novel *Devdas*, revolved around marriage contracts between families of different economic standing—like those of Anil's grandparents. When his parents were young, arranged marriages were common and certain things mattered much more than interplay of emotions between the bride and groom to be. Underlying the disparities in these stories to some degree was the controversial dowry, which a girl's family makes as a material offering, including money, to the groom's folks. But the tradition did not feature in the matchmaking in progress here. When Lalaji asked for the hand of Bauji's daughter for his son Kanhyalal Nayar, he was less interested in dowry and more in acquiring a daughter-in-law from an honest, simple, well-reputed family. Still, before granting his permission, Bauji made clear who he was and what his family was about by saying, "*Sharafat hai, sharafatan nahin,*" meaning "We have honor and modesty but not wealth." At that moment, as the story has been told, Lalaji reached out to embrace Bauji and explained

Anil's paternal grandfather Lachmandas Nayar, with Anil's step-grandmother, Pushpa, c. 1956.

that his was precisely the kind of family with whom he wished to forge a relationship. The exchange also marked the beginning of what would become a long line of non-traditional marriages in the Nayar family.

The differences between Anil's father and mother, however, extended well beyond the fiscal status of their families. As an impressionable young boy, Anil was an astute observer of these disparities and, keenly conscious of both his parents' strengths and weaknesses, he chose to embody as much as possible those qualities in each he admired most. Chief among his father's laudable characteristics were bravery and duty to family. An episode Anil had witnessed between his father and some neighborhood hooligans highlights the moment when these aspects of his father's nature became clear to him and left a lasting impression.

"The day my father chased a couple of *goondas* from our building compound, he became my hero," said Anil. "I was around 12 years old and hanging around the compound with Billy Kapur, his brother Ashok, and my brother Vijay one evening. My father had just gotten out of the car from his journey home from work when he was told by Anand, our lift man, that some older troublemakers were chasing Vijay in the compound. My father, slightly overweight and burly, took off to look for Vijay. An hour or so later, he returned home, having rescued Vijay and holding a pair of shiny metal knuckledusters in his hands. He had vanquished the two *goondas*, extracted their weapons, and saved my brother from a beating. He was a solid protector and caretaker!" There's always a flip side to a person's strengths, of course, and in his father's case the darker side of his personality often surfaced in the form of a short fuse and a fierce temper, which were often on display within the household whenever the antics of Anil's older siblings went beyond his threshold of tolerance. These lesser inspiring qualities invariably intimidated young Anil, so much so, in fact, that he always attempted to behave in ways that would spare him from his father's wrath.

The most memorable positive qualities possessed by his mother, on the other hand, began filtering into Anil's psyche from the moment he became conscious and they remained clear aspects of her nature until the day she died. Among her finest attributes were long-suffering patience, spiritual devotion, and sensitivity to those less fortunate. "My mother would read and translate the Granth Sahib and Gita," said Anil, noting that she embraced the scriptures of both her Sikh and Hindu backgrounds. "She would tell me stories of the god Krishna and the warrior Arjuna debating the merits of sacrifice and self-abnegation as prices to pay for the long-term common good. She counseled that the privileged should do service by giving to those less well off. She explained that Guru Nanak, a key figure in the development of the Granth Sahib, urged his followers to act with justice and fairness to all regardless of color, caste, or religion. I loved these feel-good stories. Through so many of them I was molded to a mindset during my childhood that may have

Anil's maternal grandparents, Chenandevi and Mulkh Raj Singh Bhalla, at the Dalhousie hill station in the Himalayas, c. 1958.

encouraged a survival instinct, rather than a killer instinct, as well as a desire to enable those around me to survive as well. I learned from her how to adjust, to be kind and polite, to give respect and to get it."

Though his mother always exhibited a strong moral core, she never displayed the outward hallmarks of, say, a Gandhian sense spirituality, such as humility and austerity, as she was keenly conscious of her own beauty and very much valued the trappings of the material elements her married life afforded her—in particular fine jewelry laden with emeralds, rubies, diamonds, and pearls and fancy *sarees*. Even the spiritual verses she composed after reading the Guru Granth Sahib were inscribed in high-quality hardbound journals with an American gold-plated Parker pen. And like many Punjabi women, she telegraphed her newfound social standing by stylishly showing off these symbols of wealth at every public occasion she attended and whenever she and her husband entertained at home.

In the world of Hindi cinema in those days, a beautiful actress called Suraiya and her co-actor, the great Dev Anand, were immensely popular personae. And Anil's mother was virtually a carbon copy of the well-known actress. With some embarrassment, Anil was regularly reminded of the resemblance between the actress and his mother during her frequent visits to his kindergarten classes, where cries that "Suraiya is here!" would be heard whenever she arrived since all generations were aware of the likeness even before the proliferation of television. (Coincidentally, Suraiya, who, like Nargis, another beauty and top actress of the day, grew up in a neighboring Art Deco building on Marine Drive and the two movie queens contributed to the air of glamour and romance that permeated south Bombay at the time.) His mother would invariably be dressed up and made up to enhance the resemblance. Yet, Anil felt that her aim to preserve her beauty was but one of the ways she sought to appeal to his father. Just as she had with her own father, she also instinctively adapted to his father's good and bad moods and worked hard to deliver the creature comforts that would keep him happy. "She was an only child from a non-vegetarian background and was treated like a pearl in her family and she married into a joint family consisting of nine siblings and the daunting presence of my grandfather and grandmother in a strictly vegetarian household," said Anil. "I saw how my mother worked on relationships as part of my father's family. With my mother's help, I also learned to navigate the moods of my sometimes combustible father, brother, and sister while growing up in Bombay."

As Anil was growing up, many observed that the initially striking quality about Anil's mother transferred to the whole Nayar family, who were blessed with a profusion of good looks. All possessed their father's intelligent, sensitive eyes, which were rather narrow and sloped downward a bit at the outer edges like shiny black buttons in neatly tailored buttonholes, and their mother's plump lips. Elder sister, Asha, seven years senior to Anil, was the first to inherit her mother's beauty. While Anil remembered with a certain uneasiness that he was his mother's great favorite and he compensated for what he imagined to be his unearned privileged position by minimizing his presence and keeping in the background during family gatherings, Asha surely was the chosen one of their father. When she was a teen, she was sent off to a finishing school at Loretto Convent in Simla, a former summer capital of the British. Anil clearly recalled those years when she developed into quite a young lady, a time that would lead to some strife in the years ahead. Asha occasionally swapped her traditional *salwar kameez* for tops and shorts, "especially on weekends, when she went to Gaylords to rock and roll," said Anil, remembering how those shorts became shorter and shorter! He also claimed that boys gathered around her in droves. While, as many younger brothers do, Anil questioned what Asha was up to, he realized later she was simply flirting casually in large doses. What was beginning to unfold in the family with Asha's bold gestures, however, was a battle between the traditional and the modern. (Apart from the modern lifestyle, Anil's sister also proved that, like her brothers, she also inherited the Nayar sports gene when she picked up a love and talent for the game of field hockey, a game in which Indians, especially in those days, boasted huge bragging rights all the way to the Olympics, and she played for the team of Sydenham College, Bombay's premier business college, in 1960 before leaving for England to learn accounting.)

Plenty was changing around the world in the second half of the twentieth century, and families across the vibrant, newly independent country were observing the passing by of traditional values with the massive influx western influences, some acceptable, others less so. The arrival of western families in their midst really wasn't seen as the problem so much, and in some ways was actually welcomed, but a daughter of the house straying towards western alliances, as Asha happened to do, was another matter altogether. She was due back from England along with her parents via Italy in 1961 on the very popular Lloyd Triestino boat MV Victoria. Two tall and blue-eyed Germans had come into her life aboard the ship and, once in India, were invited to the Nayar home as guests after they'd ingratiated themselves with her parents. As it happened, it was Ulrich Wollmann, an employee at the Bombay office of the German company Chemische Werke Huls, who was her favored one. Teenagers, as far as their elder sisters are concerned, are very observant, and Anil had noticed and suspected something significant was developing between them.

Some time later he saw Asha step out of Ulrich's Opel car near the family home one evening, and turmoil ensued as his father got wind of her budding romance and took pains to move her, with Anil tagging along, far from the family's home in Bombay in a last-ditch effort to prevent the match. So outraged was Anil's father by the idea of his daughter carrying on with a foreigner that his only choice was to put Asha under house arrest in the family's home in Dehra Dun and later in their bungalow in Amritsar, where she was forced to remain indoors under the observant eyes of the family's guards, gatekeepers, and watchmen. "They were instructed not to let her out of the compound," Anil said. To Anil's surprise, Ulrich had nonetheless learned of Asha's whereabouts and he ran into his sister's suitor at the local railway station in Amritsar. "If the men my father had enlisted as Asha's guards had found Ulrich, I imagined they would have beaten him up and left him in the open gutter alongside the GT Road," Anil speculated. "When I saw Ulrich, I told him I thought he be in danger if he were to be discovered in the vicinity. Even he if wouldn't be physically harmed, there would at the least be damaging ripple effects for him either in the German Embassy in Delhi or with his employers in Bombay." So, on Anil's insistent bidding, the German did eventually leave the city but, before doing so, he had made arrangements for an abduction coup! The next the family heard following the subterfuge was that Ulrich and Asha had gotten married in Delhi under an *Arya Samaji* ceremony. (A side note to the nuptials—was the presence in Ulrich's camp of Sohrab Godrej, the chairman of the behemoth Godrej Group conglomerate, which operates in sectors as diverse as industrial engineering, appliances, furniture, agricultural products, and real estate.)

Needless to say, when his parents received word of Asha's elopement, a meltdown in relations immediately followed. "After they married, a cold war raged between my parents and Asha for several years," said Anil. "There were overtures from Asha's friends to my parents, and my mother wanted to reunite as my father also may have wanted to do, but his pride and his posture among his friends and society kept him away until Asha's daughter and first child, Ulricke, and later her son, Hans, were born. There was no automatic switch turned on with a return to kissing and hugging. But a slow and steady path back to a new normal relationship had been opened—and ten years later, my father was not embarrassed to admit that Ulrich was, indeed, an ideal mate for Asha, as only he could contain, in a rather loving way, her volatility and strong personality."

Aside from parents and sisters, a major influence in any Indian family are brothers, particularly the eldest, especially in relation to sports. He is usually the role model and motivator, willingly or unwilling, conscious or unconscious. The Amritraj brothers in tennis, the Chappell brothers in cricket and, of course, the Khans in squash are all examples of this phenomenon. Sporting excellence came naturally to the entire Nayar family, including Anil's elder brothers, Vinod, who was skilled as a football goalie and wicket keeper, and Vijay, who was admired not only for his abilities in soccer and hockey but also for his crafty left-handed bowling in cricket. While neither Vinod nor Vijay were squash champs, both

The Nayar family, c. 1958, from left to right: Vinod, Asha, father Kanhyalal, Vijay, mother Kailash, Anil.

were excellent sportsmen in other disciplines, nurturing a fire in the belly of the youngest.

As with Asha, modern western influences also colored the views of Anil's brothers, especially Vinod, the eldest brother and six years older than Anil, who was considered a handful for his parents and found himself in a boarding school at Bishop Cotton in Simla, the hill station city in the north, where the unquestioning discipline was hoped to have a salutary effect. A six-foot-one Punjabi "*jat*," as Anil thought of him, or a salty kind of guy, Vinod was fearless in his approach to sports—and life. And, just before Asha married and to the profound dismay of his parents, he was the first to marry a foreigner, Gunhilde (Gunna) Hapke, another German and the mother of Anil's oldest nephews, Arun and Nikhil. For Anil, the sporting aspect was worth emulation—and ultimately the trend for marrying foreigners would also be replicated—though he was always overwhelmed and intimidated by Vinod, a strong man with a short fuse.

Anil's other older brother Vijay was seen as a handsome man by most who knew him—he had the long aquiline nose of their maternal grandfather. Anil described Vijay as "a clever left-arm bowler" at the time and a wizard in the game of cricket as captain of his team. Four years older than Anil, Vijay was also the head boy at Cathedral School (the Scottish-run private school in which Anil was also enrolled), no simple achievement. In Vijay, there was also an interest in squash that the younger Anil shared. At Cathedral and later as a student of Millfield school in England, Vijay turned out to be a good all-round athlete. As a squash player, Anil saw him as a "tenacious" one who would practice with his renowned partner, Sharif Khan. The awe of brother Vijay increased when Anil viewed him artfully knocking out a bigger opponent in yet another sport he excelled at—boxing. Also worth remembering at that impressionable age, the youngest Nayar would see, year after year, new girlfriends on the arm of his elder sibling when he came home for vacations—among them Air India stewardesses and a Rajasthani princess and squash player named Booty. By his own admission, Anil also looked with envy at the beautiful women his brothers, especially Vijay, would socialize with.

Most important to Anil at this point, though, was the influence Vijay had on helping the younger brother to elevate his squash skills. When Anil was 14 years old, he played squash at least twice a week with Vijay at the Cricket Club's courts whenever the elder sibling returned from boarding school in England for a break from June through August. The swelter of an August day in Bombay reaches a peak in the afternoon. So on a late-summer day in 1961, when Vijay was back at home, the budding young sportsman rose early to sign up for the 8 a.m. slot on the chalkboard of court three, his lucky court, at the CCI. It would be to his advantage to avoid the stifling midday heat in a match against his more experienced brother. He always relished playing Vijay despite the fact that the bigger brother would invariably prevail. But on this day Anil had high hopes that for once the outcome of the upcoming match might tip in his favor.

When the two teens entered the concrete court, the humidity hung like dead weight in the compact space as the blades of a rickety ceiling fan jaggedly cut through the dense air in a lame attempt to move it. Moisture clung to every surface. Some of yesterday's pounding monsoon rains had filtered through a crack in the corrugated metal roof and collected in a shallow pool on the wooden floor at the center of the court. And as the morning sun rose over the club's Brabourne cricket stadium, a sliver of its golden rays blazed through a gap in the tarpaulin stretched over the open-air back of the upper-level gallery and glistened inside the court as it grazed its sweating, pockmarked walls.

Eager to start the match, the boys paid little mind to the muggy, suffocating atmosphere and soldiered on, point after point, game after game, slicing their wooden racquets like machetes through the thick air and cracking the soft, hot Silvertown ball against the front wall like a bullet. Setting off the staccato thwack, thwack, thwack of the ball as it ricocheted round the court, the high-pitched squeaks of the players' rubber-soled shoes as they darted across the slippery wooden floor merged with the huff and puff of heaving breath as the two youths played out the familiar cacophony unique to this particular battleground. Quicker on his feet than he had been the previous year, Anil, plump and perspiring, raced to pick up the drives Vijay belted down the line and scrambled to respond to his surprising cross-court shots, often succeeding in returning an occasional devastating blow. But after four games, with wristbands, shirt, shorts, and socks sopped with sweat, Anil succumbed to Vijay's final drop shot, twisting his ankle as he slid on the floor to reach for the ball before smacking it into the tin.

Another friendly fraternal match ended as it always had—with the elder brother emerging as the victor and the younger wallowing in defeat. Of course, it wasn't Anil's first loss on the squash court, and it would hardly be his last—though at this point it was far from clear whether young player would ever become a serious contender. Yet, crushing as his loss may have been, Anil nonetheless saw the match as a worthwhile experience that stretched his chops.

So here he was—with plenty to view and absorb in the lives of his elder siblings. It was too early to tell then whether he would emulate them or take another path. "They were my competition at home and, for me, they set a high bar to meet," said Anil, who in 1961 was just 5'3" tall and weighed 135 lbs. "'Behave modern and be popular with classmates and the girls,' was the mandate initiated by my siblings." At this time in his life, though, Anil admitted that he did not have the confidence or looks or personality to follow in their footsteps. Still, he looked at the years ahead as a challenge.

* * *

PART TWO

1961-1965: Metamorphosis

CHAPTER FOUR

Bombay, Its Clubs, and Its Sportsmen

If Anil's first meaningful transition in life from the green fields and rural ambience of Chheharta to the concrete buildings and hustle of Bombay was the result of an act of men and determined by the decision-makers in his world as they moved to safer havens, his second passage, a metamorphosis of sorts—as he organically forayed though his early education toward adulthood as a teenager—was an act of nature. Fortunately for Anil, his parents were blessed with resources and capable of preparing him with options for choosing the road ahead.

Thus far, Anil's life had taken shape largely under the influences of his grandparents and his parents. He had been subjected to the vicissitudes of interactions of a large family at work and play. He had alternately looked up to, feared, and often emulated his elder siblings, and at the same time was sometimes sharply critical of them, as is not uncommon with the baby in such a family. And just as his siblings had moved on with their lives, it wouldn't be long before Anil would leave the nest and begin to explore the world in his own way, too.

As a young teenager, Anil's early success on the squash court was contributing to a change in his self-esteem that had allowed him to build a comfort zone of confidence within his core group of peers. Eager to get a clearer sense of Anil at this time in his life, I once asked his mother over a cup of *chai* to tell me about her memories of the time when he started to excel at squash. He was playing in a club tournament, she told me, and she was so nervous for him that she couldn't bring herself to watch him play, so instead went into her home temple and prayed. Later in the afternoon, she said, one of the servants came rushing into her study and shouted, "Ladoo has won the match!"

After sharing a good laugh with Anil's mother upon hearing this story, it became obvious that, while this event might have marked the beginning of Anil's brilliant squash career, his aim to excel in the sport at this point was very much driven, as he was quick to admit, by an inner need to break the "Ladoo" mold and prove himself to be something more than the rather demoralizing, if endearing, definition imposed on him by others. Indeed, one of the dominant influences in Anil's psyche at this time was the teasing he endured as a Ladoo, which continued to afflict him with significant adolescent insecurity about the opposite sex. To boot, he wore dark-rimmed glasses, which he was given after deliberately pretending to be unable to read an eye chart with the idea that a pair of spectacles would make him look more distinguished. Instead, they made him look nerdish, though he believed his cute smile spared him from being perceived as totally uncool. He had seen both Vinod and Vijay with a string of attractive young women and enjoying successes with their interactions with the fair sex. But both were considerably older, and now it was his turn.

Anil has frequently admitted that he was not much into flirting, but some of his friends believe that this had more to do with his focus on squash than shyness. "He kept a low profile and a limited group of friends," said his childhood friend Anil Kapur. "He was always reserved in his approach and style on whom to date when

Anil as a teen, c. 1961.

we were young—he wasn't a party animal. I don't know if it was shyness so much as it was his commitment to squash." Perhaps it was a combination of these aspects alongside the desire to break out of the shadows of Vinod and Vijay that prompted him to follow his own path on the dating front, taking it slowly but surely, starting with his earliest infatuation as an early teen with a girl next door. Anil recalled regularly looking out the window of his home and exchanging glances with the girl, who lived in a building across the road. The two were well aware that they were making eye contact, but their connection remained only just so for a couple of years (eventually the pretty neighbor got married to a friend of the family and Anil remembered meeting her with a knowing smile with her husband at the CCI some 20 years later).

By the time Anil was around 15 years old, his baby fat had all but disappeared, as had his glasses, which his maternal grandfather jettisoned after curing his supposed weak eyesight with a customized Ayurvedic treatment applied like a *kajal*, or eyeliner. And while his interest in females had begun to emerge (as had theirs in him), it was outweighed by his inclination to progress as a sportsman. As his fitness continued to improve, so did his squash game, and he regularly began winning club tournaments. With his parents away in England for a nine-month stay and his siblings now out of the house—all were attending school, also in England—Anil was now mostly on his own, living with his father's youngest brother, Jagdish, and his English wife, Betty. Without family distractions, he could focus on playing squash and enjoying time with friends.

A turning point in Anil's confidence occurred around this time when his brother Vijay had returned to Bombay for another visit from London, where he was attending school at Millfield. Deep down there may have been a bit of sibling rivalry, yet Anil still saw his middle brother more as an inspiration and a role model to emulate, rather than as a competitor. Nonetheless, both Vijay and Vinod had a direct effect on the mindset of youngest Anil. And with the routine matches he regularly played at the CCI with Vijay whenever he was in Bombay always ending with Anil at the losing end of the stick, Anil's expectations for a winning outcome in his next confrontation with his older brother were quite low. But this time, in 1962, when Anil was 15 and Vijay 19, they played a five-game match and the elder brother struggled to keep up until Anil overtook him in the fifth. "I didn't expect to beat him, but I did want to show him how much I had improved," said Anil. "My feelings were mixed after winning the match. I felt badly for my brother, I think he was shocked and I surprised myself, too. I didn't know that I was ready to beat him until I actually did." And so, a new die had been cast! Things were going well in the squash arena, and this win loomed large in Anil's consciousness. It was the beginning of a new—and winning—outlook.

Had his family stayed in the north or moved to a different setting, it's quite possible that Anil might never have played squash. But with easy access to the CCI, it was almost as if his fate as a sportsman was sealed. Within walking distance of wonderful restaurants and the Churchgate Railway Station, the Bombay hub of the vastly efficient local Western Railway train network, his family's home and the CCI were situated in one of the loftiest parts of Bombay when it was at its most glittering. The city also brimmed with fast cars and an abundance of other important sporting facilities—with their cricket pitches, tennis courts, billiard rooms, soccer goal posts, and even quaint rugby grounds, where the old colonial games of public schools and redbrick colleges of England found perpetuity. There were literally dozens of clubs with sporting fields and courts within the couple of square miles stretching north to south from the newly created aquarium on Marine Drive to the CCI. They were called by such names as the Bombay Gymkhana, the Catholic Gymkhana, the Hindu Gymkhana, and the Islam Gymkhana, all within salt-spray distance of the Chowpatty beach.

The remarkable couple of square miles that contained them would produce in the years ahead world champions in billiards and snooker like Wilson Jones and Michael Ferreira, epic cricketers like Sunil Gavaskar, Vijay Merchant, and Sachin Tendulkar, badminton super luminaries like Nandu Natekar and Prakash Padukone, numerous tennis personalities and table tennis aces like Sudhir Thackersey and Kalyan Jayant and, to return to the thread of our story, the squash icon and champion Anil Nayar. And, of course, he would find his playing platform at the courts of the Cricket Club of India, which his old squash buddy and a former vice president of the club Naval Pandole called "the country's biggest incubator of stellar Indian squash players and the nursery for Indian squash" at that time. Though newer than some of the city's other well-known clubs—such as the Willingdon Club, built in 1918, or the Bombay Gymkhana, constructed in 1875 and housing what are possibly the city's oldest squash courts—the CCI is regarded as one of Mumbai's most prestigious private sporting and social settings and is now a heritage property.

When it was planned, the CCI was intended to be the Lord's of India, and the popular story accompanying its creation involved India's then cricket administrator Anthony De Mello, who was said to have asked Bombay's then governor Lord Brabourne, "Your excellency, which would you prefer to accept from sportsmen, money for your government or immortality for yourself?" When Brabourne chose immortality, the CCI was allotted 90,000 square yards at a price of 13.50 Indian rupees per square yard from land reclaimed in the Back Bay scheme upon which to build the stadium and sporting club where Anil's squash career got its spirited start. And while the pet name Lucky bequeathed on him originally had other connotations, it was, indeed, a stroke of luck that landed Anil near the CCI in this magical square mile or so and he could thus set the game alight.

It's possible that Anil's trajectory as a sportsman might never have materialized had he and his family continued to stay in semi-industrial Punjab. But considering the history of his community, it is highly likely he would have lived an adventurous life either way. Among the vast pantheon of ethnic groups in India, as varied as if they had been from different continents, the Punjabis stood out for their robust joy of living, their capacity to take risks in business and in other aspects of life, which simply would not brook stagnation. The Punjab region of India was the gateway for centuries through which the majority of conquerors came, including Alexander the Great, Tamerlane, and the Mughals, until ultimately the British arrived through the ports, ruling and influencing all of India from 1858 to 1947. As such, it has always been seen as a frontier state accessed by foreigners through Afghanistan and the Himalayan passes, and so the people of Punjab had learned through centuries to adjust, adapt, fight, align, or regroup elsewhere without losing their spirit.

Before partition, Anil's landowning paternal grandfather put up a woolen and worsted textile plant in Chheharta, traveling to Japan to purchase the machinery required to operate the plant. "He was a pioneer to get industry and textiles to the Amritsar area," said Anil. "The official name of the factory was the India Woolen Textile Mills but to the locals it was known as 'Japanny Mill.'" After partition, myriad Punjabi families had come across from West Punjab to other parts of the country with essential belongings, set themselves up, survived, and, indeed, thrived. Their attitude was totally different from some of those in other Indian states who would be complacent in their clerical or government jobs, spending their lives without looking beyond the fence. Ultimately, it would become clear that this risk-taking spirit was baked into Anil's DNA.

In Bombay, Anil attended the Cathedral and John Connon School, an educational institution for snobbish expatriates and wealthy locals that was founded in 1860 and managed by the Anglo-Scottish Education Society. Here, he also was enmeshed in a vastly cosmopolitan environment that nourished his instinctively open-minded point of view. Many of his teachers were from England, others were of Anglo-Indian descent, some were Indian, and a few came from farther-flung reaches of the globe, including a Mr. Zavala, Anil's geography teacher from Peru, who, in a fit of anger before lunchtime, often threw thumb-size pieces of chalk at any student who irritated him and, in lazier moods after lunch, was also known to present surprise quizzes to keep his students preoccupied while he enjoyed some quiet time to himself.

At the same time, many of Anil's fellow students were from different Indian states, speaking a dozen languages and belonging to different faiths—Christians and Hindus, Parsis and Muslims, Sikhs and Jains and Jews. "Our prayers and hymns were Christian in school, at home my part-Sikh-part-Hindu mother read the Granth Sahib and the Gita," recalled Anil of his own multifaceted experience of the time. In this context, a person would grow up to be a well-rounded Indian rather than a provincial Punjabi or Sindhi or Maharashtrian. It was a mosaic of varied cultures and languages. And all got along essentially as equals—including the handful of European children of diplomats who attended the school.

"My Cathedral education, as disconnected as it was from our traditional ethos at home, required discipline and a lot of learning by rote," Anil said. "Most of the school exams prioritized regurgitation of the text books and doing so would have held students in good stead as they proceeded with further Indian education. Mine was the first year that the bureaucrats, in their efforts to de-link from foreign-based testing, decided to give finishing school an Indian flavor, however, so our 11th-grade finishing school exams changed from Senior Cambridge to Indian School Certificate, or ISC. I don't believe there was any change except the name in 1963. And I got a respectable First Class on this exam." Looking back at his early education, Anil saw the layered strands of culture he experienced at Cathedral as eminently helpful as he progressed through life. "In retrospect, the disconnect between my home life and schooling was a blessing in disguise," he said. "I couldn't understand the disconnect until much later when I could see more clearly the meaning and practice of inclusion that was an integral part of our education, and I thank Cathedral School for that."

Still, the sons and daughters of expatriates, largely British and mainland Europeans, would generally receive preferential treatment and, indeed, easier admission to schools and clubs, including the snobbish Bombay clubs like the Bombay Gym, whose members were largely limited to British, Europeans, and Americans until the early 1960s, and Breach Candy, which did not shed its preferential treatment for Europeans until the early 1970s. "While I saw the practice of favorable treatment to foreigners as clearly unjust and it brought with it an uncomfortable feeling of disempowerment and a sense of being 'second class' in one's own newly coined 'home country,' the experience nonetheless prepared me for my future life abroad by giving me the strength and ability to adapt and not lose myself," said Anil, who later was able to clearly see this positive side effect of his own experience as India and its citizens awkwardly waded through the uncharted territory of the era. The same held true in clubs in other parts of India, such as the

Anil, right, with coach Yusuf Khan outside the CCI courts, c. 1962.

"whites only" Cricket Club, the Calcutta Swimming Club, and the Saturday Club in Calcutta, as well as one or two exclusive clubs in Madras and Delhi. The social scene of this period, in Anil's mind, was steeped in a "post-Colonial hangover," which left undertones of doubt about how to navigate this new phase of the country's history with a redefined sense of Indian identity.

"It was still a disjointed India, yet to come to grips with its reality and make it its own," Anil said. "However, I saw balance through my father's family businesses and the people he hired." The mills now operated by Anil's father and four of his uncles required expertise not easily available in India, and so their Bombay worsted plant, Castle Mills, brought in an Englishman, a Mr. Conroy, on a contract for a few years to help with the weaving part of production. "Mr. Conroy stayed at our apartment for a few months before relocating to a residence in Thane, near the mill," said Anil. "Soon after, a Mr. Bruscoli came from Italy for the spinning department. As I remember, his financial dealings were somewhat dubious and he may have left before his contract was over, so after that Mr. Werner, a real German gentleman, managed the new spinning plant. Here we were, in an affluent Indian home, hiring Europeans in an independent country that still allowed discrimination."

Amid this multicultural context, however, many aspects of Indian traditions continued to prevail in Anil's life at home. Never taking his own success for granted, Anil's paternal grandfather began to build a relationship with a trust in Punjab run by the Bawalalji group, a family of gurus, or *pandits*, known in the Gurdaspur district near Batala for their good deeds and social work in the community, to which he donated each year a certain percentage of profits from the business concerns to fund schools, infrastructure, hygiene, and general uplift of the area he had left behind in rural Punjab, where several relatives continued to dwell.

"I was fortunate enough to meet one of the leaders of the Bawalaji group, Mahant Ram Parkash Maharaj, a truly benevolent Brahmin priest with kind yet piercing black eyes," said Anil. "Everyone in the family would listen to him. He was our extended family's consigliere." In Bombay, however, the family's rapport with the Brahmin, or priestly, caste was less intimate—and not altogether easy. The *pandits*, who were often referred by friends of Anil's parents and came to the family's home at St. James Court, could roughly be divided into two categories: professional *pandits*, who performed rituals on auspicious days, like Diwali and Hindu new year, and at important events, such as marriages, *mundans*, births, and deaths; and astrologers, who would devise charts and predict the future.

Anil didn't think much of the former type of *pandit*, particularly the one chosen by his mother to perform rituals on holidays and at ceremonial events. "He just seemed shifty-eyed and greedy," said Anil. Yet, he managed to keep his distaste for this fellow quiet over the years, and the very same *pandit* oversaw his own Hindu marriage ceremony to me, his second wife, as well as that of his brother Vinod, also the second time around to his wife, Joanne, Anil's nephew Niki to his English wife, Samantha, and Anil's son Sanjay to his American wife, Amy Nicole. "My mother got a lot of comfort from his presence and from the fact that we were following the rituals as laid out by our Maharishis," he noted. Anil does have positive recollections, however, of the type of *pandit* in his family's sphere who would foretell their futures and were often consulted by business families before making investment decisions. Among the most memorable of this category of holy man was a dumb and deaf *pandit* who came to the Nayars' home for a span of ten years starting around 1960 and predicted that Anil would emerge as a champion player and travel around the world. "He always wrote on a small black slate with chalk and also predicted my life overseas," Anil said.

Anil also recalled some of the darker remnants of the Hindu social hierarchy as he saw it evolve during his youth. He was well aware that the members of his own family were *Kshatriyas*, the landowner class regarded as society's ruling and military elite and the second of the upper castes behind the *Brahmins*. Conscious of his place within this ancient social system, he witnessed its effects play out and slowly erode among his family members as they interacted with people of the lower rungs of the social order—the *Vaishyas*, who were merchants and traders, and the *Shudras*, who were unskilled workers and servants. While his father regularly worked with *Vaishyas*, who played critical roles in the distribution system of the family's business and purchased its goods to sell in cosmopolitan centers throughout India— from Bangalore, Calcutta, and Delhi to Kanpur, Lucknow, and Srinagar—his mother struggled somewhat with the *Shudras*, as well as the fifth caste, the *Dalits* or *achhoots*, who were seen as untouchables and are now referred to as the Scheduled caste and often continue to remain victims of extreme bias. "The ones who were ostracized were the *jamadars*, a subcaste of the untouchables known as the sweepers, and my mother made it a point to keep her distance from them when they came into the house to clean the bathrooms, especially when we were in Batala, where they would go to the lower levels to physically remove the excrement and put it into baskets that they would then carry out on their heads and transport to a pit nearby," Anil explained. "Early on after our move to Bombay, the sweepers always came into the apartment through the servants' winding staircase and entry. In those days, the older *jamadars* would walk away from us backwards and never show us their backs. But over time, Bombay's secular effect on my mother softened her stance toward sweepers, as well as Muslims, with whom she also had issues after partition. But both were later allowed to come through the front door to the apartment, and the sweepers eventually adjusted their behavior as society made progress toward a more egalitarian structure and the restrictive and inhumane barriers to social and economic access began breaking down."

A reset of interactions among Indians of varied religious backgrounds post-partition also had an impact on Anil that would shape his broader outlook. "Before partition my maternal grandfather's loyal servant was a Muslim," Anil said. "However, after partition, there was often talk of Muslims turning on their masters and Bauji did not want to take that risk, so soon after partition he was let go to both the relief and feelings of guilt by all those he had served. Muslims, I was often told in Batala and Amritsar, were the most loyal of workers and the deadliest of enemies." Indian Christians and Jews, on the other hand, were regarded in a much more hospitable and welcoming light, as were Parsis, Jains, and Sikhs. "Prominent Indian Jews were very important to our family business as distributors and sources of liquidity when we needed it," said Anil, who was also friendly with some of the children of the various Jewish families who lived in his family's building. "Christians, who often worked as employees in hospitals or in our family's household as help, were regarded with a feeling of trust." And these early perceptions of people of diverse backgrounds served as stepping stones to a cosmopolitan sense of open-mindedness that would become a central part of Anil's world view in the years ahead.

* * *

CHAPTER FIVE

The Golden Age of Indian Squash

For Anil and his fellow sportsmen, one of the handicaps of the '60s was the struggle to acquire adequate equipment to play sport—whether it was tennis racquets, cricket bats, golf clubs, or balls. The lexicon of squash is one of rails, boasts, and languid lobs, swift volleys, quick kills, and three-wall nicks, deft drop shots and deceptive reverse corners. To craft poetry with these motions, a player not only needs a coterie of highly honed skills—savvy, strength, speed, stamina, and style—but also the tools to execute them—shoes, racquets, and balls. When Anil was emerging as a player, however, India was going through a foreign exchange crisis, and scarce currency was required for essentials like energy, infrastructure, raw material imports, and, often due to unpredictable monsoons, for food grains, medicines, and medical equipment. Sports equipment was regarded as a non-priority item, especially for "frivolous" games like squash.

In those days, there were no Nike, Puma, Reebok, or Asics sneakers, only the indigenous canvas Bata shoes were available. In addition to not being easy to come by for logistical and economic reasons, the government also did not allow the import of racquets as they were supplied by Indian makers, such as Menzel, even though their products were subpar. Furthermore, the heat and humidity would take a toll on the racquets, which were then made of wood. And the racquet strings made of local guts would fray and often break. Restringing would cause the frames to weaken and a racquet might crack in just three or four weeks. To eke out a few more weeks of usage, the cracks would often be wrapped with more gut. Those who lived through that era also remember the limited number of Dunlop squash balls that were allowed to be imported. The license to import lay with India's Squash Rackets Association, which rationed out the balls to actual user clubs and institutions. Anil recalled that even the serious players relied on the few balls available long after they'd gone "bald" and sometimes patched them with tape to get an extra 15 minutes or so of play.

The Nayar family, c. 1962, (left to right) Vijay, Vinod, Asha, father Kanhyalal, mother Kailash, Anil.

While the Indian players made do with the balls, the racquets were much more personal, especially to the committed players. So even though the import of racquets was not permitted, itinerant travelers were always being requested to bring them back to India from abroad and resources would somehow be made available not just for squash racquets, but also tennis racquets, golf clubs, and cricket bats. Commercial currency was rationed out and restricted, and so much depended on the generosity of a friend or relative. As such, Lillywhites, which sold Grays of Cambridge, Dunlop, and Slazenger racquets on Piccadilly Circus in London, did brisk business. And so, quite frequently, did the Indian customs officers! As for shoes, Bata sneakers would have to do. No import was permissible at all. And inadequate shoes and improper sports gear as well as non-scientific training would cause significant wear and tear on the body (Anil noted that Yusuf Khan, later in Seattle, another younger fellow player, Ananth Nayak, now in California, Anil Kapur, currently in Washington D.C., and Naval Pandole, who remains in Bombay, are all now suffering from knee- and hip-related ailments as is Anil himself).

The CCI courts the young Indians played on were also rather rudimentary. As in the rest of the country, they had no air conditioning, only ceiling fans attached to a metal roof which absorbed the heat. "No matter the time of the year, the temperature varied from hot to hotter and humidity varied from 50 to 100 percent," said Anil. "As a result we all oozed sweat and during a match droplets of perspiration smattered all over the court, which generally were wiped off after a game. After a long game or match, our socks, shoes, shorts, shirts, and headbands were usually drenched. The English-made leather racquet grips were not designed to absorb that level of sweat, so wristbands were a must to prevent moisture from seeping into the grip. We also often wrapped the grips with torn bath towels to absorb even more sweat."

Despite the less-than-ideal context in which Anil emerged as a sportsman, he pressed on to face new challenges. After overcoming his brother Vijay in the friendly match at the CCI, he went on to play in various tournaments in western and central India, coming close to victory as a runner up in the western India junior tournaments to Cadet Narain in 1961 and to Sanjit Roy in 1963. He also played the men's national tournament in '63 and came in second to the then five-time prevailing champion Captain K.S. Jain, who like Narain, learned the game in the army cantonments where the earliest Indian players mastered the game as part of their fitness regimen. In the central India junior tournament in 1963, he played and prevailed over a player named Digvijay Singh, later building a "competitor" friendship with him for a time.

Anil credited his coach with giving him an edge in these matches. "Yusuf taught me and other fellow players, such as Fali Madon, Dinshaw Pandole, and Pheroze Contractor, classical play," said Anil, who also acknowledged his fellow players in helping him elevate his standard of play. "He gave us skills in positioning, balance, swing, and—to some extent—strategy." His practice with Khan began to pay off a year later. "I went off to a mid-level tournament in Indore, the central India championships, and entered both the boys under 18 and the men's events and won both tournaments," Anil remembered. "I came back home with a carton full of trophies and remember greeting my parents just after they had finished their morning tea, presented them with my box and told them I'd brought back a bunch of mangoes for them to enjoy. They had such a look of surprise when they opened the box and saw these large trophies." At this point, they weren't quite sure what to make of his squash fixation or his successes.

During these years, Anil's game was clearly ascending, yet he admitted that a few players in the draws always worried him—and Sanjit "Bunker" Roy was one of them. "Sanjit was a tall young man with a terrific reach who had learned to play mostly on his own and was therefore an unorthodox player," said Anil. "When he had a ball at the center or three-quarters deep in the court, he would often hide it with his body and there was no telling where the ball would go—down the line, cross court, or to the highly deceptive reverse corner. I was convinced that no one could beat him the first time they played him. And I didn't when I played him in 1962 and '63. Sanjit hit those reverse corners so quickly and deceptively off his forehand that, unless you were ready for it, you were caught flat footed."

Seeing Anil's trouble with Roy, his coach Yusuf Khan noted that Roy adjusted his thick grip each time he hit a backhand and urged Anil to try to make him uncomfortable by hitting a few deep forehands and then a quick shot to his backhand to extract an error or a loose ball by doing so. After observing him hit the reverse corner from the same position again and again, Roy's deceptiveness became predictable, and Anil soon learned to sprint to the front of the court and counterattack quickly with a drop, hard cross-court, or parallel shot and eventually he beat Roy in a semi-final match in the western India/all-India junior tournament in 1964 before moving on to the final where he triumphed over Fali Madon to win the championship title.

Once he started winning matches, Anil admitted he began to reinforce this streak with superstitious gestures. "During tournament times, I made sure I had the same racquet, same grip, same socks, and same wristband as I did for my previous win," he said. "That usually meant doing some hand-washing overnight for the next day's match, an arduous task if one was traveling. I remembered the Samson and Delilah tale, so I also never cut my hair or shaved. And sex (not that we had choice in those days) was taboo—it took away the focus, vigor, strength, and adrenaline required to win a match. And of course, no alcohol—not that it was available to us in the early 1960s anyway!"

Ultimately, 1964 turned out to be a transformative year for Anil. While nursing a fractured left hand in a plaster after getting hit with a stick playing field hockey, he also faced down K.S. Jain, who by then had upped his rank from captain to major and had reigned supreme in Indian squash for six years. Anil's earlier matches laid a strong foundation for the prestige battle he fought against Major Jain during the western India/all-India men's tournament held simultaneously with the junior tournament at the CCI that year. He had done enough to merit being the favorite for the junior version of the championships, which he'd won against Madon. But, in the senior's tournament, this privilege was firmly in the court of the older Major Jain (Anil was just 17 years old at the time). Over a six-year period, the army player had won everything in sight. So where does an opening lie? "He was fit, strong, consistent, and, to my advantage, a predictable and risk-averse player," said Anil. "I was the opposite—fast enough to create a crisis and benefit by it."

According to Anil's fellow squash player Naval Pandole, who witnessed the entire match, "Lucky went in as the underdog, but we all kept hoping a miracle would happen." And while from the beginning the Major did a good job of consistently pushing Anil around the court, the younger player amazingly managed to hold his own and the first game went to Anil. Yet it was apparent during the one-minute break that the effort had not taken much out of Jain. Anil was flat out on the cool cement floor struggling to get his pulse back to normal and gathering his breath. So at that point, Khan exhorted his ward by saying, "S*abber se*," (Play patiently).

The second game was packed with drama. "Major Jain had Lucky running all over the court—from one corner to the other, from one side wall to the other," said Pandole. But after taking heed of Khan's advice, Anil played the long points and got into rallying, thus containing errors. He was determined to play one point at a time so that he would not entertain, prematurely, thought of possible victory and instead remained focused. In one rally, however, the Major held the upper hand and, when he saw Anil pinned to the back corner after the junior player made a weak shot to the front wall, he opted to reply with a drop shot in the opposite front corner knowing that the ball would be virtually impossible for Anil to retrieve. "Well, that's the end of that point," Pandole remembered thinking. "But something happened and Lucky decided to take off, to take the chance that maybe the drop wouldn't be good," said Pandole. "And not only did he take off, but he also reached the ball and slammed it back as an outright winner." Major Jain then turned to the gallery with his jaw dropped in disbelief only to see the crowd burst into laughter and applause and thereby affirm the reality of the junior player's astonishing feat. "It was a huge turning point," said Pandole. "From that point on, Major Jain was mentally destroyed, his body language changed, he knew that he was a beaten man." And Anil staggered off the court after winning game two and collapsed once again on the cold cement floor outside the court, breathing hard. "I wondered if the Major's pulse rate was around 80, compared to mine, which felt like 180!" he said.

Now came the crunch—Anil kept up the rallies with consistent aggression and shot making. His game had ascended to a whole other level, and, maintaining the momentum, he readily clinched the match in the third game. "Anil beat the Major convincingly," said Pandole's brother Dinshaw, another fellow player eight years Anil's senior who also witnessed the tournament. "That match dispelled any notion of the Major's invincibility." The match also marked a turning point in the history of Indian squash: It was the very first time a junior player would win both the junior and senior national titles in the same tournament in the very same year.

Anil has been asked innumerable times whether he would consider the successes of later years as closely related to remarkably dethroning a seasoned opponent. "Yes, it was a spring leap to another level of confidence and play," he said, noting the match proved to be another important turning point in his career. "Words can't describe the elated feeling you have after a tournament win. It's as if you have conquered the world, especially after the first few victories. Though there was a release of all this pent-up energy, as after most wins, my body was still pumping so much adrenaline that I could not sleep the night of the victory." An offhand compliment from his coach—"*Tu Hashim ke jaise bhagta hai,*" meaning "You run like Hashim"—also did much to elevate

Anil's sense of confidence after this match, for Hashim Khan, the patriarch of the stellar Pakistani Khan dynasty and arguably the greatest squash player of all time, was the idol of all young squash players, especially on the subcontinent, at the time. "It was the best compliment Yusuf could have paid to me after my win against Major Jain—I don't know if Yusuf realized the effect it had on me," he said. "That—and the surprise win—gave me a huge boost of confidence."

A side effect of this victory: After Anil had managed to dent the invulnerability of Major Jain, Sanjit Roy, Anil's peer and formidable foe, also managed to get the better of the army player in the same tournament the following year. And Dinshaw Pandole later overtook him in a playoff match, gaining him a place on the Indian team along with Anil, Sanjit Roy, and Fali Madon when they would later play in Australia and New Zealand in 1967 and beat Pakistan for the first time in Sydney.

* * *

CHAPTER SIX

England and the Drysdale Cup

Given the shortcomings of equipment on the one hand and the severe government control of sports on the other, it's hard to imagine an athlete embracing a sport like squash in India in the mid-1960s. Yet, such limitations did little to stop Anil and his fellow player Fali Madon from excelling at their chosen sport. And it was amid this environment that the two young players were selected by the Squash Rackets Association of India (later renamed the Squash Rackets Federation of India) to go to the U.K. to get foreign tournament experience in 1965. Madon had aged out of the junior group and so would play a few local men's tournaments, while Anil, at the age of 18, was to focus on the Drysdale Cup tournament in London, then regarded as the world championship event for junior players.

The tournament itself was envisioned by all-round sportsman and Cambridge graduate Dr. Theodore Drysdale, who was said to have had a "bee in his bonnet about juniors" when he joined the exclusive Royal Automobile Club in 1919. The RAC's then rather new clubhouse in Pall Mall, which opened in 1911, housed three squash courts and Drysdale not only won the RAC's first open championship held there the year he joined, but also went on to become one of England's leading amateurs as well as the first honorary secretary of the Squash Rackets Representative Committee of the Tennis and Rackets Association, then the organizing body for the sport in the U.K. Widely regarded as the "grandfather" of British junior squash, Drysdale was prepared to donate a trophy for the junior championship event he attempted to organize with a sub-committee he chaired in 1925. Although Drysdale died unexpectedly before the tournament became a reality, a group of thoughtful friends put together a considerable sum of money for a fine silver trophy now known in his memory as the Drysdale Cup, which was first awarded to C.J. Wilson at the inaugural competition hosted by the RAC in its Pall Mall clubhouse in 1926, the year after Drysdale's death.

In his book *A Celebration of 100 Years of Squash at Pall Mall*, British squash player and author John Hopkins described the Cup as "the most magnificent-looking trophy of them all." The spectacular trophy continues to be awarded each year, Hopkins wrote, "to the winner of what has come to be known as the premier boys' annual event in the world—the under 19 competition at the British Junior Open Championships." The four-sided trophy is "well over a foot high," and "is much bigger and much heavier, for example, than the claret jug given in golf to winners of the open, the oldest professional major championship in the game."

So this is the prize that Anil would be vying for as he prepared to set out for England to play at the Royal Automobile Club, where the tournament would be played. Anil remembered that there were strong opinions in the squash circles that approval by the Indian government for the pair of players was pushed through by one Mr. Ahmed Peermohamed, then the secretary of the Squash Rackets Association of India, who, although a scion of a wealthy business family, might also have been motivated by the prospect of his own government-paid trip to hobnob with the renowned British squash official John Horry and do some pub crawling, or so thought the young squash players. So alongside the two youngsters was the official, and thus it was that the precious foreign exchange for the three was made available for their excursion.

London of the 1960s has more literature on it than the entire era stretching from Dickensian darkness to the Victorian Puritanism. It was the time when English rock bands like the Beatles and the Rolling Stones were winning plaudits for belting out variations of the rhythm and blues of the American black musicians, such as Muddy Waters, John Lee Hooker, Chuck Berry, and Jimmy Reed, who inspired them. The Pop Art movement, largely a British and American phenomenon defined by icons like Andy Warhol, Roy Lichtenstein, Jasper Johns, and David Hockney, was well underway with the vanguard appropriating images from the street and supermarkets and presenting them in their art. The British artist Richard Hamilton, who incorporated magazine imagery in his collages, defined the movement as "popular, transient, expendable, low-cost, mass-produced, young, witty, sexy, gimmicky, glamorous, and Big Business," to stress its everyday, commonplace values. The first of the James Bond series of movies—with Sean Connery starring as the international man of mystery—were hitting the big screen, which set the swinging tone of '60s British cinema and heralded London's emergence as the epicenter of hip music, fashion, and art. It was the Mad Men era, when mini skirts, colored tights, and thigh-high boots redefined the fashion of the day.

There was another rather forgettable part of London life in those days that Anil was conscious of. Apart from the RAC, which would serve as the tournament's venue and which he described as "aloof, white, and proper," there were distinct racist attitudes prevailing in Britain, where Indians and other non-European foreigners were often lumped under the categorization of "coloureds." Newsagents and other retail outlets where residences for foreigners were universally advertised would follow ads for "bedsitter available" or "room for short let" with phrases like "no coloured please" or "white only." This largely affected the student community with the shortage of student accommodations in the big city and, of course, could also trouble short-term visitors like Anil and Madon, but they had already looked after their lodging and arranged to stay in a hostel. This trend would largely disappear in the aftermath of the D'Oliveira affair and the brouhaha surrounding the mixed-race cricket player, Basil D'Oliveira, who had been selected to represent England in a series to be played in South Africa in 1968, and the noisy anti-apartheid movement. And of course, in the years ahead, there were strict anti-racism laws passed by Parliament under Harold Wilson's Labour government to ensure that Britain did not follow in the footsteps of South Africa.

Indeed, the old English world was ending as Sir Winston Churchill passed into history and the pretty young monarch Queen Elizabeth had become the new, if still relatively traditional, symbol of the times. Yet it was the stuffier, old-school world of England that would hold more direct sway over Anil's experience there. But that world would soon begin to change, too, thanks in part to his own presence—and spectacular accomplishment—in one of its hallowed halls.

After traveling to England on his first trip abroad aboard a newly acquired Boeing 707 Air India aircraft, Anil and Madon got their first taste of the British cold shoulder upon their arrival at the elite members-only Royal Automobile Club, where they were quickly turned away after showing up at the door to ask for permission for practice time at the courts. As it turned out, they weren't the only ones who were barred from entering the courts before the match. Chris Orriss, an English squash player, who also played in the tournament that year and is currently the vice chairman of the squash committee at the RAC, said he, too, was prohibited from practicing on the courts ahead of the match as only members were allowed. "It was my first excursion to London from Yorkshire and my first visit to the RAC, which was quite an adventure for a young lad from the hinterland," said Orriss, who lost in an early round of the tournament in 1965 yet emerged as the winner and claimed the Drysdale Cup the following year. "I remember going to the club the night before and being struck by the fact that it was quite formal and stuffy, requiring a jacket and tie—it was also a men's only club at the time. It was a period of post-colonization, and these kinds of clubs were still discriminating against everyone, especially females, and only members were allowed in the pool as there was no requirement to wear swimsuits—it was truly a male sanctum that is anachronistic nowadays."

As an Indian, Anil remembered never feeling altogether at ease in England on this particular journey, yet the road to the top of British squash tournaments for foreigners had already been paved by an elder from his part of the world—the legendary squash player Hashim Khan, the first Pakistani to win the men's British open squash championship tournament in 1951 after a string of Egyptians had held the number one spot since 1932.

To Anil's good fortune, his brother Vijay was then studying at Southampton University and was friendly with another Pakistani squash player, Sharif Khan, Hashim's son, who arranged for the Indian visitors to practice at the New Grampians courts, run by Sharif's uncle Azam Khan. As it turned out, another stellar player, Jonah Barrington, also happened to be at the courts while the two young Indians were there, and Anil was able to benefit from an additional stroke of good fortune by practicing a few games with the legendary Irish player and subsequently with Sharif Khan, who later emerged as a star player himself. So although these courts weren't quite the same as those they were designated to play on, the two young squash players did get in some quality practice time before the big event.

The day the tournament began Anil admitted he felt a certain sense of hostility and aloofness in the air as he went into the first round match. "Arriving at the Club the day of the tournament, I felt like a fish out of water," he said. "I didn't know the protocol and felt we were strangers and we weren't made to feel comfortable. I kept thinking of the colonial era and, even though this was a post-colonial time, I had apprehensions about being in England. London was uncomfortable to say the least, but part of it may have been due to my own lack of understanding about English social norms. I was looking out to be slighted at every exchange that would validate my complex." An article about the tournament in an issue of *British Lawn Tennis and Squash* magazine written by John Horry, the prominent English squash promoter and writer who was secretary of the Squash Rackets Association at the time, made note of Anil's outsider status and the low expectations for his performance, stating that "Nayar was something of a dark horse and was not in consequence seeded." Nevertheless, he managed to breeze through the first four rounds without dropping a single game. Bryan Patterson, who had won the tournament the year before and was expected to win again, lost in a semi-final match to Warwick Sabey. And, as Anil was rather easily knocking off his competitors round after round, Orriss recalled that many were getting the clear sense that he would play Sabey in the final round and take the top prize.

But Anil's semi-final match against Philip Goodwin wasn't as effortless as the other rounds had been. Once on the court, his discomfort continued unabated. "In no game at that stage was I confident of winning," he said. The reporter on the tournament summed up the match as follows:

> "Goodwin, having lost only 10 points in four rounds, was possibly short of worthwhile opposition. Certainly the Indian played beautiful squash to win the first game, but lapsed into errors the second. His greater variety of shots brought him to match ball in the fourth and in all he reached this enviable position no less than five times before Goodwin squared the match."

The particularly vexing problem for Anil at this point was the fact that his opponent was habitually obstructing him from making a shot instead of following the rules and stepping aside to allow

Anil a clear path to the ball. "I came 7,000 miles on government money and I can't lose because the guy I'm playing is unfair," Anil remembered thinking at the time. "It's a testament to the game of squash itself that it usually brings out the best in players, not just in terms of their level of play, but also as a reflection of their sense of fairness and ethics," said Anil as he considered how seldom he encountered players who were inclined to cheat. "There are plenty of opportunities, with or without a referee, to pick up balls after double bounces, to dispute an obvious red line fault, to purposely come in an opponent's way to distract him, or to move away just a bit slowly after hitting the ball to prevent an opponent from setting up in time for his turn to strike. Surprisingly, with two players playing their hearts out in such close quarters, the unfairness of play is minimal. And in a tournament, a marker and referee are there to call out unfair or fault play." But when a referee cannot or does not see a particular event of unfairness, such as not clearing after striking the ball as was happening here, the offended player's only remedy is to lift his racquet and turn to the referee and say, "Let please." The ref then either awards a replay or a stroke, or he denies it.

After requesting a let once or twice and getting denied as his opponent continued with this unsportsmanlike form of play, Anil finally took matters into his own hands and directly cautioned the player to move out of the way to allow him a clear approach to the ball. "The officials still were not able to 'see' that I was being affected, so the other least attractive option to ensure you're granted your right of way is to hit your opponent with the ball until both he and the officials realize that there is a problem that needs to be addressed in the spirit of the sport," Anil explained. "And at that point, I told my opponent, 'The next time you come in my way, I'm going to hit you with the ball.'" But Goodwin kept up with his obstruction strategy, leaving Anil with no choice but to hit him with the ball, softly the first time and harder the next. "I had to hit him a couple of times to get the points," Anil said, noting the ref eventually duly acknowledged the rules of fair play when Anil wasn't given right of way and gave him the points. Ultimately, Goodwin got the message, and according to the writer "there was never any doubt about the fifth game in which Nayar reeled off winner after winner" in a match that lasted for an hour and a quarter. "I got a lot stronger in my head after that," Anil said.

Warwick Sabey, the finalist from the other half, was described as "an intelligent player whose boasts are a delight to watch." So one-sided was the final, however, that the writer could only say that Sabey "defended stubbornly and at least showed us that he possessed a good drop shot." But he was compelled to state that Anil's opponent "had not the pace of shot to cope with the severe attack launched by the Indian and was in consequence almost entirely on the defensive," adding that the "final was brief and the result never in doubt...once Nayar had completed his softening up programme, he proceeded in the third game to show a bewildering variety of brilliant strokes which had his opponent helpless" and enabled him to clinch the match.

History had been made! Anil was the first Indian to win the coveted Drysdale Cup. When I asked if strategy played a role in

Anil, after winning the Drysdale Cup, the trophy for what was then the world junior championship tournament, in 1965.

his ultimate win, or if he just played his heart out, he remembered the result being more about heart. "I had never seen foreigners play before and never played with one, so it was really a matter of hunger," said Anil. "I'd done hundreds of hours of work and hit the same drop shot hundreds of times, and I was strong and so quick at the time that I felt I could practically climb the walls. But I also had the feeling of vulnerability without a lot of time for correction, so I knew I just had to do my best."

For support, a British friend named Collin McAndrews, who worked in the British Consulate in Bombay, came to watch him play in the tournament. After Anil won the final, McAndrews, who was a member of the Royal Automobile Club and something of a contrarian, rushed up to him, grabbed the Cup, and said, "Let's show these guys." Together they proceeded with Madon to the club's lobby where McAndrews filled the Cup with champagne, and all drank together from the massive trophy to celebrate Anil's extraordinary triumph. "I never really drank much alcohol before that day, so I woke up the next day with the worst hangover of my life," admitted Anil, who had also just achieved the greatest victory of his life.

Three months after the tournament, Aziz Currimbhoy, a respected Indian sports journalist of the time, got around to writing an account of Anil's win in *The Current* under a screaming headline—"Anil Nayar—India's Best Squash Player—Wins Celebrated DRYSDALE CUP"—spread across three columns. "So good is Anil and so easily did he win the Drysdale Cup that he has actually been invited by the authorities to come back to England and participate in the All-England Open Championship to be played at the end of the year," he wrote. "Whether he goes or not depends on first his studies and secondly the Education and Foreign Ministries." The writer went on to explain the justification by the Squash Rackets Association of India to send Peermohamed as manager, stating that the secretary had made a convincing case that "youngsters are high spirited and lacked the know-how of correct behavior in tournaments, especially abroad. In foreign lands, the glamour life is so totally different that boys do need guidance," Peermohamed was reported to have said. Currimbhoy noted that both boys had later been invited to play in Stockholm and Amsterdam as well, and also received an invitation to play from the King of Greece, a great squash enthusiast, but had to turn these invitations down, as they had permission from the Indian government only to play in England. In those days, nothing could be taken for granted when it concerned overseas travel.

The same year that Anil won the Drysdale Cup, the producer-director team of Indian-born Ismail Merchant and American James Ivory released a poignant film in the U.S. called "Shakespeare Wallah," which cemented their relationship with the notable author and screenwriter Ruth Prawer Jhabvala. Loosely based on a true story about a traveling family theater troupe of English actors who perform Shakespeare plays in towns across India amidst diminishing demand for their work and the rise of Bollywood, the picture revolves around the short-lived love story between Lizzie Buckingham, an English actress in the troupe played by Felicity Kendal, and an Indian playboy, Sanju, portrayed by the stellar Indian actor Shashi Kapoor. (In real life Kapoor fell in love with and married the actress's sister, Jennifer Kendal, and the couple later became close to Anil's brother Vinod and his first wife, Gunna.) A review in *The New York Times* applauded the film's delicate portrayal of the transformative cross-continental currents flowing around the world at the time, noting that the story "managed to convey a countless number of strong implications and subtle hints that quiver with irony, sadness and benign resignation to change."

Inevitably, perhaps, some of the bittersweet chords struck in this offbeat film would not only resonate with Anil's own experiences of the crumbling traditions in India and England, but also in America, where broader cultural changes would soon affect his life in ways hitherto unimaginable to his adventure-seeking forebears.

* * *

PART THREE

1965-1971:
American Dream

CHAPTER SEVEN

Harvard

Not unlike upper crust British boys, whose lives are chalked out for them—starting with an education at Eton or Harrow followed by Oxford or Cambridge and then by a career in finance, banking, commerce, or politics, a flat in Belgravia, polo, exclusive clubs like White's, Brooks's, or the Royal Automobile Club, country weekends in the Scottish Highlands, fox hunts, and lots of Bertie Wooster-style adventures—there was also plenty of pre-destination for boys born into the elite, wealthy families in India's Punjab—such as registration on the day one is born at Doon School (or other such institutions gifted by colonial rulers) followed by a choice of college at St. Stephen's in Delhi or the further-afield Military Academy in Dehra Dun or, for those so inclined, Oxford or Cambridge in England. And, whether you were the son of a wealthy landowner, a prince of Jaipur, Gandhi, Jinnah, or Nehru (who, in fact, began his British education at Harrow School, the British boarding school for boys where the sport of squash was born in the 1870s), many years would likely also be spent in mother England, acquiring the British mannerisms, accent, and way of life.

In contrast, however, to the predictable progress of an Indian boy from a well-to-do Punjabi family in the mid-20th century, so much of Anil's childhood experience had been shaped by the winds of chance following partition. So, instead of boarding school at Bishop Cotton or Doon in north India, he attended the cosmopolitan Cathedral School in Bombay. And by the time he traveled to England to play in the Drysdale Cup tournament, he had enrolled in Sydenham College of Commerce and Economics, the oldest business college in Asia and affiliated with the University of Bombay (now Mumbai), where he saw the quality of his education as a step down from the schooling he'd received at Cathedral.

Inspired by his siblings, who had all been encouraged by his parents to get an elite international education in the U.K., Anil also had set his sights on attending college at a top academic institution outside the country. Following his graduation from Cathedral, he had applied to Cambridge but was asked to wait a year before being admitted, and so spent his first year at the Bombay business college, which is located on B Road. Sydenham was one of the best commerce colleges in India. Prominent businessmen, government sector economists, chartered accountants, politicians, and some very famous actors and actresses (remember it is in Bollywood country) graduated from the college mostly with B.A. degrees in economics but also with Masters degrees in commerce. "But as respected as Sydenham was then, the teaching level was just not the same as at Cathedral," said Anil, recalling his dissatisfaction with the quality of his undergraduate education there. "The professors, although quite experienced in their field of work, just did not expect nor did they get the same level of respect that the teachers at Cathedral received. Perhaps it was their vernacular accent or their dress, or perhaps it was because they were teaching in a government college and saw themselves as government servants who were dispensable cogs in a large bureaucracy."

As a result, many students did not take their studies seriously and often relied on other classmates, who saw an opportunity to generate income from their less academically inclined peers, to sit in for them at class. Attendance was required of the 40-45 students in each class and their presence was confirmed with a standard roll call. Knowing the professors proceeded with this exercise as a bureaucratic routine and rarely looked up while names were called, students soon realized that others could respond for them, enabling them to skip class without detection. "Thus was born the title of 'Proxy King,'" Anil said. "There were a couple of boys sitting somewhere in the middle of the classroom, answering 'Present,' for six or seven other students in voices that imitated those they represented, including a couple of girls. It wasn't a culture of learning then, but of passing time in class and, at the end of four years, getting a certificate—though I did get a First Class for the first-year exam."

Disenchanted with his local college and eager and to move on with his life, Anil decided to take matters into his own hands. Still intrigued by the possibilities of broader international experience in squash—bolstered, of course, by his recent win of the Drysdale Cup—as well as the benefits of an education abroad, he turned to his coach Yusuf Khan for guidance on how he might pursue an education in America. Though he knew little about Ivy League universities in the U.S., he'd heard about Harvard, Yale, and Penn, and with Khan's help, Anil said, "We hatched a plan on how to go about getting me into one of them."

As luck would have it, his coach's connection to Mohibullah Khan, another of the legendary Pakistani Khans who dominated the squash world at the time, turned out to be critical to his access to Harvard. Mohibullah, who was indirectly related to Yusuf, had met President John F. Kennedy during an exhibition match at the Pentagon squash courts in 1962 and later was introduced to Kennedy's brother Ted, who enabled Khan to secure his position as the squash professional at the Harvard Club in Boston. Yusuf sent him a letter written in Pashto, which Mohibullah then translated and shared with a member of the club, who subsequently suggested that Anil send his own letter. This was a time when Harvard was one of the few Ivy League universities developing a more culturally diverse student body in the wake of the civil rights movement that unfolded across America throughout the 1960s. So with a prompt from Mohibullah, Anil wrote his own letter addressed to the admissions committee and sent it to the Harvard Club coach, who later forwarded it to his contact to deliver to Eric Cutler, a Harvard admissions committee member.

Within a very short period of time—thanks in equal parts to chance, Anil's squash talent, and the good offices of Khan and Cutler—a new twist of fate would once more alter the course of the young sportsman's life in a direction he'd barely begun to consider. It was as if destiny were making the big decisions on where he would go and whom he would meet and he was chipping in with his sporting brilliance and the hard work that admission to any top university entails. Cutler followed up with a letter to Anil and explained that he'd need to take the SAT tests before being considered for admission. After learning that Anil scored reasonably well on the SATs, Cutler sent Anil the admissions form and Anil told his parents, who were puzzled by his plans, that he was going to mail in his application to Harvard. Since the Indian government did not allow any foreign currency exchange for undergraduate students, Anil came up against another hurdle: He wouldn't be able to pay for his tuition unless he could get a scholarship. Back in touch with Cutler, Anil recalled him saying, "We'll see about a scholarship if you come, but to qualify you'd have to do some part-time work," to which Anil readily agreed. Then, in June of 1965, Anil received a telegram from Harvard, which stated he'd been accepted and the term would start in September.

After a send off by a group of squash buddies and schoolmates who joined him en masse at the airport to wish him well before he departed for the states that fall, Anil landed at JFK airport in New York before transferring to another flight to Boston where he got his first taste of America as he traveled to Harvard in Cambridge in a taxi cab. "It was dusk and the fall chill had set in," he said. "As I traveled along illuminated Mount Auburn Street, I peered down the small dark lanes that intersected it at right angles and

Anil, surrounded by friends and coach Yusuf Khan (to Anil's left) and his brother Vinod (whose hand is on Anil's head) at the airport, before leaving for Harvard in 1965.

noticed the dimly lit, low rows of houses with a few modern highrises stretching up behind them. It was very strange. I had never seen this type of architectural scenery. My experience of residential buildings revolved around South Bombay's Art Deco buildings, which were ideally suited to a place with plenty of air and light and contrasted with the city's older British colonial structures, such as the majestic Victoria Terminus and the Rajabai Clock Tower. Here in Cambridge, the smaller brick structures were just the opposite and designed without verandas and with smaller windows to protect their occupants from the snow and cold that dominated much of the year."

Upon entering his dormitory room in Strauss Hall at the perimeter of Harvard Yard, a grassy open space surrounded by a collection of mostly 18th- and 19th-century redbrick buildings at the heart of the university's campus, Anil had only a limited grasp of the history of the elite institution that lay before him. He knew that it was widely regarded as the top university in the world and one among a small group of colleges in the northeast known as the Ivy League, a term said to have stemmed from the custom of students of America's older colleges of planting ivy in front of their buildings each spring. But it wasn't until after he'd arrived that he learned it was the oldest university in the nation, the first institution of higher learning in the British colonies and founded by the clergyman John Harvard in 1636. He didn't know that its alumni included several U.S. presidents, dozens of heads of state, and scores of Nobel laureates, Pulitzer Prize winners, Olympic medalists, and founders of companies around the world. He wasn't aware that the nickname of its athletic teams was Harvard Crimson or that its motto was Veritas, the Latin word for Truth. Nor did he realize how unusual his presence on campus would be—he was the only Indian from the subcontinent in his class and just the second person from India to play on the Harvard squash team (the first was Muggy Mugaseth, a Parsi cricketer who also participated on the squash team in the early 1950s). Viewing the university from the eyes of an outsider, Anil would soon learn how access into an elite institution like Harvard shaped the sense of privilege among his American classmates and, in turn, would influence the trajectories of their lives as well as his own.

Indeed, little about Anil's life was conventional to this point and his entree into Harvard was no exception. A week after he'd arrived, J. Dinsmore (Dinny) Adams, then a senior and the captain of Harvard's squash team, was one of the first of his college mates to meet him—and in a most surprising way. "It was September 1965, my senior year—at that time Harvard had freshmen playing on their own separate team," remembered Adams. "I was slated to be Harvard's weakest varsity number one in many years, so I started playing as soon as I got to Cambridge. Jack Barnaby was then both the squash and tennis coach, and in September he still worked down at the tennis facility across the Charles River at the other end of the Harvard campus. I went down there to speak with Jack and he told me that John, the custodian at Hemenway gym, Harvard's squash facility, reported to him, 'There was some freshman kid from India at Hemenway who could really hit 'em,' and he wanted to know if I knew who he was. I replied, 'No, but I'll find out.' The next time I practiced at Hemenway I asked John about him, and he said, 'The guy's been on the court for half an hour.' So I just waited and watched. It was in court three, the lefthand gallery court, and Anil was hitting the ball around by himself. I was amazed by his fast speed and flexibility as well as his ability to hit the ball with great pace. And Barnaby didn't know he was in the school!" Anil and Barnaby later learned that Cutler had kept his admission a secret from Barnaby as a way to have a little fun with him. "Imagine getting into Harvard as the butt of a joke," said Anil. "Well, I did and I felt complimented! That, in a sense, was quintessential Harvard—it could always lighten up on its serious self."

Though nothing like it had happened before or since, Anil's path to America—and to one of the greatest universities in the world—was duly noted by his fellow Indians and emulated by some, including his friend Anil Kapur, who applied to Penn at Anil's urging, as well as a younger generation of Indian squash players, such as Dinesh Nayak, who also went to Penn, and Adrian Ezra, who later played on the Harvard team in the 1990s. It also served as a wakeup call to squash coaches, who soon began to refine their recruiting strategies to attract top caliber foreign players to enhance their teams. And while it is now commonplace to find players from all over the world on college teams, at the time Anil's admission to Harvard—as well as his subsequent introduction to Harvard's head squash coach, Jack Barnaby—was so unusual that his tale has become something of the stuff of legend, particularly in squash circles, and is regularly recounted by alumni and sports reporters, who have retold it in various iterations in journals and books. American squash player and writer Rob Dinerman, for example, described the story in his book *A History of Harvard Squash 1922-2010*:

> It really WAS "news"... and a sign of how much has changed in the ... half century since 1965, that Barnaby didn't even know of Nayar's existence, much less his remarkable pre-Harvard accomplishments prior to learning about them from Adams. By contrast, [today] every current college squash coach meticulously monitors junior tournament results all around the world online and carefully calculates which players to recruit. It would be unheard of today for a great American- or foreign-born junior player to simply materialize without fanfare on campus as an out-of-the-blue gift to a major squash power, as happened...in the case of Nayar, who in addition to his superlative physical skills, possessed a dazzling smile, impeccable court manners and an ingratiating personality that swiftly endeared him to everyone in the Harvard squash community.

Rather than "ingratiating," those who know Anil well would likely use a different adjective to describe his personality—"charming," certainly, or "playful," or "genuinely curious" more readily come to mind. In any case, another variation on the tale of Anil's introduction to the Harvard squash scene appeared in a piece written by Craig Lambert in a 1997 edition of *Harvard* magazine:

> Let us begin with a period piece: a story that was startling when it happened, but today would be beyond startling because it could not occur. In the fall of 1965, at freshman registration, Jack Barnaby, '32, the head coach of tennis and squash, sat behind his table at Memorial Hall, hoping to interest these freshmen in racquet sports. A young man who had come to Harvard from Bombay, India, approached and greeted Barnaby politely in British-accented English: "My name is Anil Nayar

and I would like to try out for the squash team." The coach learned that Nayar had played squash, and invited him to Hemenway Gymnasium to hit a few balls and talk further. At the gym Barnaby asked Nayar if he had played competitively. The freshman said yes and Barnaby inquired, "How did you make out?"

"I won," was the simple reply.

"Oh, were you the junior champion of India?" Barnaby asked.

"I have been the men's champion of India," Nayar explained, "for the past two years."

After Barnaby recovered his composure, he assured Nayar—who went on to play number 1 for Harvard and won the national intercollegiate singles championship three times—that there was a red carpet in the squash office and he would be glad to roll it out at any time. Later, Barnaby asked the admissions officer why they had kept the young champion a secret. "We thought you'd find it a pleasant surprise," was the answer.

While Anil enjoyed reading Lambert's variation on his story—he noted for the record, the factual inaccuracy claimed by the reporter in one of his quotes, clarifying that he had been both the men's and junior champion of India in 1964, rather than the men's winner for the past two years. Also, Anil recalled that his first acquaintance with the squash community at Harvard actually occurred on the day his two roommates, Michel Scheinmann and Steve Devereux, arrived at their dormitory room at Strauss Hall. Having flown in from India and settled in a week earlier than the other students in order to fulfill his obligations on the dorm crew, the cleaning team he was to work with as a condition of his scholarship, Anil had already chosen the best room for himself by the time his roommates arrived.

"Steve and I played tennis together in high school, since we were at Phillips, and you could choose your roommates at Harvard, so since we knew each other we chose to room together, but we knew we would have another roommate," said Michel Scheinmann, who remembered entering his dorm room for the first time and being curious about who his other roommate might be. "Anil wasn't there when we arrived and he had already claimed the single room for himself, so we had to share a room with bunk beds. But we looked around at his stuff, and saw a book in Hindi, I think it was the *Bhaghvad Gita*, and being somewhat provincial, I thought, *Oh my God, we're going to get some crazy intellectual student as a third roommate*. Then I opened the book and saw his name and saw that it was foreign. I pronounced it 'Anal Nay-er' and thought, *It might be a difficult year*. Looking around some more I saw his squash racquets and thought, *Maybe it won't be so bad after all*. Then, to my relief, shows up a handsome young Indian with jet black hair and pearly white teeth. And I said to him, 'I see you play squash.' He flashed his pearly white teeth and responded with a British-tinged Indian lilt, "A little."

After his initial introduction to these two players, Anil remembered meeting his Harvard squash coach, Jack Barnaby, the next day at an orientation event at Memorial Hall, when he introduced himself to the coach and explained that he was a squash player. Barnaby responded with some pleasantries and Anil believed the exchange didn't really register with the coach until the next time he met him at Hemenway. When Anil met Barnaby again at the courts the next day and repeated his interest in playing, Barnaby said, "'We'll get you a game or two,' and then directed me to a squash court to hit some balls by myself," according to Anil. It was there that he remembered catching the eye of Dinny Adams. With Adams' insistence, Barnaby decided to take a peek. "Everyone was playing with hard Cragin-Simplex balls, which were totally different than the soft balls I was used to, so I was over-swinging," explained Anil. "As a freshman, I couldn't play for the varsity team at that time, but at that point Jack and Corey Wynn, the assistant coach, took interest in me and after that I got the attention I needed to adapt to the hardball game."

The following day, Anil's squash circle expanded when Dinny Adams stopped by the freshman's dorm room. "Dinny was a well-known figure on campus and everyone looked up to him and respected him, especially the tennis and squash players from Andover," said Anil. Adams, who was then the captain of the team at Harvard also had been the captain of the squash team at Phillips Academy, the Massachusetts prep school also known as Andover that Scheinmann and Devereux had also attended. "Since we knew him, we were surprised to learn that he wasn't coming to visit us, but instead to see Anil," Scheinmann said. "I then realized what Anil had said earlier about his squash abilities must have been on the modest side or Dinny wouldn't be coming to check on him. Jack Barnaby had probably asked Dinny to drop in on Anil to see how he was acclimatizing." Feeling fortunate to have the interest of a big man on campus, Anil welcomed his presence. "If Dinny didn't like someone he wouldn't have anything to do with them, but because he liked me, I started to like him, too," said Anil, noting that over time Dinny would become like a protective older brother as well as an important friend.

Since the squash season didn't start until a couple of months after the school year began, Anil had had a little time to practice with Adams and some of the other freshmen players before the varsity players started coming around to the Hemenway courts. "He was learning to hit the hardball, but because of his history playing with a softball, he hit it so hard that it was like a rocket," said Scheinmann. "Your eyes couldn't even see the ball. It was frighteningly fast." So by the time he met Rick Sterne, a stellar sophomore player on the team who'd gone to prep school at Deerfield in Massachusetts, Anil had gotten used to the hardball, though he hadn't quite mastered it—and playing with seasoned players like Sterne pushed him to a new level with the American game. "Anil was more of a happy-go-lucky, friendly, good guy, not a killer squash player," said Sterne, who, over time, also became a supportive friend to Anil. "Everyone thought he was going to be good, but they didn't know just how good he was going to be. When I first played him a few times in the early days, I was able to outsmart him, hitting corners that he wasn't used to seeing, and I thought it was going to take him a year or two before he'd be good, but it only took about three months."

Soon Anil would become the number one player on the freshman team, never losing a single game in his matches against players on the teams of opposing schools that year. Although his skills and the quality of his hardball game accelerated quickly his first year, none of his rapid progress seemed to go to his head as his fellow players are quick to point out, observing his gracious court manner and spirit of fair play as readily as they do his speed and racquet skills.

"He was a joy to watch, but also a joy to play against," said Scheinmann. "He always behaved impeccably on court and never seemed to sweat—it was psychologically killing to an opponent, which made him fun to watch." Scheinmann noted that Anil was fun to play because no matter who he was playing, he would play down to their level. "Even if you thought you were playing at a decent level, and you'd think, *Maybe I can beat him this time*, and you stepped up your game, he'd start playing a little better too, and then if you'd start playing even better, and you thought, *I can beat him*, he'd play better, too. And at the end of the game, after he'd win, you'd come out feeling pretty good and think, *Maybe I will beat him next time*, but it never happened," he said. "Even so you enjoyed the game, and he would make it seem as if you were in the game, even if you were never in the game. It was completely different than playing another guy, Larry Terrell, who, if he could beat you without you scoring a point, he'd do it. This was a time when it was a 15-point game and you would get a point on every exchange, not just when serving. It was the killer in Terrell that just wanted to smash you into the court. It was different with Anil, who really appreciated the beauty of the game."

The 1966-67 Harvard squash team, including Anil, standing next to coach Jack Barnaby (far left, back row), and his friends Michel Scheinmann (second from right, back row) and Rick Sterne (third from left, front row).

Adams remembered the fun of playing with Anil with a slightly different take. "Anil couldn't have been more charming and sportsmanlike, but the other notable thing about him was his mobility. When the ball got behind him on the backhand, he seemed nonetheless to be able to hit the ball cross court. It defied the laws of Newton. Obvious and most wonderful, though, was the just plain joy Anil took in playing. When you fooled him he got just as much of a boost out of it as when he fooled you," Adams said. "Anil was like the Roger Federer of the squash court," Scheinmann added. "When you looked at him, you could see that he's out there because he really enjoys the game. Not that the rest of us weren't enjoying ourselves, too. But there was a beauty of the shots, and Anil would be moving you around the court and getting you to your last shot and it didn't matter what it would be because you weren't going to get the shot. He played in a way that wasn't about winning at all costs, but winning beautifully."

Indeed, Anil's squash buddies formed the nucleus of his early support system in America, which quickly and easily developed with their common interests and passion for sports. But Tom Webber, his dorm crew crony and the first student he'd met at Harvard, added a different dimension to the coterie of Americans with whom he would develop lasting friendships. Like Anil's other new friends, Webber came to Harvard through the private school route, in his case Collegiate in New York, but instead of sports, his passion was music, and his background was unlike anyone else's. His father was a congregational minister of Dutch and English descent, who was interested in supporting the country's disenfranchised black and Latino populations. So instead of growing up on the Upper East Side or in a suburban estate behind a manicured hedge in New England or Philadelphia like most of his classmates, Webber grew up in a modest apartment in a public housing project in the heart of Spanish Harlem. As a result, he was not only open to a diverse range of people, he readily welcomed the company of people from different walks of life.

"We had the same kind of sense of humor," said Webber, who got to know Anil while they were sweeping dorm rooms and swishing out toilets together in preparation for the students who would come to campus the following week. "Anil and I just got along immediately and I was very interested in him because he was from India. I had never had a friend from India. I was hoping I would meet some foreign students when I went to Harvard, and there he was the first day." Given their compatibility and mutual desire to expand their world views, they swiftly developed a special bond that enabled Anil to see America through a different kind of lens. "Indians often gauge friendship intensities through informalities, jokes and plenty of gestures," said Anil. "Without the drama that characterizes Indian relationships, I found it difficult to gauge the degree of friendships with my WASP friends. But in the very beginning, fate put me together with Tom Webber, a blond, blue-eyed Robert Redford-type WASP, on a dorm crew team as part of my commitment for the scholarship I received. Tom was polite, non-intimidating, and absolutely the most appropriate ambassador to my introduction to America! I wanted to be accepted and understood. I wanted to assimilate and yet be separate. Who else could make this easier for me than this all-American young man who grew up in Spanish Harlem?"

The two disparate students made a good team. "We started dusting the mattresses and cleaning rooms and bathrooms—ugh!—with a great deal of gusto," remembered Anil. But after sprucing up a few rooms, he admits a certain ennui began to set in. "Tom's Protestant ethic allowed him to slow down only partially, but my Hindu *Kshatriya* upbringing brought me to a complete halt," he said. "If I had told my mother what I was doing she would have been flabbergasted and probably would have commanded me to come back to India. People in my caste did not clean bathrooms—the darker-skinned *Shudras* and untouchables did. The irony was that here I had teamed with a white boy going through the routine of bathroom cleaning with no historical or social misgivings. What a different world America was! It was just displeasing work though, caste system notwithstanding. In Tom's Protestant view, I imagine he thought of it as character building. I never did believe in the caste system. Unwittingly, I believed more in the Buddhist line of thought and I was then, as I continue to be now, sensitive to those not born into privilege. Nonetheless, I couldn't carry on with this job, it was completely inconsistent with my former life and, by the third or fourth day of this, I made up an excuse that it was just too much of a culture shock and was reassigned some other kind of odd jobs doing bookkeeping or clerical work, while continuing to develop my friendship with Tom."

Anil also felt compelled to appear and be social in this new context. "For Tom and I, keeping each other company was a wonderful if not mutually expedient way to feel less lonely," Anil said of his budding friendship with Webber, who, on occasion, took out his guitar in the evenings and sang Beatles or Motown tunes. "What a treat! It was just like I had seen in the Hollywood movies in Bombay. I told Tom he had the best voice in the world. My mother loved to sing Bollywood and spiritual songs on a harmonium at home to relax and enjoy. And here was Tom, some 8,000 miles away, doing the same with his kind of music."

For his part, Webber was really never attuned to his preppy classmates and recalled feeling his own sense of status in aligning with Anil. "He was a big shot—we were two pretty handsome, pretty self-confident guys," Webber said. "I didn't want to have just white friends. I wanted to show that I was different from the regular preppy student. He was a different kind of guy, it was status having Anil Nayar as your close friend. But he also never took himself that seriously. I mean here he was this superstar, he wasn't the football star, but there was a whole subset of folks who recognized him and did see him as a superstar. He was very humble and got along with everybody and he had a wonderful smile and quick laugh."

Luck, as Anil had become accustomed to seeing, had generally been on his side. And among the greatest strokes of good fortune he'd encountered upon his arrival at Harvard was the almost immediate appearance of these four fellow students—Webber, Scheinmann, Adams, and Sterne—who would eventually become and remain some of his finest friends and supporters. And with his core group of friends in place—and his hardball skills getting honed—the ascendant squash star's first year of college was off to an enchanting start.

* * *

CHAPTER EIGHT

Jack Barnaby—A New Mentor and Coach

Just as Yusuf Khan had been a transformative influence on Anil in his early years as a squash player, so would be Jack Barnaby as Anil transitioned to a new level of match play with a new kind of ball on the narrower American court. "Once Jack Barnaby saw Anil play, his eyes kind of got big," said Adams. Indeed, as recounted by the authors of *The Third H Book of Harvard Athletics: 1963-2012*, one of a series of tomes on Harvard varsity sports, after Anil convinced the coach to allow him to join the team, Barnaby immediately observed that he "was a rare species of player" and later offered his own thoughts on Anil's abilities upon witnessing his on-court skills for himself. "Moving with the litheness of a Bengal tiger, perfectly poised at all times, flattening out like a snake to reach unreachable front wall shots, possessing already a bullet-like English forehand and a deft feathery drop shot, all he needed was an improved backhand and a little knowledge of American tactics," wrote Barnaby of his earliest impressions of the stellar young Indian player. So, after recognizing Anil's remarkable talent, Barnaby started coaching him in earnest, modifying his softball strokes to accommodate the faster American hard ball. "The ball came back three or four times faster than the international softball," said Anil, noting that he needed to take shorter back swings and shorter follow-throughs to adapt for timing and control. And with Barnaby's help, said Adams, "Anil shortened all his backswings, but could still hit the ball with tremendous pace. His ability to hit it very early or quite late enabled him to be deceptive—an opponent often felt totally fooled or nailed to the floor by Anil's counterpunches."

Harvard squash players of Anil's era invariably marvel at Barnaby's intellectual yet non-intimidating approach to squash—and especially his ability to tailor his advice for each player to their distinctive skills. "Jack Barnaby made Harvard the winningest college of any college coach," said Scheinmann. "He was larger than life. He wasn't just a coach. He was an appropriate person to be a Harvard coach because he understood the role sports plays in university life at Harvard. He was perfect. But he didn't plan to be a squash coach. He graduated in 1932 around the time of the Great Depression and there weren't a lot of jobs around in the real world, so the position of assistant coach was better than no job."

Barnaby started his career by serving as assistant coach to the legendary Harry Cowles, Harvard's first squash coach, who was taught the sport by a world champion Englishman by the name of Tom Pettitt and was hired to coach squash at Harvard in 1921. In his book *Squash: A History of the Game*, American squash player and author James Zug describes Cowles as "the Knute Rockne of squash, the first squash genius," and the man who "created the prototype of future squash coaches: the excellent player, the genial taskmaster, the quiet technician, the unflappable leader." According to Zug, he also changed the nature of squash in America. After getting its start at St. Paul's School in rural New Hampshire in 1884, when the school's master, Jay Conover, the father of American squash, built four open-air squash courts behind the schoolhouse next to the woods, squash eventually spread to the newly built and luxurious clubhouse of the Boston Athletic Association in 1888, when a few of St. Paul's alumni started playing the game

The untouchable 1967-68 Harvard squash team, including Anil (second from left in front row) with team captain Rick Sterne (center) and Jose Gonzalez (seated to right of Sterne), posted the best record (14-0, 5-0 Ivy) in program history. Coach Jack Barnaby stands next to Anil's friend Michel Scheinmann (both at far left in back row).

on its courts, and later to the Racquet Club of Philadelphia, where other St. Paul's graduates among its membership held a tournament in 1901 to determine the best squash player in the club.

As interest in the sport blossomed around other parts of the Northeast, courts started appearing in more elite private clubs, where members included the highest echelons of society, and as the inchoate sport evolved so did its rules and structure and by 1904, the United States Squash Racquets Association, the sport's first American governing body, was founded by a group of its most passionate players. Once past the embryonic stage, the sport moved to the collegiate sphere, emerging at Harvard in 1908, when the first courts were constructed in its athletic building and it quickly became the preferred winter sport among freshmen and later upperclassmen. After Harvard brought in Cowles to coach its fledgling teams, he led a seemingly endless string of the greatest of America's early collegiate players, such as Beek Pool, Germain Glidden, and Ben Heckscher, to extraordinary heights and made Harvard the unbeatable number one collegiate team in America for decades until he had a nervous breakdown and retired. Barnaby, another legendary sports figure and squash mentor at Harvard, stepped into the void as head coach in 1937 and stayed in the role until he retired in 1976.

"Jack was a sports coach, but he was also a life coach," said Scheinmann. "He had been through so much turbulent history. It was wonderful to learn about life from Jack. We went on roads trips with him and would have long discussions about what was going on in the world, and how squash relates to the world on a broader level. He also reminded us that it's just a game and he gave us a good sense of how to create balance. You know, today we hear a lot about 'work-life balance.' Well, we were learning about that from Jack in college. Technically he was a fabulous coach, but what was more important was his primary philosophy that 'you cannot beat the court.' In other words, even the best player cannot win if he makes mistakes by getting too close to the tin, for example. You beat your opponent by learning techniques that allow you to minimize your own errors and maximize your strengths. He also helped you develop a strategy so that you could move your opponent around the court until there was no risk for you. It's different from classic coaching, which is oriented toward trying to beat the court. And he would adapt to you. It wasn't a cookie-cutter approach. He would analyze you and talk to you in your language in phrases that would light up in your mind until you got it. He took each player separately and taught each differently with purpose to address different skills. It was his genius. He taught us that you need to analyze your opponent to come up with a strategy to do the opposite of what he was building in you—to magnify his weaknesses and minimize his strengths."

"The beauty of Jack's coaching was that he assessed your play and built upon it," agreed Anil, who deeply appreciated Barnaby's seasoned experience, astuteness, and capacity to break situations down to their basics and deliver effective and understandable advice. "Rarely, did he make radical changes to style, balance, and grip. He told me earlier on as I tried to master the reverse corner, 'No point in practicing the reverse corner, put your speed to use and use your Hashim-style feathery drop shot as a counterattack.'" His personalized approach to imparting practicable wisdom with references to styles of other players also worked well for Anil. "Jack had so much history behind him that when he spoke of Beeky Pool's hard serve, or Glidden's deft racket movement, or Hecksher's quickness all his analogies felt real and doable," Anil said. Barnaby, and his assistant coach, Corey Wynn, also taught Anil to develop a strategic approach in order to make him an effective hardball player, rather than rely so heavily on his athleticism, which had served him well in his softball matches.

"Anil's tremendous natural ability was the most fertile possible environment for Jack's creative squash genius," said Adams. "One of the things that Jack also did, over the course of a year or so, was teach Anil to be a better shot choice player, a better observer and strategist." Lithe and quick as a cracking whip, Anil was so much more athletic than his contemporaries when he arrived at Cambridge that he didn't have to really pay much attention to what they did because what he was doing worked so well. But later, when he got to the very top of the amateur American game and was playing with aggressive older players, such as Sam and Ralph Howe from Yale and Victor Niederhoffer from Harvard, they were almost as athletic as Anil was and much more experienced. "So, Anil had to think harder about strategy and shot choice than he did as a freshman," said Adams. "In softball, Anil could afford to make a sloppy shot and then compensate for it with his retrieving ability. But when he played Sam and Ralph and Victor in American hardball he couldn't get away with that sloppiness."

During his freshman year, when Anil quickly rose to number one on the freshman team, he rarely practiced with freshmen. "The freshmen couldn't hold a candle to him," said Adams. Instead he played sophomores Jose Gonzalez, who had been the U.S. national junior champion, and Rick Sterne, a star left-handed player, as well as Adams. "I got beaten quite a bit in the first few months," recalled Anil. "But I was learning the golf-like bounce of the ball, and Corey Wynn, the freshman coach, was helping to some extent. But I needed Jack's attention, which I did get once he was convinced I was a candidate for next year's team. Harvard players had a ladder, with regular challenge matches taking place between players on either side of you. I started to move up the ladder and was on auto-control for a while. Soon, I was to play the left-handed player, Rick Sterne. I saw him play but didn't quite comprehend the severity of his attacking game. I wasn't prepared for his aggressive low volleys or his reverse corners. Time and time again he surprised me with his relentless shot making. I lost and was totally taken aback. I still remember this loss as one of lack of preparedness in hardball play."

But it wouldn't be long before all that would change. "By halfway through the season, Anil was a sure winner over Rick, Jose, or me," said Adams, who also attributes Anil's quick grasp of the hardball game to Barnaby's coaching. "Jack was such a virtuoso coach that he could watch you play once, and then he'd noodle about it and figure out what the best squash game would be for Anil Nayar or Dinny Adams or Jose Gonzalez. Those three squash games would be irreconcilably different. He would invent a squash game to maximize each individual's greatest assets and correct or minimize his greatest liabilities and combine them in a way that was the best game for you."

Anil receives his first national intercollegiate championship trophy as fellow players Matt Hall, Craig Stapleton (far left and left), and Jose Gonzalez (far right) along with freshman coach Corey Wynn (to Anil's right) look on.

Anil remembered well Barnaby's approach to his playing partner, Jose Gonzalez, an outstanding yet "weighty" player who was number two or three on the Harvard team at the time. "He honed in on and improved his tremendous shot making and shot selection abilities," said Anil of Gonzalez, whom he remembers as the kindest player to his racquet he has ever seen. "While I broke four or five racquets per season, wooden Bancroft racquets at that time, Jose probably broke one—he so finely hit the ball without ever engaging the wall."

According to Adams, one of Anil's key skills that Barnaby tapped into to exploit was his extraordinary mobility. "You know what kinesthetic sense is?" he asked. "Anil had that at a genius level, just naturally. When his body was off balance or going in the wrong direction he had such control of his body that he could change direction and maintain perfect balance. He could be going full tilt in one direction and you could fool him, but then he could recover and retrieve a ball you thought was a winner. Those traits made him a tremendous counterpuncher. So one of Jack's strategies with Anil was to teach him to provoke a mixed-up crisis in a point: Reduce it to a punch-counterpunch athletic contest. That eggbeater style was the strategy Anil used with the classic American big stroke players like Sam Howe. Howe was a great champion. If you gave Sam two or three good chances he could hit a drive or a drop shot that nobody could get. But Anil provoked crisis points, so Sam couldn't hit his best shots. Anil also retrieved many shots which were masterpieces. He simply loved to run for the ball."

While Anil valued the extraordinary personal support he received from Barnaby, he also admired his approach to coaching a team, which served Harvard so well while Anil was in college. "Jack had a reputation for making squash players out of tennis players and of making players of non players," said Anil. "He repeated often that each of the nine-man team's win counted equally. Number nine and number one players both got one point for a win. He spent a lot of time grooming numbers six through nine on the team and that was one of his strategies for such a successful career. Jack, like Yusuf, also made many national champions. He was a cerebral coach, a master tactician. He had a gift to hone in on and analyze a player's and the opponent's capabilities during a match and, more often than not, give match-winning advice."

Anil believed that Barnaby, with his thoughtful and strategic approach, was exactly the right coach at the right time for him at this point in his life. "I was fortunate to have Yusuf Khan and Jack Barnaby in my life at the times they appeared," he said. "I needed the soft and fuzzy encouragement I got from Yusuf while growing up. After all, I never dreamed of being a champion—I was a Ladoo, and if Jack had seen me then I doubt he'd have encouraged me in the same way. It was a perfect 1-2 combination."

Khan, with his classical approach to footwork, balance, racquet preparation, and drills on a basic variety of shots and fitness, and Barnaby, with his targeted player-directed strategy and simple commonsense approach to coaching and error reduction by aiming higher or focusing on serves, made Anil a champion. And both instilled in him an ethos of fair play, which contributed greatly to who he became on court and in life.

* * *

CHAPTER NINE

Lessons Learned

That he was able to immediately bask in the glow of his shining stardom on the squash court was a great boost for Anil in his early days in college, but excelling in academics is also expected at an Ivy League institution like Harvard, where Anil chose to major in economics. Yet finding his footing in the classroom context required some extra effort for the squash champ, especially at the start.

In contrast to the rote and sometimes uninspired teaching he received at Cathedral and Sydenham, the illustrious professors who delivered lectures on varied subjects at Harvard brimmed with seriousness and energy. "It was not the environment of proxies," said Anil. "It was one of giving it your 100 percent and more." His first introduction to a liberal arts education was encountered in a one-year course called Humanities 2 taught by a Professor John Finley, who was known for his spirited lectures as he walked back and forth across the dais of Memorial Hall and told riveting tales to a rapt group of 200 or so students about Odysseus, Achilles, and the gods of Greek classics and mythology, which Anil readily absorbed, finding many similarities between the Greek gods and goddesses and their counterparts in Indian mythology. Both Hindu and Greek gods, he realized, "were wise, playful, loving, mean—no different than humans no matter what their ilk."

Initially, he couldn't see the relevance of this course to his focus on economics. "But I realize now my Humanities education has stood the test of time, just as have the lessons on Shakespeare I learned in English literature classes at Cathedral," he said.

This course required a tremendous amount of reading, however, and a composition course he took at the same time required significant class participation. "I was intimidated by both the preparedness of my fellow classmates and the teachers," Anil confessed, noting that his education at Cathedral and Sydenham had not primed him to interact with professors in the formal-informal way in which American students did at that time. Nor was he ready for the voluminous weekly reading assignments. "I was and still am a slow reader," admitted Anil. "I was told by my expository writing instructor to take a speed reading course provided by the college for students like me. It helped significantly with this problem. It was impossible to get by on the rote system here. One needed to apply the information that was taught, not just learn it."

His shyness posed a different problem for him in the comp class. After a brief introduction by the teacher, each student in the class was asked to speak about what occurred to them when they heard the word "freedom." According to Anil, "Many students talked about freedom of thought or freedom in philosophical or religious terms. This was way too intense for me. All that occurred to me was the feeling of freedom as it related to Indian independence—in other words 'freedom from colonials.' I felt embarrassed that my idea didn't seem to resonate with the teacher and class, and I sensed they didn't feel my meaning was deep enough, so I decided to move to a similar class with another teacher and soon learned that that class was no less intimidating. In retrospect, years later, I felt that my answer then was as good as any of the others and it was a reflection of my history and background. Even though my answers were as good as any others, I often felt intimidated by fellow students and professors. I was not able to speak up in a small or large group."

Another handicap was the fact that Anil had never learned to type and his handwriting was virtually illegible. "American students had learned how to type in high school and were used to submitting their assignments in neatly typed form," Anil said. "Initially, I alternated between writing my papers and typing my papers depending upon whom I could find to type them for me. Either way, I went through numerous iterations before I could submit a paper."

As he progressed at Harvard, however, Anil adapted and ultimately enjoyed the classes he took, a few of which he remembers vividly, partly because they related to his background or interests. One of them was an advanced course on empirical studies in emerging countries and was taught to a small group of ten or twelve students by Professor Simon Kuznets. "He was frail then, in 1968, but his discussions were as simple and clear as only a person with supreme understanding can present," remembered Anil. Professor Kuznets spoke softly, with a slight Lithuanian accent, and the challenge was to get a seat at the front row to hear him well. The class was enthralled as he simplified trends and numbers and offered data to make forecasts without being a statistician. "Class presence was not required but no one missed it," said Anil. One of his discussions revolved around agricultural developments in emerging countries with a focus on the Indian farmers, who, throughout the ages, had continued to make tools more efficient as new technologies became available and, as a result, earnestly continued to transform traditional farming in their county to the extent they could with limited resources. The simplest and latest development at the time was the move from wooden wheels to rubber wheels to reduce friction while rolling. Professor Kuznets later won the Nobel Prize in economic sciences in 1971 and, when he did, Anil sent him a telegram to congratulate him. He also remembers mourning his inspiring professor's death in 1985. "The world lost a true academician with a heart," he said.

As it turned out, one of Kuznets's assistants was an Indian by the name of Dr. Subramanian Swamy, with whom Anil formed a courteous and amiable relationship. "I admired Dr. Swamy for his forthrightness in his views and his patriotism towards India," Anil said. "To the chagrin of many naysayers in the economics department then, Dr. Swamy informed the students of the developments taking place in India, including the White Revolution, which involved massive increases in milk production, and the Green Revolution, which focused on rapid increases in wheat and rice production, especially in Punjab. Most of his department members were looking south towards Brazil or finding interest in China, perhaps because, as Dr. Swamy pointed out, their numbers were unrealistically optimistic!" Dr. Swamy undertook a detailed analysis of the numbers presented by the governments of the latter countries, especially China, which were not in sync with the supporting data published by the government. Dr. Swamy, as many in India know, is now a member of the Rajya Sabha, the upper house of parliament, and is known as a maverick and a deterrent to Indian politicians and business people who veer toward the path of corruption and bribery. Hated by the fringe and loved by others, he is also currently a prominent member of the ruling Bharatiya Janata Party.

Another course Anil remembers well was Professor Roger Revelle's seminar relating to demographics in emerging countries. "It was a six- or seven-student seminar," said Anil. "And like Kuznets, Revelle was appreciated for the simplicity of his delivery of complex information, and the discussions among students at the table during his lectures often went on far past than the scheduled close of the evening class. "There was an important and fundamental feature to most efforts relating to population control. The Khanna project, which was funded by the Rockefeller Foundation to study the relationship between education and birth rates, was started in Khanna, Punjab, a wheat *mandi* on the Grand Trunk Road that links

Delhi to Ludhiana, Jullundur, Amritsar, Batala, and areas further west and north to Pakistan and Afghanistan. The project started before the Green Revolution that Dr. Swamy so insistently said was taking place and it examined the birth rates and infant death rates before and after the revolution," said Anil, noting its findings became the basis of present development over almost all of India and revealed that sending the young girls to school and sometimes to college when the farming families had gained more disposable income resulted in reducing the girls' fertility span, increasing their awareness of better birth control methods and hygiene, and yielding both lower infant mortality rates and lower birth rates. Anil noted that Revelle was also an influential mentor for former U.S. vice president Al Gore, who was also a Harvard student in Anil's class. "Though I don't recall Al Gore in my seminar or having met him, I later found out we have some mutual friends and it's interesting to know that Revelle was so deeply influential in awakening Gore's concerns and inspiring his activity relating to climate change," Anil said.

At this point in his life, Anil is now struck by the fact that Professors Finley, Kuznets, and Revelle, as well as Dr. Swamy, have left him with lifelong memories. "Professor Finley's class encouraged me to enjoy otherworldly emotions, weaknesses, strengths, and experiences and to see them reflected in our real-world heroes and heroines," he said. "In Professor Kuznets's lectures about the poor Indian farmer, who was mistakenly believed to have been left behind in time, he illuminated the fact that the farmer was actually working hard at getting more out of the land and was as innovative as he could be given the resources at hand. It gave me a new appreciation of the farmer as I travelled back and forth on the Grand Trunk Road from Delhi to Amritsar by car or by rail later in the 1980s."

Anil was similarly reminded of his lessons with Professor Revelle and Dr. Swamy when he passed Khanna on the GT Road several times by car after he graduated from Harvard. "Before I went to Harvard, Khanna was one speck of a village passed by in a blink of an eye," he said. "After I came back from Harvard it had developed into a huge *mandi*, burgeoning with wheat or rice heaped along the side of the road and bustling with men, women, and children going about their business. I felt connected like I never had before. I could also imagine young girls going to school, some pressuring their way into college despite family objections for fear of not being able marry off their daughters at an early age. I could imagine resistance, too, from the young female graduates to bearing multiple children early to ensure the birth of as many males as possible and that at least a few would live to adulthood. And when I periodically go back to Batala and Chandigarh, where I am now involved in school programs, who do I see bringing their kids to school but the mothers and grandmothers!" Dr. Swamy also left Anil with a fresh perspective on India. "With his involvement in the government, I could see there was hope that we Indians do have ethical monitors who are not afraid to speak out," he said. "How ironic that Harvard would alter my connection to India with such lifelong effects."

At the end of four years, Anil finished Harvard with a B grade average. "Certainly not stellar, only a modest finish," he said. "But squash did take time with afternoon practices and, during the season, weekends away playing other colleges or at Harvard's Hemenway squash courts. From my sophomore year onwards, my playing schedule also included amateur tournaments to gain experience. Usually, the tournament settings were at beautiful clubs in cities and suburbs where the rich and powerful were members. There were never issues of being welcome though. I was always welcome. That, I thought, was the beauty of Americans. They embraced excellence and my background and color made me all the more interesting at that time."

While squash demanded a lot of his energy, he did make time to study. "I believe I would have done much better by singularly focusing on academics," said Anil. "But Harvard encouraged students to do more than just study. Harvard wanted its students to explore, experience, learn, and engage in social activities," he said. And so he did.

* * *

CHAPTER TEN

American Counterculture

Anil's formative years in college in the U.S.A. were stormy ones for the country—and the planet. So much was going on. In Vietnam, a distant land almost 10,000 miles away, Americans were getting more and more embroiled in a war that the U.S. could not win. The events in Vietnam were destroying the fabric of U.S. civil society and one of the most significant effects was on the education system. Colleges were in turmoil, with outbreaks of violent protests, rebellions against the system, anti-war sentiment in universities across the country—from the Ivy League to Kent State—and mass protests and occasional violence were the order of the day. These were also the days of Rock 'n' Roll icons from Britain—The Rolling Stones, The Beatles, Donovan, The Who, The Kinks—coming to America and American musicians like Jim Morrison, Janice Joplin, Bob Dylan, and Jimmy Hendrix completely transforming the music scene. At the same time there were antiwar folk singers like Joan Baez and Arlo Guthrie, and there were open-air rock concerts like Woodstock, where free sex, drugs, and hippies reigned. It was also the time of Hell's Angels, of Abby Hoffman, of anarchy in the streets as a total breakdown of communications between generations and between citizens and the body politic unfolded.

But the popular culture of the day hardly resonated with Anil. "Elements of the art and music scenes of America were all but passing me by until I was able to revisit them after my active squash career at the beginning of my second marriage to my wife, Jean," Anil admitted. "I never really understood Vietnam. I thought the domino theory and the theory of pre-emption as applied to Vietnam were false propositions. I saw using power and might versus spirit and understanding as an ineffective way to show leadership. Why couldn't America stop spilling American blood and wasting money in Vietnam and instead deploy resources to benefit those who were left behind in its own country? Didn't the folks in D.C. understand that colonial-style subjugation and propped-up puppet governments were just one big waste of resources and doomed to fail? They didn't understand this then and certainly have not understood it since."

During his second year at Harvard, when Anil was rooming with his friend Tom Webber, he got a firsthand view of the post-traumatic suffering of a neighboring roommate, who had fought in Vietnam. Both of them have vivid memories of this student screaming, banging against the wall, and jumping on his bed. Many in the student community had heard of such happenings. A radicalized contingent of antiwar activists began to emerge while Anil was at Harvard, and campus tensions reached a tipping point in the spring of 1966, when hundreds of students led by a group called Students for a Democratic Society mobbed then defense secretary Robert S. McNamara, who'd been invited to Harvard to speak as the first honorary associate of the Kennedy Institute. After the secretary had declined a request by the SDS to participate in a debate about the war, the group organized a protest against McNamara in the Quincy House courtyard. And while McNamara was leaving the campus after giving a talk to a preselected group of 120 students, he was mobbed by the student demonstrators, who forced

McNamara to abandon his car and climb onto the hood, where he agreed to take only three questions from the student protestors. With tensions mounting as McNamara became belligerent in the face of the students' resistance, the confrontation ended with the arrival of the police, who whisked McNamara away.

Another of the many strands of social change affecting the lives of college students at this time, was the women's movement, which played out in distinctive style among American women and on a smaller scale at Harvard, and some of its early effects would have an impact on Anil while he was a student. A visitor from India could be quite stunned by the vision of bras burning and demands for equal treatment and equal pay. Just before Anil arrived at Harvard, important legislative strides had been made to address the inequities American women and minorities faced. In 1963, Congress passed the Equal Pay Act, promising equitable wages for the same work, regardless of the race, color, religion, national origin, or sex of the worker. And this legislation was reinforced with the passage in 1964 of Title VII of the Civil Rights Act, which prohibited discrimination on the basis of race, color, religion, sex, and national origin in employment. The Equal Employment Opportunity Commission was also created that year. By the time Anil arrived in 1965, the Supreme Court established the right of married couples to use contraception. And in 1968, president Lyndon B. Johnson signed an executive order prohibiting sex discrimination by government contractors and requiring affirmative action plans for hiring women. And in 1969, the year Anil graduated from Harvard, a Wellesley College graduate named Hillary Clinton became the first female student to address the graduating class at commencement.

While the women's movement wasn't especially high profile on campus, it did set Anil thinking about the plight not only of American women but also of Indian women, having grown up in a home with traditional Indian values. "I could see that women felt that they were not understood, despite the plethora of magazine articles and literature that was being published at the time that might have helped men," Anil acknowledged. "The women's liberation movement encouraged me to appreciate and embrace the possibility of non-traditional roles for women and to gain an understanding of the degree of deprivation they had undergone throughout history and in all cultures." At the same time, as a freshman, he felt there should have been more of a two-way conversation on the issue. "I didn't see that there was enough of an attempt by women to understand men—and there was no literature around to help them," he said. "Over time, I began to see this as a monumental battle for change with an evolving reset required by each of the sexes in understanding the other to defeat stereotypical thinking that still continues to a significant degree in the present. In the 1960s, I also thought males and females were out of alignment in their thinking about sex. Males generally had a more casual attitude toward sex than females did. There seemed to be a disconnect about the signals being sent by women, who were showing their thighs and cleavage, and what was going on in their heads versus how men were interpreting these visuals."

Ultimately, these cultural and social changes contributed to Anil's sense of feeling somewhat out of sync with American social norms of the day, as he was still quite entrenched in the attitudes of his own country and upbringing. As cosmopolitan as he was, there was a retro air to his tastes and ideas that wasn't quite in tune with the fashionable trends of the day in America. "In India, when I was growing up, we watched local or national Bollywood movies, and sometimes Hollywood movies, we listened to popular Indian music, and our entertainment sometimes involved dancing," he said. As for music, he recalled clearly the sound of his mother singing aloud prayer hymns and periodically playing the harmonium to please her husband and herself. "We also heard songs by Elvis and some Rock 'n' Roll and Cha-cha-chá and sometimes we saw titillating cabaret shows or listened to Anglo-Indian crooners singing songs that were frequently played by Radio Ceylon in a few restaurants," said Anil. "We also fantasized about getting close to our female classmates, but until we were in the ninth or tenth grade, the school-organized socials were always under teacher supervision. In any case, for me, Hollywood and Rock 'n' Roll and Cha-cha-chá never quite stuck. It felt artificial to dance with a girl I didn't know. Besides, I just didn't have the moves. What did stick with me all my life was calypso, Harry Belafonte, Miriam Makeba, and, for romance and fantasy, Caterina Valente. With Rock 'n' Roll, while I sometimes liked hearing the music, I couldn't follow the words and so the songs didn't stay with me. So, here I was in America, with my ears virtually deaf to the music I was listening to. It was foreign."

The American, mostly WASP approach to social interaction Anil encountered at Harvard was also a novelty to the young Indian—and something that took some getting used to. "Certain interactions were precise," Anil said. "A straightforward 'No' was not considered brusque or rude, as it would be in India, while at the same time, when someone issued a directive or offered an opinion on preferences, the messages were often indirect. In contrast to the Indian way of providing direction where someone would simply say, 'Do this or that,' Americans would do so in a suggestive manner and say something like, 'Try this or that.' Also, I noticed that small talk or a sense of casualness in conversation or behavior seemed to be all but missing by Indian standards."

Furthermore many of his classmates were very much at ease with one another already having had a shared history that stretched back to their youth in private prep schools. "I really didn't know much about American private schools, such as Andover and Exeter, or who went there, or that they were the traditional stepping stones to the Ivy colleges," said Anil. "The loyal friendships I witnessed among my fellow students that began in their teenage years effortlessly seemed to continue into their twenties and, I later learned, beyond. It almost seemed that Harvard for most students was like déjà vu from their earlier school days." The similarity in their experiences and their tastes left him feeling somewhat disconnected from the status quo, with something as basic as the food in the dining hall posing a quandary for him. "I wasn't sure whether I should like or dislike the foreign food that I ate," he said. "Should I like milk, which my friend Michel drank from multiple glasses neatly lined at the edge of his tray? Or, should I suffer the once-a-week meatloaf served at dinner time that would send me the nearest bathroom around midnight? I tried for a while to conform to the lifestyle and patterns of interaction of my roommates and college mates, until something became uncomfortable enough for me to just accept my own tastes and live with them."

Nevertheless, Anil did his best to fit in—and for the most part enjoyed himself at the parties, mixers, and squash events that would occupy his free time—and he occasionally dated American women, though he admitted that most of the "Cliffies" and young Wellesley girls who attended college in the 1960s were oriented toward marriage material—in other words, American boys—and generally didn't give him the time of day. "Michel and I would organize parties and invite young girls from various schools around Boston and Cambridge," Anil said. "Wrongly, perhaps, we and other young men around us felt Cliffies would be way too serious for the mood we wanted to set, and so they seldom got invited. I think in hindsight we were intimidated by their intellect. This was a time when Radcliffe students had separate dorms a mile or so away from Freshman Yard. It was also the time when parietal rules required all girls to leave our dorms before 11 p.m. The administration probably assumed this would discourage sexual activity, though I'm not sure of the effectiveness of this archaic policy in 1965. In any case, the administration did encourage socializing with girls but on somewhat regulated terms. Harvard and other colleges had mixers to which invitations were sent en masse to freshmen at certain colleges to get together, mingle, dance, and chat. I found this system quite strange but nevertheless attended two or three with no success. I was different and didn't have many connection points or experiences to share, and in those times most of the girls had sights on white boys. So my brief dances usually terminated with my partner making an excuse to go to the restroom and never coming back."

Anil pointed out that there were few if any Indian women amidst the Harvard scene. However, he did remember meeting a young Pakistani woman by the name of Benazir Bhutto during his senior year when he was coaching the female squash players at Radcliffe as a way of giving back on a pro bono basis. "I'm not sure how many people knew she was the daughter of Zulfiquar Bhutto, then the leader of an influential political group in Pakistan known as the Pakistan Peoples' Party who later was elected prime minister," said Anil. Though his meeting with her as a coach on the squash court was brief, he remembered her as very passive. "She surprised me. She was meek and docile, I couldn't see strength in her. That came to her after her father was executed," added Anil, noting that she later went on to become the prime minister of Pakistan herself. He didn't remember seeing her again, but he did recall that the fact that there were so few women from his part of the world around campus meant he would ultimately turn his attention to the American women who were open to spending time with a foreigner from a completely different culture—and, without question, he managed to find a few.

Aside from the need to adapt to myriad social, political, and cultural norms, acclimating to a new culture invariably involves understanding commonly celebrated holidays, which can be lonely for a foreigner in a strange land. So Anil was grateful to spend many a Thanksgiving at the family home in South Dartmouth of his friend Michel Scheinmann, or at the Spanish Harlem home of his friend Tom Webber. "Michel was an ideal roommate in my freshman year and became like a brother later on," said Anil. "Squash was a major connection point. He, like my friend Tom, was patient, understanding, and he had a sense of humor that we could both enjoy. And he welcomed me into his life and so did his parents, André and Claire, who thought of me as a second son and treated me with love and affection. I, in turn, thought of them as my American family." At the Thanksgiving weekends he spent with the Scheinmanns, a meal often included fresh lobster picked up from the nearby fishing stations in New Bedford or South Dartmouth, and Scheinmann's mother showed Anil how to eat the lobster without letting even a morsel of its soft, tender meat to go to waste. "Over time, Michel and I had a ritual set up," said Anil. "To build up our appetite for the Thanksgiving meal we would eat very little earlier on in the day, then around noon we'd go play squash at what I remember to be the coldest courts in North America, come back, shower, and get ready for a sumptuous Thanksgiving dinner. I felt so at home."

In some ways, the fact that the Scheinmanns were recent immigrants to the U.S. probably contributed to Anil's comfort with them as well as to their inclination to welcome him. Scheinmann and his parents moved to America from France when Scheinmann was only four years old. "I had an American experience, except that we spoke French at home, so it was like living in a European household. And we often went back to Europe, even though it wasn't that easy to travel overseas then. Most Americans never left their home state let alone went overseas. It wasn't common either to speak a foreign language. I grew up in an environment that was open, unprejudiced, unbiased, non-discriminating with a bigger world view that was framed by my parents' experiences before and during the war. So we were open to meeting someone as foreign as Anil," remembered Scheinmann, whose mother had spent the World War II years in England working with the Royal Air Force Intelligence Service and whose father had served in the French army, joined the resistance, ran a spy network, was caught, and then sent as a POW to a concentration camp in Dachau until he was released at the end of the war after Scheinmann's grandparents had perished in Auschwitz. "My parents didn't discuss it until I was 15 or so, they didn't want me to be exposed to any prejudices until I was capable of drawing my own conclusions—it was very powerful," said Scheinmann. He admitted though that he knew little if anything at all about India. "I had never really read anything about India except *The Jungle Book*—how provincial we were. But others were even more so, and I remember one student from Pittsburgh, who believed Anil when he told him he went to school riding an elephant when he was growing up in India. Anil had an innate sense of practical joking, but in a nice way, not hurtful."

Another memorable Thanksgiving at the family home of his friend Tom Webber was a completely different yet equally heartwarming experience. "Tom was empowered by belief," said Anil. "He and his parents and four siblings lived on 102nd Street in East Harlem. Tom's father, a reverend, had built a church for the local Hispanics and blacks and he ministered to the underprivileged. At the first Thanksgiving I spent at Tom's apartment, I noticed with some awe how this family spent so much energy and effort being kind and generous to those around them who did not have enough. It was not the dramatic emotion you might witness in India, but it was cool, sincere, and profound. I was part of this holiday celebration in which young girls and boys from the neighborhood also joined. I began to see Tom as my moral compass in a country where there were so many distractions of money, women, sex, drugs, individualism—all so different from the conservative social and cultural background I came from." Reflecting now on these particular friends, Anil sometimes wonders whether meeting Webber in dorm crew was a mere co-incidence, or if rooming with Scheinmann, a young Jewish man of French origin, was simply serendipitous. "Probably not," he concluded. "Harvard makes decisions purposefully, effectively, and usually well thought through."

Just as Anil's core group of friends eased his initiation into America, Anil would serve as the conduit for these exceptionally bright, but mostly sheltered American friends to their first direct taste of his completely foreign culture, too. Over time, some of his American friends would also visit Anil in India to get a firsthand sense of his own upbringing and family as well as the current culture on the subcontinent. One of the memorable visits to India by a college mate then was the journey made by his teammate Rick Sterne on the occasion of the wedding of Anil's brother Vijay to his then-fiancée, Meera, in 1966. "Rick was working for TWA at the time and could travel at little cost," said Anil. So the two decided to rendezvous in Bombay, where Anil would host him at his parent's flat on Marine Drive. "An Indian wedding in those days wasn't understood in the West like it is now to anyone who has seen the movie 'Monsoon Wedding,'" noted Anil.

"I'm sure I knew some Indians, but I didn't know any squash-playing Indians, and I didn't know the difference between Bombay and New Delhi and if I had any impressions of Bombay it was a place where David Rockefeller was going to run out of dimes trying to give people money on the street corners," recalled Sterne of his thoughts about visiting India before he landed. But when he arrived at Anil's home on the Queen's Necklace overlooking the sea, his view of the country changed a bit. "It was not as backward as my impressions of it before I left," Sterne said. "Anil led a very fancy life in comparison to most people, but I was a little worried when he was driving around and coming close to running over the poorer people who were sleeping on the street when they weren't getting out of the way."

While the wedding proceedings were quite glamorous, they were completely unfamiliar to anything Sterne had seen before. "It was a three-day wedding and we went to the various services, but they were not ones I fully understood and no one explained them to me and so I just went through the process," Sterne said. "From my perspective, they were basically big cocktail parties, where everyone was moving around and talking while the ceremony was going on." He was also struck by the wedding procession that typically precedes the ceremony on the street. "Anil's brother was blindfolded, sitting backwards on a horse or an elephant, and tying up traffic. Other than the food, it was a lot of fun," said Sterne, who is known to favor classic American fare and left India three or four days earlier than he'd planned because the many spicy meals he'd eaten had wreaked havoc on his stomach. "Rick enjoyed the rituals and celebratory aspects of Vijay and Meera's wedding," said Anil. "But he was not used to a context in which the rich and poor coexist as neighbors. The food didn't suit him either and he was very apologetic for his early departure. I totally respected his decision. Still, his visit had drawn us closer."

The highlights of Anil's social scene in America, however, invariably revolved around the frivolity of the squash parties and events he attended—many of them black-tie affairs at country clubs like the Merion Cricket Club, the cradle of Main Line American squash in suburban Philadelphia, or the Rockaway Hunt Club in Cedarhurst, Long Island. It was at some of these gatherings that he inhaled the most rarefied of squash air and met the loftiest of the squash world's old guard WASPs, who took him under their wings and fêted him in great style. Among them, he remembered fondly Stewart Brauns, a former president of the United States Squash Racquets Association, who hosted a party one evening at the Gaslight Club in Manhattan when Anil's parents had come to New York for a visit. "About forty people had been invited, and he thoughtfully arranged to have small American and Indian flags set at each place setting to make my parents feel comfortable," said Anil. "He also had the best collection of cuff links I've ever seen." Other notable elders in his sphere included Seymour Knox III, a philanthropist and sports entrepreneur who owned the Buffalo Sabers hockey team, and Treddy Ketchum, a decorated WWII veteran and another former USSRA president, who later, in the 1970s, invited Anil to become a member of the Jesters Club, a prestigious international squash and racquets sports club.

The Jesters Club was established by a clubhouse-less touring band of schoolboy rugby fives players in England in 1929 and slowly evolved into one of the squash world's most exclusive and influential international organizations, eventually launching branches in the U.S., Canada, South Africa, Bermuda, and Australia. His Royal Highness, the Duke of Edinburgh, is the patron of the club, and being a member of the Jesters is one of the highest honors a squash player can receive. Although membership in the club is granted only to a select few on the basis of their skills, sportsmanship, and contribution to the game, its members are expressly encouraged to emphasize enjoyment over the serious nature of competitive games, as suggested by the name of the club itself. In fact, the second of the original club's rules stated that "the purpose of the Club shall be to play in a spirit not unworthy of the name of the Club." Since that spirit comes very naturally to Anil, his particular brand of sportsmanship, along with his skills, made him a welcome member, though for years, membership was limited to only the WASPiest of players.

At the events held by the Jesters at some of America's fanciest private clubs, Anil gained a clear sense of the lifestyle of the country's aristocrats. "I was used to wealth in India but not the extent of the wealth I witnessed among members of the elite social clubs in America," said Anil, recalling the occasions when he was invited to stay at their homes when tournaments took place nearby. "Our family was very wealthy in the 1960s, but I just had not seen this kind of opulence before. My family didn't spend money lavishly, despite being Punjabis, who have the distinct characteristic of trying to appear as though they have more wealth than they actually do. Very few of our friends in Bombay knew that my family owned five buildings in downtown Bombay and large manufacturing facilities in Bombay, Delhi, Amritsar, and Dehra Dun. But here, in the surroundings of these American clubs, wealth was ubiquitous. I had never before seen a wealthy suburb, never witnessed the abandoned manner in which the American rich and famous celebrated and enjoyed themselves. During these parties, I witnessed the slight cracks in some of the relationships, the growing frictions between men and women at that time. I did not quite realize it then, but decades later, after I saw Ang Lee's

"The Ice Storm," I could see that, in some cases, there were serious fissures taking place, fissures that marked the beginning of a major reset of the relationships between men and women as they struggled to find equal footing, not unlike the men and women who were undergoing different yet parallel changes in India during the Green Revolution. Ironically, but not surprisingly, the cracks in relationships would sometimes become more apparent during times of merriment, dancing, and drinking at these very high-style parties." Ironically, too, these parties often took place the night before a finals tournament the next day. With his fitness level at its peak at this point, he was able to finesse the balance between partying and match play relatively easily. Though later in life, he admitted, the festivities and sport became harder to juggle.

As Anil's squash skills swiftly developed, he was also tapped to play in exhibition matches and national tournaments that required him to travel and exposed him to other parts of the country—and a wider audience. "Anil was a phenom," said Adams. "As time went on, he was playing competitively with the best U.S. amateur players—Sam and Ralph Howe, and the Canadian national champion Colin Adair. Everyone knew who Anil was and wanted to see him play."

Both Adams and Anil recalled the first exhibition match Anil played as a freshman, which not only gave him a taste of the appreciation he'd encounter from American fans, but also opened his eyes to the bleak and bone-chilling New England winters he'd be contending with in the years ahead. "In late autumn 1965, Bowdoin College had opened a new field house with six or seven courts," remembered Adams. "The college's coach called up Jack and asked that he bring a couple of players up to Maine to show how the game was supposed to be played and give a clinic—and Jack chose Anil and me."

Anil agreed to participate in the match with great enthusiasm, knowing he'd be riding with Barnaby and Adams together in Barnaby's car. "A highway trip in a comfortable car—what better way to see the country?" he said he thought at the time. Soon he would learn that the automobile he'd be riding in was a red two-door VW Beetle, which wasn't quite the comfortable highway car he'd imagined. "I took the back seat as I was the junior member of the group," Anil said. "Jack drove and drove and drove his somewhat vintage car, which probably had clocked more than a hundred thousand miles by the time we took this journey—and the back seat ride got harder and harder as we headed north and the air got colder and colder. So, I opted for a blanket, as the heater didn't seem to work well enough against the cold."

Along the way, Anil was struck by the many Howard Johnson's motels dotting the edges of the highway, just like the ones he'd seen in a Hollywood film at the Eros Cinema in Bombay. There were also quite a few Valle's steakhouses, where they eventually stopped for a meal—one of the first of many steaks Anil would gradually grow accustomed to eating (any form of beef is still widely considered an off-limits dish for a Hindu hailing from the land of the Holy Cow). "I was astounded at the portions of food that were served," he said. "More miles and more Ho Jo's and Valle's steakhouses later we finally got to Bowdoin and I experienced my first real, cold weather. It was cold outside and the court was cold, too, so cold that the ball hardly bounced."

According to Adams, Bowdoin had a medium-size gallery court, where he and Anil were to play two exhibitions, which were artificially constructed to be five games each and the crowds were very enthusiastic. "But apparently the word had gotten around the Bowdoin campus about this exhibition," said Adams. "And there were many people who couldn't get in to either match. So damned if the coach didn't ask us to play a third time. We had to, although I was plain exhausted. But Anil arranged things. He was so accommodating and such a good sportsman that we played five games the third match, too. Only Jack, Anil, and I were aware of the 'fix.' Neither Anil nor I can remember who won, although I have a pretty good guess. To Anil it didn't matter."

Anil remembered bonding with both Barnaby and Adams on this and other mid-winter road trips they would make together, which allowed them plenty of time for devising sophisticated strategies to cope with formidable opponents and drilling deep into the finer points of squash. "I was so glad that Dinny, a really bright, cerebral young man, befriended me," Anil said. "His sense of humor, sometimes, was so clever, I lost track of the joke—so I learned that you really had to pay attention to Dinny's line of thought to understand and enjoy his personality. We were very different, he from an educated elite WASP background, and I from the village of Chheharta via Bombay with not a lot of educational inventory in my family. But we bonded through squash from very early on in our relationship and that has carried through to this day."

By the time Anil was a sophomore, much of his shyness with respect to women had faded away to an extent that he acknowledged that there were female fans, who often found Anil's exotic air to be quite compelling. Adams recalled a particular match in Chicago that highlights how college girls began to gravitate to many of the matches Anil played. "Everybody was excited to see how well he would do when he went to the nationals in Chicago," Adams said. "Anil played Don Leggat, a great big strong Canadian, whose principal weapon was his cannonball hard serve, which didn't exist in softball. Don really wasn't fit to hold a candle to Anil, but he beat Anil with that hard serve in the first round. Nevertheless, Anil was very curious to meet some of the corn-fed blonde Midwestern coeds from Chicago and Northwestern. Anil had probably never seen anything like those coeds, but they'd never seen anything like Anil. And I remember a late evening game of mixed triples—Anil and I and four women playing in a doubles court at the Lakeshore Club, several of us in pajamas. Definitely my most memorable doubles experience."

In fact, oftentimes when Anil and I meet his college friends to this day, they cannot resist dropping a comment on the affect that

Anil had on women during his college years. Elaborating on this tournament in Chicago, Adams explained the stands were virtually empty until Anil walked in, then suddenly filled up with an expansive crowd, most of them young women. Jay Umans, another squash-playing contemporary at Cornell, recalled a similar scenario at a tournament in Pennsylvania. Anil always dismisses these stories as exaggerations, but I have a feeling that so many classmates testifying to similar stories in unrelated contexts must have a closer recollection of reality than Anil pretends to have. As his wife, I'm also uniquely privy to his particular charms, including his twinkling eyes and electric smile ever ready to light up a room. And I'm well aware of his knack for avoiding topics that don't interest him by deploying what he calls a "MacGuffin," a Hitchcockian device that he often uses to redirect the storyline of a conversation he doesn't like by injecting distracting non sequiturs. He was also known to use a variation of this concept in physical form on the squash court, where he would subtly control a rally by hitting a roll corner or a drop shot to throw his opponent off stride or "precipitate a crisis," as Adams and Barnaby described such play, and push an on-court plot toward a conclusion of his liking. Techniques like these, as Scheinmann explained, can be maddening to an opponent, or a spouse, yet incredibly effective in getting one's way.

* * *

CHAPTER ELEVEN

Civil Rights and Unrest

To be sure, Anil had plenty of good times at Harvard, but his college years were hardly without challenges. The decade of the 1960s was also an era of political assassinations—with president John F. Kennedy perishing in a hail of bullets in 1963 and his brother and presidential candidate, Robert Kennedy, getting gunned down in 1968. At the same time, the civil rights movement, helmed by diverse organizations—from the NAACP to religious congregations to Black Power groups—had emerged to claim maximum attention on a national level with the Reverend Martin Luther King taking center stage on one end of the spectrum and Stokely Carmichael, Eldridge Cleaver, and Malcolm X commanding the spotlight at the other extreme.

To get a sense of Anil's view of this phenomenon, it's useful to bear in mind that his history in India exposed him to extreme grassroots poverty, which was pervasive on the subcontinent, where millions did not have a roof over their heads and struggled through their lives with perhaps a single inadequate meal a day. Medical treatment was almost non-existent and the infant mortality rate was probably ten times that of the U.S.

In contrast, in the U.S., where the government was actively making an effort to look after the African-American community by providing affordable housing, welfare sustenance, food stamps, and eventually the passage of anti-discrimination legislation, including the Fair Housing Act, at the urging of President Lyndon B. Johnson, racism and inequality were their central issues, rather than access to square meals or basic shelter. The conflict was different—"Black pride" emerged as a rallying cry to move the community's psyche beyond the remnant humiliations of slavery and the historical emotional and mental mistreatment of the country's African-American population. Anil noted that while he was growing up he was plagued by what he thought of as "a post-colonial hangover," but it was something very different than what American blacks were enduring under the shadow of the slave era. "Yet the psychological damage of both slavery and colonialism was similar in that it resulted in a culture of subservience and disempowerment that has affected groups of people over the course of generations," said Anil.

In witnessing and attempting to understand their experience, Tom Webber was a wonderful sounding board to Anil, who by now was quite immersed in Gandhi's readings, and his emphasis on "experiments with truth," which echoed then and, according to the great squash player, still do. "Tom knew of Gandhi and was well-read on Martin Luther King," said Anil. "I believed in the thinking of Gandhi and, though I never was a part of any grassroots socially uplifting movements, at all stages of my life I have been a sympathetic supporter and contributor to certain social causes. Tom and I had shared feelings about these world changers. We agreed that they were products of their environments, which allowed them to become leaders of important social movements. Especially Gandhi, and later Dr. King, taught us the meaning of sacrifice, of selflessness, of *satyagraha*. These heroes acquired strength through belief. And I believe Mahatmaji and Dr. King had inner voices that allowed them to thrive on their sacrifices."

Inspired in part by their interest in participating in authentic social change, Webber and Anil decided to move off campus to live together in the housing projects of Roxbury, a largely black section of Boston, during their junior year. "A lot of the black kids, certainly most of the ones in our class, were from middle class or upper class backgrounds and had gone to private schools," said Webber. "And the Black Power movement that Stokely Carmichael started in 1965-66 was really strong on black separatism and black rights and black studies and learning about Africa, so blacks started having their own clubs and started sitting together in the dining hall, and these were mostly prep school kids who, for the first time, were identifying themselves as black. This was very strange to me, because the black friends that I had were public school kids that didn't give a damn and I related to them more, because we all grew up in a really poor neighborhood or in the projects, while the upper class black folks didn't want to have anything to do with me."

Webber remembered concurrent movements that were happening at the time that didn't resonate with his experience either. "Black Panthers were also coming up, but Black Power was about black people having to do for themselves, black people having to have their own organizations," Webber explained. "This is when the black students at Harvard were pushing for a black studies department, it was very different from the Vietnam movement. White radicals were involved in that. Women's rights was another whole issue. I didn't relate to the Black Power movement, but I felt the same way about some of the white radicals who were upper class people and you questioned whether they were rebelling against their parents or trying to make a statement about how cool and hip they were by being more radical than the next person. I never got into that. I always felt you had to prove yourself. I felt alienated by the very wealthy, upper class Harvard snottiness. I hated that. I think Anil sort of did, too. That's why we moved to Roxbury."

At the time, however, students at Harvard were not allowed to live off campus unless they had a reason. So Webber put forth a thoughtful effort to justify the move. "I desperately did not like being overwhelmed by Harvard, and this Black Power movement, and everybody saying white people have to stop working for black people. My father started a church in East Harlem, his parishioners were all black and Puerto Rican. With the Black Power movement, black people wanted to be running their own churches, running their own businesses, running the welfare office, they felt black people should be the officers on the beat in Harlem instead of white officers, there should be a black mayor instead of a white one in Chicago, or Detroit, or Cleveland because they were mostly black cities. I remember one speech where someone asked Malcolm X, 'What's the role of white people in the black struggle?' And he said, 'Well, if white people are really sincere, and I don't know too many who are, they should go to white Appalachia or down to the South and convince white people to change their racist ways.' They didn't want white people working in a black organization or in a black community. I grew up in East Harlem, I wanted to be around black people, and I wanted to work in a black community. But I couldn't join the black organizations, they didn't want me, they felt they were looked down upon to be associated with white people. So I wanted to get out of Harvard. I was messed up in a way. I was so involved in my identity as a white boy from Harlem, I thought maybe I was black," Webber said. "More than singing the Beatles I would sing Motown and Marvin Gaye. I was just too relating to blacks. I wanted to move, I wasn't allowed to maintain my identity at Harvard, so I thought, *Like my father moved to East Harlem, I'm going to move to Roxbury*. I had to convince the Harvard authorities to let me move. And I suggested to Anil, 'Why don't you move with me? It'll be a lot cheaper, but also, we'll be off campus and we can do what we want.' In those days you couldn't have a woman in your dorm after 11 o'clock. You would get kicked out."

The latter part of Webber's argument might have ranked high in Anil's list of reasons for moving out, but he told the authorities at Harvard his rationale for wanting to live off campus revolved around cultural dietary issues, which conflicted with the food served at the university's cafeterias. "I don't know if he had to get a doctor's note stating that he had to cook his own food, but I know my father wrote a letter that my commitment to working in Roxbury was sincere and he supported it, and Harvard agreed. We were probably the only juniors who weren't living in a dorm that year," Webber said.

So in 1967-68, the two friends moved into a public housing project for $45 month. "I got a job at the Roxbury neighborhood house and the director said he could get us a place there easily," explained Webber. "We met the financial requirements because neither of us made any money. So I got out of dorm crew when I got this job and I remember being upset that no one ever told me I could work wherever I wanted for 15 hours, I didn't have to work on the dorm crew." For Webber, who had grown up in Spanish Harlem, the experience was not all that alien and he was relatively comfortable with the surroundings. But he did share with his Indian counterpart some precautions to take while living in a black neighborhood. And Anil remembered developing a sort of 360-degree radar sense, which was instinctive to Webber after living for years in Harlem. For a while they lived in Roxbury relatively peacefully. But a few months after they had settled in, Martin Luther King was assassinated and soon the neighborhood was on fire with rampant vandalism, arson, and gunshots.

"It was a very tough neighborhood, the toughest in Boston," said Webber. "The day Martin Luther King was shot, I remember being very nervous about going home. The trains stopped running at 11:30 p.m." Both he and Anil had the option of staying in a dorm on campus called Dudley House, and they crashed there for a night or two before going home to Roxbury. Anil recalled a knock on the door shortly after they returned, and opened it to find a black neighbor checking in to see if all was well with the two disparate youths. In many ways that experience went a long way towards clearing some of the cobwebs that had clouded Anil's mind about American blacks. "They said they'd take care of us, I think the people in Roxbury actually liked us," said Webber.

The following year, Webber moved to a house in Cambridge after marrying his college sweetheart, Andrea Bertocci, a German languages literature student at Radcliffe, and Anil roomed in a house with a group of other friends near Central Square. In many ways, their shared experiment in Roxbury was more meaningful to Webber than it was to Anil. "I didn't identify with black people," said Anil, who saw this phase as a social experiment and a chance to deepen his friendship with Webber. "And I understood even less why lower income blacks needed extra help more than food stamps and a subsidized place to live. From my Indian vantage point, I saw their situation as lower middle class, an economic level that the grassroots poor Indian would be lucky to achieve. Yet, with Tom's help and my own subsequent interactions with blacks I understood to some extent their need for social and psychological support in a very wealthy country that had an embedded history of slavery and racism." So the experience did shed some light for Anil on the African-American view and their experience of discrimination, which, in fact, contrasted sharply with his own.

"I am often asked how America treated me. It is sometimes anticlimactic for those who ask the question when I don't get dramatic and outline all the insults played upon me by Americans. Americans generally appreciate merit and are open-minded enough to suspend judgment of the unknown. I was a champion squash player, I was at Harvard, and I was neither black nor white nor a Jew. I was from India, and most Americans didn't know much about its history, geography, and culture," Anil said, noting aspects of his own experience were not unlike that of the great Pakistani squash player Hashim Khan, who often praised America and how good its people had been to him. "He, as a champion of champions, arrived in the 1950s, was accepted, made so many friends, and had so many supporters. He, a true champion, left behind a goodwill that will last for several generations after his departure," said Anil, who is critical of some of his fellow squash players of South Asian origin who he believes have unfairly cried discrimination where it didn't exist.

"I have seen referee decisions, or exclusions from a team, or just certain behavior towards them described as 'discrimination,'" said Anil. "Perhaps, it was the case, but it might also have been the right decision or it might have been that the decision-maker just didn't like the person involved. It's easy to bash America by using the discrimination card, as that is an area of vulnerability in the U.S., where discrimination lawsuits might smudge the reputations of those who really are not racist at all and instead are in a dispute relating to merit or social behavior, or some other reason. The race card is a most convenient fallback for certain groups if things are not going in one's favor. It's such a fine line, especially for a non-black, between personality dislikes and color discrimination."

Ultimately, his experiences with people of all walks of life during his college years, including the people he met in Roxbury, deepened Anil's broader views on discrimination, which he had been sensitive to even as a child. "Benign activities in India could also be classified as discrimination by way of caste and color," he explained. "It was well known in Amritsar, where I was born, that the one common thread amongst the beautiful young girls on Lawrence Road was buxomness and skin of a lighter complexion. Middle class Indians purposely avoided the sun if they could. They didn't want to get that darker pigmentation. One of the Tata companies made a fortune on the sale of Lakmé bleach cream as did Hindustan Lever with a cream called Fair & Lovely that were and still are used by both men and women of a darker pigment."

Though loath to support reckless accusations of discrimination in any context, Anil was certainly exposed to the challenges that

The Indian squash team for the world open amateur tournament in Australia in 1967. From left to right: Sanjit Roy, Anil Nayar, team manager A.R.V. Peermohamed, Fali Madon, and Dinshaw Pandole.

true forms of social injustice posed to sportsmen and everyday citizens alike in his experiences around the globe. His experience in Australia, when he was part of the team representing India at the World Open Amateur Championship in 1967, is a case in point. The prior year, England Squash hosted a conference that led to the formation of the International Squash Rackets Federation and Australia, Canada, Egypt, Great Britain, India, New Zealand, Pakistan, South Africa, and the United States sent delegates. By August of 1967, ISRF started the men's World Team Championships with six teams playing in Australia.

"We were drawn against South Africa and we were lamely instructed by telegram through the Indian sports ministry two days before play started not to play the South Africans due to their apartheid policy," Anil remembered. "This was sport, not politics, and even though the South African government followed this inhumane, detestable policy, everyone on our team felt the white South African squash players must feel differently. We were all sportsmen. Our common language was one of stamina, boasts, drops, lobs, kills—nothing to do with color." The Indians later ran into the South African team at nearby restaurant and after a few uncomfortable glances, Anil decided to break the ice. "I introduced myself and the team, sat down with them, had couple of beers, talked about issues and soon we became sports friends," he said. "We pretended we didn't know of the ministry's message and played against them the next day. I had the satisfaction of winning against a big strong Boer, Darvie Botha, a stronger stockier version of my Harvard teammate Fritz Hobbs, who later became an Olympic rower, and I can't say I didn't relish this win despite the entente that took place the night before."

Following the Indian team's less-than-stellar performance at the men's world team championship event in Australia, "where we beat Pakistan to the team's and the government's joy," said Anil, but tied with Pakistan in fifth place overall, they toured New Zealand to play in a series of club matches in cities like Wellington, Rotorua, and Auckland. Anil got a taste of the changes occurring at the time on the multicultural front Down Under during his billeted stay with a player on the All Blacks rugby team. "The rugby professional was a Maori with a white wife," recalled Anil. "He was a strong, imposing, fit man, who was also polite and respectful. It was not yet time for mixed marriages in New Zealand, but here was a topnotch athlete who was not only a minority on the well-known, ironically-named All Blacks professional rugby team, but also a pioneer, leading the way to diversity at a pivotal time in New Zealand. I was fascinated by him and, at the same time, he was fascinated with my racquet and mobility skills. Sport was the ultimate unifier!"

While Anil remembered feeling very much accepted in America with squash playing a large role in reinforcing that sentiment, he

The Indian squash team goofing off at dinner in Australia in 1967.

does recall that Victor Niederhoffer, a topnotch Jewish champion player a few years his senior, encountered a completely contrary experience in Chicago in the mid-1960s, when, even as the national champion, he was shunned as a member at all six of the Windy City's prominent squash clubs. In his book *Squash: A History of the Game*, James Zug sheds light on Niederhoffer's exclusion, which Niederhoffer believed was due to the fact that he was Jewish:

> To some extent he was right. Squash was still very much a Protestant, Christian sport in America.... In the spirit of the countercultural sixties, Niederhoffer decided to make a public statement. In the autumn of 1966 he wrote a letter to the

USSRA declaring that he would boycott the 1967 nationals unless a Chicago club asked him to join.... The Chicago Clubs called Niederhoffer's bluff and did not make a move. Niederhoffer "retired." He did not play the 1967 nationals, and stayed away from singles tournaments for five years.

Whether Niederhoffer was excluded from the clubs because he was Jewish, or because his screwball attitude and spirit of play was out of sync with Stewart Braun, Seymour Knox, and other "grand panjandrums of squash," as Zug refers to the reigning elders of the sport at the time, is debatable. Niederhoffer was known for his histrionics as well as for thumbing his nose at squash's blue bloods by wearing mismatched sneakers to black-tie dinner dances, which, according to Zug, contributed to making him "the most unclubable man in squash."

In contrast to Niederhoffer's offbeat and often brash demeanor, Anil's sunny disposition, charm, and brio on the court gained him easy access and a warm welcome to all of the clubs throughout the Northeast, where his star was rising at the very same time. "I felt safe in the Northeast, at Harvard, in Boston and New York, and have no memories of discrimination leaving any toxic scars," he said. "This was my experience, but at no stage would I ever intend to minimize the existence of discrimination in the U.S." He also pointed out that by the 1970s more clubs had begun to open to non-WASP members, and by the 1980s the numbers of Indians in America had increased three- to fourfold since he first came to Harvard in the 1960s. "They were there in all walks of life—cab drivers, corner candy store operators, white collar professionals, doctors, and techies—and were respected for their hard work and intelligence," he said. "It was no longer a novelty to interact and socialize with the snake charmers and elephant riders of the days gone by."

* * *

CHAPTER TWELVE

Winning, Losing, and Sporstmanship

The most important lessons Anil learned during his college years revolved around character, and many of them unfolded on the squash court. Ask any squash player whether it's possible to glean insight into a person's psyche on the squash court and virtually all would agree that the tight quarters and mano-a-mano competition involved in squash provide a view into the nature of an opponent unlike any other sport. "With the small court, you can tell a lot about a person's personality by the way they play and act," said Scheinmann. "It's amplified, there's no place to hide your emotions or how you tick. For example, Rick Sterne, if you ever played squash with him you'd know he was a winner and that translated into his professional life. You just knew if you had to count on somebody, it would be Rick. You could see his character." Anil agreed with Scheinmann's assessment of Sterne, who eventually became an exceedingly successful investment banker in New York and a national masters hardball champion in the 40+ age category. And several memorable matches over this period revealed much to Anil about his fellow players—and himself.

Anil's first meeting with the charismatic southpaw Mohibullah Khan sheds light on the unique qualities that propelled so many of the legendary Khan clan from Pakistan to the very top of the squash firmament in the 1960s and '70s, when Anil was at his peak. Feeling he owed Khan a word of thanks for his role in forging a path to his admission into Harvard and wanting to congratulate him on winning the world championship tournament the year before, Anil called him at the Harvard Club of Boston to set up a time to meet about a week after he'd arrived at Cambridge. With an air of standoffishness, Khan reluctantly invited him to the club, and Anil remembered arriving to see him give a lesson to a B player. "Mo was playing the typical club pro game of running the member all over the court and leading him to exhaustion," said Anil. "I watched in awe as he glided across the court with ease, making it just hard enough for his opponent to get to the ball and make a weak return. I thought of a cheetah going at an easy trot ready to unwind into a gallop at any moment. Mo was fiercely strong on the court, a force of nature waiting to explode. His choked grip, his sprawl on all sides of the court, and his total deception if by chance you hit the ball anywhere near the T, I had never seen anything like this and I knew I had to learn from him and the way he played."

After the lesson ended, Anil descended from the gallery to meet Khan at his pro shop. "He was surprised to see me and his very first question threw me off guard," Anil said. "'You from India?' he asked. This probably was the first time I had met a Muslim from Pakistan and Khan was a Pathan from Peshawar. As a Hindu from India, there wasn't much to like and warning bells went off in my head to be careful. Pathans, especially those who grew up in Peshawar and Pakistan, were volatile at best and the general feeling among Hindus was they were not to be trusted at all in relationships and close quarters."

Anil said Khan didn't remember contacting Eric Cutler about considering him for admission, so he presumed that Khan might have mentioned Anil to a member, who probably followed through with Cutler. In any case, though their chat was brief, Khan did make a date to play with Anil a week later and the squash pro readily beat him. "He was way too fast, too awesome in his movements, and his forehand power psyched me out," said Anil. "But there was hope because I was fast, too, and at the time I hadn't developed effective hardball shots. A few times I wrong-footed him, and I thought, *Ah! I think I can get him.* But I didn't."

The last time Anil played Khan was at the Saucon Valley Country Club in 1968. "By that time, Mo was getting vulnerable," said Anil. By then, Anil had also learned to take advantage of the lefty's weak backhand, which Anil's fellow Harvard player Larry Terrell described as reminiscent of a lame chicken wing, and he managed to score several points against the domineering professional player by doing so. "The gin and his unsporty lifestyle showed in his weight gain and in his slower stride and reaction time. I was 2-1 up in games when, in typical Mo fashion, he started allowing balls that he could have retrieved with his backhand to hit the back wall and then he would turn around and smack the ball with his forehand at rocket speed right down the center where I was standing." With ample room for Khan to hit a clear backhand, Anil knew his opponent's intimidatory tactic was uncalled for. Whether Khan's intention with this maneuver was to compensate for his own weak backhand swing or to dragoon Anil into altering his play and force errors, the stratagem produced the desired effect, as Anil sprawled to the floor a few times to avoid getting pummeled by the ball and lost the points and lost focus. "I was imagining the hardball hitting my back or head at bullet speed and going straight through me and it did once hit my leg," Anil said. "The referee could have warned him and penalized him for these intimidatory tactics, but he himself was intimidated by Mo. I lost the match, but consoled

The 1968-69 Harvard squash team with captain Anil (at center in front row) flanked by Larry Terrell (left) and Fritz Hobbs (right).

myself that I had been victorious at some level against Mo. I had forced him to play unfairly in the match." Anil remembered being surprised by the disappointing level of sportsmanship Khan had displayed and questioned him on his antics once they were off the court.

At the same time, Anil also remembered with gratitude the techniques he learned from Khan that enabled him to significantly elevate his own game. "I learned by visually observing him, and I adapted quite successfully his sprawl to the corners after taking one or two quick steps—I was quick enough to do that well," Anil said. "I also learned to choke up on the racket and wait and use the wrist more to deceptively change the direction of the ball at the last moment, which was especially effective with the hardball—just a flick of the wrist would send the ball careening in an unanticipated direction, similar to a flick by the master batsman, Sachin Tendulkar, past slip and gully—an analogy my young commonwealth brethren would appreciate. But, there was just no way for me to learn how to replicate the powerful 'animal' spirit Mo often showed on the court. He was a killer in his heyday! In fact, Imran Khan, the current prime minister of Pakistan, has been known to have said during one of his first visits to India, 'There are two kinds of players, *insaans* (humans) and Pathans.' Mo certainly lived up to the Pathan reputation."

Another experience with Hashim Khan—a completely different kind of Pathan—left Anil at the same losing end of the stick. "Hashim and I played in a tournament when Hashim was around 60 and I was probably 22, after having recently won my first U.S. men's nationals in 1969," recalled Anil. "Hashim was the one player I dreaded to play. I was nervous and edgy and Hashim was comfortable, hitting his drop shots from every impossible angle in the court. I lost, but at the same time felt honored. I had lost to the best of the best. My only solace was the thought that I would have done better if we had a replay. I needed to overcome the 'awe' factor, and for me it often happened the second time around."

In other matches, Anil was thrown off early on by his inexperience with the speed of the hardball or certain players' style of play. In one of his first American tournaments, a U.S. nationals championship in 1966, he was drawn to play Don Leggat from Ontario. "A fine, polite gentlemen was Don," said Anil. "However, once he got on the court, he unleashed his hard serves at me. The ball coming at me reminded me of beamers being bowled at cricketer Vinoo Mankad by Wes Hall at the CCI. I was not prepared for this kind of 100 mph ball coming at me and more often than not, I didn't react quickly enough to get my body away from the ball so it could hit the back wall on the fly. Needless to say, I lost in three games and was thoroughly humiliated, but I did get my revenge and won the second time I played him."

Anil also recalled certain players in club leagues or tournaments who would possess the nettlesome habit of obstructing his path or blocking his view of the ball at the last moment. "It generally happens on the left wall where most of the rallies take place," he said. "It may or may not be intentional, but the effect is of the hitter seeing that ball a split second later than he could, resulting in a weak shot or an error." Anil's coach, Jack Barnaby, warned him of such a player, Ralph Howe, whom he played in an early round after beating Tom Poor at the 1969 U.S. nationals in Rochester, New York. "Sure enough, I was drawn against Ralph, who had recently beaten Mo Khan in an open championship," Anil said. "Predictably, in the very first point Ralph hit the ball along the left wall and stayed there that extra microsecond before he moved to the center. He did the same in the second and third points, and I was losing patience. I knew what was happening and finally I asked for let, which I got. The next time it happened, I asked for let again and I got it, but I feared I might lose focus in winning the points and the game by constantly asking for lets and not being allowed to play my strokes. So I told Ralph of my discomfort and soon after that I swung my racquet over his head and asked for a let—along the left wall. Ralph, I think, got the picture and from then on we played a fair match. He even sent me a note congratulating me on my win against him and then later his brother Sam in the finals in the same tournament. This to me was a very fine gesture of a fine sportsman and athlete."

So impressed was Anil with Howe's gracious letter that he preserved it among some squash keepsakes from this period of life. Indeed, its quaint and clever charm offers a view into the high level of sportsmanship and grace that characterized squash players then—and, in many ways, continues to today. It also provides a refreshing counterpoint to the debased level of discourse that often prevails in the political sphere, and sometimes in sporting arenas, in the current polarized era:

Dear Anil:

Heartiest felicitations on your fine victory over Tom Poor in Rochester! While I "de facto" accept your other victories, I shall reserve my enthusiasm out of sheer selfishness. No I shan't! Seriously, you have captured, in my opinion, one of the great squash titles—of which you may always be proud. I salute your solid victory over me—I can't (in recent time) remember losing three consecutive games without getting to 10. You and Sam must have had a ding-dong affair. Hope to see you on the doubles circuit. Again well done!

Sincerely,
Ralph E. Howe

During his college years at Harvard, Anil won every intercollegiate match he played except one, when Harvard was playing the Naval Academy at Annapolis in 1967. Interestingly, that match is one of the most often remembered not just by Anil, but also by many of his teammates.

"We arrived on a Friday to play on Saturday and when we went to practice there were five courts in a row with no separation in the gallery between the courts and no one was there," said Anil's teammate Michel Scheinmann. "While we were practicing and loosening up, I was the only one who knew that Anil had the flu. After we practiced, we went to eat in the midshipmen's dining room. On our side was the coach, the manager, and nine of us on the team, and on the other side there were hundreds of midshipmen, and all through the lunch they were doing a wave, like you see at a football game, and screaming, 'Go Navy!' The sound was reverberating through the dining room and the noise never stopped the whole time."

Under the weather as he was, Anil remembered feeling overwhelmed by the atmosphere. "The midshipmen didn't quite care for us Harvard folks, especially when some at Harvard were not only anti-Vietnam, but were also against much about U.S. foreign policy at the time," said Anil, who felt targeted by their antagonistic tone. "Strong guys these young men, and here I was with my Harvard team, playing number one, but feeling intimidated by the shouting amongst the midshipmen. I was brown, not white, and I was number one. So I stayed close to Fritz Hobbs, a tall, strong player on our team who later became an Olympic rower, just to feel safe."

By the time the squash players got back to the courts the rowdy atmosphere was amplified. "The gallery now was like Madison Square Garden, with standing room only," said Scheinmann. "Unlike the gentlemanly WASP tone we were used to on the squash courts, the midshipmen were screaming their heads off. I remember playing at one end, and I was number nine of nine players, and I couldn't focus because of all the noise and I couldn't remember the score, but I managed to win. So I went down to watch Anil playing his match, and I knew he had a 102-degree fever. He was playing Scott Ryan, who wasn't as good as he was, but it turned into a five-game match, and Anil lost the match 15-12 in the fifth. But I never once heard Anil tell anyone else he was sick, because he didn't want his opponent to think that his win was any less valid because he wasn't well."

Aggravating his fever, Anil recalled the courts and gallery being overheated, too, as Navy was reported to customarily do in preparing its courts for a match. "It felt like 90 degrees F inside and 30 degrees F outside. The court was so hot that the balls behaved like golf balls—super fast off the front wall and often rising high above one's head," he said. "We might as well have been playing racquetball. And as was the tradition at Navy, the galleries were packed with midshipmen whose sole purpose was to boo the opponent after each point and create so much noise that you could not hear the ball hit the front wall."

Though Anil lost the match that year, he's more often remembered for his team spirit by his fellow players and Harvard friends.

"Since he was number one, if he hadn't played, everyone else on the team would have had to play stronger players up the ladder," said Adams, noting that Anil was always a thoughtful team player. And in fine health the following year, Anil and the team had the opportunity to get their comeuppance against Navy. "Navy was soundly beaten 9-0 the next year when they played us at Harvard," Anil noted. "And a year later at Annapolis, we had made sufficient preparation mentally and physically to beat Navy definitively again 8-1."

The wider athletic community at Harvard saw in Anil the same high standards of sportsmanship his fellow squash players had experienced with him directly. At an annual dinner at the Varsity Club during his senior year, the Varsity Club's board members chose to honor Anil with the William J. Bingham Award, which

Anil with tournament chairman Derek Drummond and Colin Adair after defeating Adair in the Canadian national championship final in 1968.

is named after an outstanding former director of athletics for Harvard and was first awarded in 1954. By its own definition of standards, the Varsity Club gives the award annually to "one male member of the graduating class of Harvard College, who, through integrity, courage, leadership, and ability on the athletic fields, has best served the high purpose of Harvard as exemplified by Bingham." It is also recognized as the award that goes to Harvard's single most outstanding male athlete each year. In 1969, Anil was recognized as that athlete and the award was handed to the surprised recipient in the form of an engraved Omega watch.

After graduating from Harvard in 1969, Anil continued to play in regional and national tournaments in the U.S., Canada and Mexico, and he earned the national champion title in all three countries several times between 1969-71. Among the more challenging players he came up against during this period was Victor Niederhoffer, the formidable and eccentric Jewish player who was known for his calculating approach to the game and had returned to the sport after moving to New York in 1971 and joining the Harvard Club with the intercession of Charlie Ufford, an influential senior player at Harvard. "Victor had just come back from his long layoff and I was fortunate to catch him before he got much better," Anil recalled of some of the matches he played with the elder Niederhoffer, who by this time had gained a bit of weight. "I remember beating him in four games at the Joseph Lordi Memorial tournament in New York City. Victor had a reputation of being a master strategist, and when we got to the fourth game, as he was tiring, I realized that I could have lost if he had been 15 percent fitter." Anil, on the other hand, "was as fast as a Bengal tiger and had an innately sharp court sense," wrote James Zug, echoing Jack Barnaby on the quality of his play at the time. "His bread and butter was a forehand cross-court kill."

Following this tournament, however, Niederhoffer would spend a lot of time practicing by himself on court, where he seemed to be playing out a match in his own head. "I saw him practicing three-wall nicks, imagining the position of his opponent in the court, or making a drop shot after a visualized exchange of a few rallies deep in the court," said Anil, noting that this visualization was part of his strategy in fine tuning his accuracy. "It was a very effective combination and it allowed him, in later years, to conquer the indomitable Mohibullah Khan." According to Anil, Niederhoffer was also very confident in assessing his chances to win. "I remember talking to him in a Midwest city at a U.S. professional tournament in the early 1970s while we were watching Mo play an early round from the stands," Anil said. "He leaned over to me and simply said, 'I'm going to beat Mo.' And so he did by dissecting Mo's game convincingly, though it's important to mention that by then Mo was in the sunset years of his career as a champion and he was becoming undone. He was slower on his feet, he had lost the sting in his shots, and his choked backhand grip had lost the torque needed to get both power and accuracy and was thus becoming a liability." Reflecting further on this match, Anil observed the completely different strengths of these players and clearly saw that the time was right for Neiderhoffer to astutely exploit Khan's vulnerability as his strength waned with the passage of time. "It is the natural order of squash succession," he said. "A powerful player whose overwhelming strength is cheetah-like speed loses just a bit of his quickness and becomes the victim of a slower-footed yet strategic predator. It happened to Mohibullah, it happened to me, and it has happened to many others."

Later in 1971, Anil met Niederhoffer again at the Gold Racquets tournament, the nation's oldest invitational tournament hosted at the Rockaway Hunting Club, a beautiful country club in a seaside setting amid a scenic golf course in Cedarhurst, New York, with, perhaps, 25 tennis courts. "This was a much acclaimed tournament, one of three topnotch tournaments, which most players would play before competing in the nationals," said Anil, who had won the Gold Racquets tournament at least once or twice before. This time Niederhoffer was ready for Anil. "He made me work really hard, often making me run those extra two or three steps due to his shot placement," Anil recalled. "Victor is a big person on the squash court and sometimes did not make sufficient effort to give me a fair view of the ball. It was a five-game match and he won 3-2. He had beaten me and, as I remember this match, I could see how he had analyzed my game enough to keep me moving as much as possible so as not to allow me the time and position to make effective shots."

Occasionally thinking through the match in the years that followed, Anil still has questions about why he lost. "Did I let him beat me? Was I not strong enough mentally? Had I lost my confidence or passion to win? Did I not have enough focus? Was I too concerned with the fear of losing versus doing what I did best, which was to concentrate and play a point at a time and enjoy the process? Did I fail to learn his game well enough?" wondered Anil, who no longer had his trusted coach Jack Barnaby at his side to help him. "I should have telephoned Jack to chat before my match—he always gave the simplest, customized, and most implementable advice of anyone I had known." He also wondered if he'd have fared better if he had called his old coach Yusuf Khan, who by then, with an assist from Anil, had moved to Seattle, where Khan coached at various clubs, including among others the Seattle Racquets Club, the Bellevue Club, and the College Club of Seattle, and sometimes played exhibition matches with Anil at places like the Seattle Tennis Club or the Multnomah Club in Portland whenever Anil visited him on the West Coast. "I didn't prepare fully, I was not mentally ready to play this match," he concluded, knowing he might have won that match against Neiderhoffer, who later went on to play the professional circuit, with a little more forethought or a boost of confidence from Barnaby or Khan.

By this time, after having won the U.S. nationals in 1969 and '70, the Canadian nationals in 1968 and '70 and the Mexican nationals in 1970, Anil had also had a ski accident in Stowe, Vermont, where he sprained the ligament in his right knee. "I was out

Anil with Craig Benson, Canadian junior national champion, after winning the men's national title in Canada in 1970.

of commission for several months and when I did go back to play the nationals in 1971, I lost to John Reese, someone I should have beaten," he admitted, noting his physical condition might have also contributed to a loss of confidence, which, in turn, may have contributed to this particular maddening loss. "I wasn't fast like I had been before. I had lost that additional split-second edge and I had failed to adjust my game to one of more conservative, conventional play. A loss, when it does not happen often, creates a cycle of self reflection and self doubt. No matter how much I tried to rationalize the losses with my physical condition, my confidence had been eroded."

While the hard knocks of Anil's tough losses surely contributed to some character building during his college years, a few notable wins gave him a clear view into the strengths of some of his toughest opponents—as well as his own. "The mental state is undeniably the hardest to manage, but I remember clearly when I felt I played the best squash of my life—it was like I was playing an instrument to perfection," said Anil, whose name in Sanskrit means spirit or wind. And, recalling what he believes was perhaps the ne plus ultra match of his career during the Canadian nationals in February 1968, Anil covered the court as smoothly as a cool breeze on a summer day. "I played Colin Adair, a strong competitor and somewhat physical person on court. He would nudge or push during rallies, not too much but just enough to unnerve a newbie. I had played him in 1967 and lost in three games at the Montreal Athletic Association championship," he said. After beating Sam Howe in four games in the semi-finals, Anil's match against Adair was classic squash. "My balls went deep into the corners, sometimes at medium pace, sometimes quickly. I had Colin picking up balls in the corners and allowing me to hit volleys, three walls, or drops, all the time keeping him off balance. I don't think I ever felt so in control of a national finals. I won 3-0. Mental and physical in sync, the ultimate winning combo!" he said, noting that the key to his success here was his positive mental attitude.

"It takes hard work to stay positive," he stated, adding that following this match he replayed in his mind all the things he did right, visualizing every high point. "Where did I excel? My amazing retrieval, my superb anticipation, my counterattack before my opponent could finish his follow through, my three-wall nicks that I could pull off from awkward defensive positions, my aim to be as fast as Hashim, who legend has it, was volleying drop shots!" he concluded, recalling as well his concerted effort to "think positive" to remain in good mental shape.

As Anil reflected on this match he also saw it as one of the few times when he found himself in a space where mind and body meet in a kind of sacred harmony that sportsmen often refer to as "the zone." "The mind takes over, the mind commands the body, the mind sees the imminent next play, the mind tells the body 'you will have time to heal later but now you must suspend the feeling of pain'—a spirit overtakes you," he said. "It's singularly the most enriching and beautiful moment of being—and it can come for a split-second as an exceptional retrieve or an aggressive counter or it can last for the entire a period of a game. But it always goes away as quickly as it comes. And it comes rarely."

Other memorable matches involved a good measure of luck. One was at the men's nationals in February of 1969 in a seesaw battle between Anil and Sam Howe. "It could have been anybody's match," Anil said. An article by Ike Shynook in the local newspaper *Democrat and Chronicle* described the tension-filled match and emphasized Anil's "cat-like agility" in defeating the former two-time title holder in five action-packed games when it was 2-all in the fifth:

> Howe was able to gain a 12-12 tie in the fifth and deciding game when Nayar dropped his racket during a brisk rally. The match ended dramatically after each man had scored a point to make it 13-all, with Howe twice driving low into the front wall to end the hostilities.

Anil had come out victorious for the first time in a U.S. men's nationals tournament, capturing the men's singles crown. "The score was 12-all in the fifth game, then 13-all, when Sam opted to play to 15, hoping he could ace me a couple of times and win the match and the nationals title," said Anil. "He went for the winners but hit the tin twice. It was my match and my first U.S. nationals win. It was eventually luck, but to get to 13-all in the fifth did require grit amongst both players," he said.

In a story in *The Harvard Crimson*, A.J. Daly described the match in more detail:

The already legendary Nayar, who is perhaps the best individual performer in any sport Harvard has ever had, climaxed a perfect season with a narrow 3-2 victory over Sam Howe in the finals. After winning the first game 15-11, Nayar lost [the second game], 13-15, but came back strong in the third to win, 15-5. Howe eked out a 15-14 victory in the fourth game, but Nayar persevered for a 15-13 win in the deciding game. The victory is one of a long string of title victories for the talented Nayar, whom Harvard coach John Barnaby has called "one of the half-dozen best collegiate squash players of all time."

Without question, though, the most memorable moment in which luck loomed large was during the semi-final match against Spencer Burke at Yale the following month, when Anil was playing his third national intercollegiate championship tournament in New Haven. It was astonishing to Anil then that Burke would call his own shot—one that appeared to be a sure winner—down at match point in the fifth game of the grinding match. "Spencer was the only one who could see the ball," said Anil, adding that another player in the same position might have acted differently. With victory just within reach for Burke, his honest gesture at that tense moment was significant in the annals of sports history in that it turned the tables of fortune in Anil's favor and enabled him to not only win the semi-final with a tremendous three-wall nick, but also to subsequently claim the final match and capture the tournament's crown.

Over time, however, the magnitude of Burke's honorable act has become entrenched for Anil on a personal level, as the lasting memory of that fateful moment has crystallized his measure of the man. "Character and fair play in squash, as in life, can be judged on two levels, when there is no pressure and when there is pressure," said Anil. And he saw Burke's choice to call the ball as he saw it at such a critical point as a shining reflection his fellow

Philadelphian player Sam Howe holding the U.S. men's national champion cup with Anil, who won the event in 1969.

player's true nature. When Anil met Burke again more than 30 years later at the wedding of his friend Dinny Adams to his current wife, Nancy Hopkins, a molecular biologist and professor emeritus at MIT, he thanked him again for his sportsmanship and wondered aloud whether Burke ever felt that he had actually achieved the more laudable win that day. "It was a match for the two of us to remember," said Anil. "My name was on the record board, yet he was the hero. Spencer's highest level of sportsmanship has always stuck with me as the gold standard."

Other players who saw and remember the match have often asked Burke to replay his thoughts on that pivotal moment when the possibility of victory slipped from his grasp. Why did he report the fact that his shot nicked the tin when no one else saw it or

Winning, Losing, and Sporstmanship | 157

heard it happen? Every time the question comes up, Burke said his response is the same: "You think I'm going to cheat somebody? It's a sport. I saw the ball caress the top of the tin and float up before it dropped to the floor. There was no question that it hit the tin, and my reaction was spontaneous. There was nothing to think about."

While Anil reflected on the match with gratitude for Burke's supreme sportsmanship, he also looked back at it with a healthy measure of self-reproach for own his lack of preparation. "I had always prepared for an important match by playing out in my mind how I'd respond to an opponent's attacks," said Anil. "I knew that Sam Howe, for example, would usually hit a backhand reverse corner from around the T and that I would have to prepare myself to run to the left front wall before he hit the ball and my response would usually be a roll corner or a drop shot or drop nick. Before a match, I would usually lie on a bench in the locker room away from the traffic flow, and just think about my drops, think about aiming 6 inches above the tin to reduce the margin of error. I'd also envision a hard, low shot, or a cross-court shot that would bounce off the side wall a foot or two behind the service line so that the ball would die in the corner before my opponent could reach it. I'd think about a rail that would hit at a certain height with a certain force to enable the second bounce to end up at the back corner. Or, I'd picture a deceptive roll corner in the front or a head fake and a cross-court to wrong-foot a strong opponent, like Colin Adair, a tough retriever who played the long point and often nudged here, sometimes pushed there. I would get lost in playing out a match in my head for five or ten minutes. This was the kind of meditation I used to help mentally settle me before and during a match." And by taking too much for granted before going into this match, Anil knew the outcome could have easily have gone either way before he finally unleashed the rare three-wall nick that got him out of trouble in the end.

Has Burke ever lost sleep over the choice he made to call his own shot down that day? "Not one iota," he said. Instead, the star

Anil with the intercollegiate and men's national trophies in 1969.

Penn player remembered that he played his very best squash during the match. "That match was the performance highlight of my life—it was an out-of-body experience and I played at a level I had never played before. Many of us were irritated that the preppies had a lock on the sport until Anil came along. He played a different kind of squash than the rest of us and it added to his mystique, his luster," said Burke, comparing Anil's style of play to that of other great players of the day. "Anil played with such incredible ease, he was like a cat, a cougar, he was so different than someone like Victor Neiderhoffer, who was also an incredible player, but on court looked more like he should be driving a truck. Anil was an amazing athlete who came here and was playing our game and beating us at our game. I have absolute respect and admiration for him and what he did for the game, because here's a guy from India who's killing everybody with his unimaginable, breathtaking talent. You had all these legacy people who thought they owned the game, and Anil shows up and not only does he show them that they don't own the game—he does, but also that he's also a great guy. There are a lot of jerks in the game, yet Anil is someone you enjoy being around—he's a gentleman, he's professional, he doesn't take himself too seriously, he's not arrogant. So it was an honor to be on the court with him." For Anil the feeling was mutual.

The third time luck factored heavily in a match for Anil was at the U.S. men's nationals at the University of Pennsylvania in 1970, when he was up against Sam Howe again in the finals. "The gallery court is around 40 degrees F, and Sam is a master stroke player and I am not good in the cold," remembered Anil. "Before I could count to 10, Sam had deftly stroked his way to a 2-0 lead and I am barely breaking a sweat. *I'm done this time for sure,* I thought. But my coach Jack Barnaby offered me good, simple advice after the second game: 'Hit the ball hard and keep hitting hard—don't give Sam time to hit his shots.'" With speed being one of the more lethal weapons in his arsenal, Anil readily absorbed Barnaby's advice, upped the tempo and relentlessly belted the ball. "I hit and hit and hit hard and got Sam off his rhythm until it was two-all and near the end of the fifth," Anil said. "As I get ready to serve, Sam loses his contact lens, goes around searching for it, finds it, and puts it back on. It's a distraction for him and it helps me win the next few points, the match, and the championship. I may have won with or without the contact lens episode, but luck certainly did help."

Later that month, an article in *Sports Illustrated* by Roy Blount, Jr., described that nationals tournament in vivid detail:

Over the long Washington's Birthday weekend, when the national amateur championships of squash racquets were held at the University of Pennsylvania, it was a sport with a good deal of tang. It had speed, human interest and, most of all, an Indian named Anil Nayar.

Granted, squash has its stodgy aspects. Almost all of its leading amateurs rise naturally, like cream, from the posh prep schools and private clubs of New York, Boston and especially

Philadelphia. And when you ask a squash follower what a given player does for a living, the answer is almost invariably, "Oh, investments." At Penn's Ringe courts for the nationals, most of the spectators—no more than 250 of whom could be accommodated—were fitted out uniformly in aquiline noses and camel's hair. In fact, the whole tournament had the air of an annual reunion, complete with a formal dinner dance and luncheon entertainment provided by the Orpheus Club, a harmonizing group of substantial Philadelphia businessmen. But beneath all that upper crust, considerable life was beating. One thing about squash is that in time the ball—black rubber and slightly larger than a golf ball—comes alive.

After describing a heated and exciting match between Colin Adair and Charles Ufford in an early round in which Ufford, the considerably elder and sentimental favorite player, won the match in overtime, Blount went on to write:

The two big guns of the tournament were advancing toward each other: Sam Howe, 31, the Philadelphian with the build of a large mama's boy and the squash strength of two good-sized daddies; and Nayar, the former Harvard student and last year's champion, who is currently in the import-export business out of New York. Howe, the 1968 champion, is a product of Merion Cricket Club, which means that people accuse him of having been playing squash since he was 5; his strength is his classic, sweeping, always-appropriate Philadelphia-brand shots. Nayar plays Pakistani-Indian style, scrambling helter-skelter all over the court, slapping low-skimming bullets with a racquet held nearly halfway up the handle, returning impossible shots with even less possible shots and, above all, going like crazy all the time.

Reprinted courtesy of SPORTS ILLUSTRATED: "A Spicy Day at Penn by Roy Blount Jr. March 9, 1970. Copyright © 1970. ABG-SI, LLC.

Shortly after Howe beat Ufford in the semifinals, Nayar eliminated Canadian Peter Martin, perhaps the most fit and agile college player—outwitting and out-agiling Martin to such an extent that Martin turned red in the face and cried, "I don't know how you do that! How do you do that?" After observing that exhibition, Howe—himself already beaten twice this year by Nayar—said: "Anil is too fast for me, too quick for me."

And old master Henri Salaun seemed to agree. Speaking of the Khans (there are Mohibullah Khan and Sharif Khan as well as Hashim) and of Nayar, Salaun said, "They have a different chemical makeup than we do. I don't know whether their blood is thicker or what, but they don't get tired." The prevailing theory is that playing at 7,000 feet in 100° heat with the less springy English ball day after day in their boyhoods breeds in the players of the East a superhuman endurance. The consensus is that Nayar is still no Khan (he has never beaten one of them, and seldom meets them in competition because they are professionals), but he dominates the amateur game now as no one has in many years. "These American players have decided they just aren't going to beat Nayar," says Penn squash racquets Coach Al Molloy. "He's a great champion, but they don't challenge him, won't alter their games to cope with him. He plays too sloppy, because they don't press him enough."

Howe pressed him in the finals, however. Nayar had hardly stepped onto the court when Howe had him three points down. In fact, Nayar led only once in the first two games, which Howe swept—flushed but otherwise expressionless—15-11 and 15-8.

Then Nayar became aroused, and you had two explosive players dashing across that small enclosure, slashing with racquets and rocketing the ball within an inch or so of each other. Point after point, the two spun into position and stretched drastically to scoop the ball off wall or floor, not just getting it but hitting what should have been winners. For long stretches during the last three games of the Nayar-Howe match the red-hot ball

Anil, as pictured in Sports Illustrated *magazine, on court at the University of Pennsylvania during the 1970 U.S. national championship.*
(Photograph by James Drake/Getty Images)

never rose above the players' knees. Nayar bore down harder and harder and came back to win the three decisive games 15-9, 15-6, 15-11.

Molloy noted afterward that Howe had, as a matter of fact, taken measures to offset Nayar's strengths—had tried to throw the Indian off his stride by lobbing the ball at strategic moments. But it had not been enough. "Anil gets the pace going so that you feel yourself on a treadmill," said the vanquished Howe. "You wonder when it's going to stop, and it stops when Anil wins." So squash in this country had better learn to adapt to a dash of curry.

Blount had no way of knowing then that the particular blend of spice Anil had brought to the American squash circuit would be soon disappearing from the table, however, and, in consequence, would actually leave the sport in the U.S. a little blander—at least for a while.

* * *

CHAPTER THIRTEEN

Turning Point

Later that spring, Anil's close friend Tom Webber and his wife, Andrea, invited him to a brunch party, where a fresh twist of fate would soon lead the young Indian in a new direction at another critical turning point in his life. "Tom and Andy had recently gotten married and were hosting a get-together," said Anil, noting that Andrea's older sister, Linda Bertocci, had already come to the event with a Puerto Rican Harvard grad named Angelo Giordani by the time Anil arrived. *She should be dating a better-looking guy than that*, Anil thought upon seeing the pretty young woman, who, he was later told, had majored in French literature at Emory. He had a few brief intermittent chats with her at the gathering and left the event thinking she was beautiful. A few weeks later, he considered calling her, but had doubts about whether it was the right thing to do. "So I called Tom and asked him if he thought it would be OK," Anil said. "I remember saying to him, 'If Andy's great, she's also probably great.' So he and Andy had a pow-wow and he called me back and said, 'Call her.'" Knowing she was working at a local bar in Boston, Anil instead decided to drop in when he knew she'd be there and pretend to run into her by accident. "She served me a drink," he said, and within a year the two were engaged to be married.

By this time, Anil had made a failed attempt to launch a clothing import business with Bob Hellerson, a fellow squash player. "I was trying to get the sportswear company off the ground when I had a falling out with my partner," he said. Anil's friend Dinny Adams, who was by now an accomplished lawyer and eventually became the president of the Harvard Club of New York, helped him get out of the dispute in a quick and efficient manner. "His compensation was a profuse thanks and perhaps a meal," Anil said. "On a more important, bigger level, his assistance helped me realize the strength of our friendship." After regrouping, Anil opted to go to Harvard Business School for an advanced degree, which bought him some extra time in Boston.

With plans to settle for the long haul in Boston, he explained to his parents that he was engaged to an American, but was met with a frosty response. A familial tug from his parents, who urged him instead to return to his homeland, placed him at a crossroads. "My parents' explicit disapproval of Linda was painful," Anil remembered. "I pleaded, prayed, and begged them to change their minds—to no avail. Both my parents, equally adamant, were not going to relent on their last chance to get at least one of their children married to someone of their choice. They wanted to be a part of the decision making—they were willing to be modern and liberal by Indian standards by not taking total charge of my choice of a mate. But there was little flexibility as far as caste and family status was concerned. Although Linda's father was a well-respected academician, which might have been acceptable to them if she were Indian, Linda was foreign, from an Italian-Finnish family, and so did not belong in any preordained caste in the Indian sense, and they couldn't support her as my choice."

As it turned out, Anil chose the path that all of his siblings had taken—and decided to carry on with his plan to get married despite his parents' disapproval. In attendance at his bachelor party were several of his college buddies as well as some childhood friends from India, his childhood coach Yusuf Khan, and the host of the party, Mohibullah Khan, with whom Anil had developed an offbeat friendship over time. "I had an uneasy, but at times enjoyable relationship with Mo," said Anil. "He was meteoric like my brother Vinod. But Mo was at his dynamic best at my bachelor's party in 1970. He had rented a hotel room somewhere on Commonwealth Avenue and supplied the liquor and wanted to host my American and Indian friends, some of them from Bombay, including my friend Premal Shah, a diminutive fellow appropriately nicknamed Tit by grade school friends, who chose a British term used to describe small birds as his tag. The night progressed and, of course, we all drank excessively, moving on to a new bottle of liquor as each one was finished. Around 1:00 in the morning, Mo and Tit got embroiled in an argument about which of the two had more prowess with women. Mo flared up and, upon deciding to throw Tit out of the second-floor window, he caught him by the collar and dragged him to the sill. With typical Gujarati courage Tit did not let up and continued to defy and taunt Mo. Of course, no one allowed him to be shipped out of the window, and to stop matters from getting worse, the Indian boys packed themselves in a car and went home."

Anil remembered staggering to the Emmanuel Episcopal Church on Newbury Street in Boston the next day, just sober enough to follow through with the nuptials. Later he worked on softening up his parents, who had opted not to attend the wedding. Eventually he organized a visit so that they could meet his new bride as well as her parents, Angelo Bertocci, a professor of comparative literature at Boston University, and his wife, Aili.

"I had witnessed my parents' disappointment before with all my siblings—with their displays of anger and disconnection to demonstrate their position to their friends and relatives," Anil said. "I could also clearly see their internal feelings of frustration when they were unable to marry off even one of their children to a mate of their choice. First came silence, then the threat to cut off and disown their children. Over a period of a year, after they had made their disapproval known to their friends and family, they always realized they really did not want to lose their child and would gradually end the cold war with the help of several mutually known intermediaries. They saved face and the children couldn't wait to reunite. That's how it had happened with my other siblings and I prayed and hoped it would not be different with me. To my relief, it was not. A year later they came to visit us, on foreign turf where they did not have to be faced with societal pressure. No matter, it was great to be together again."

But it wouldn't be long before the pull toward India would prevail. "I just couldn't deal with the full-time demands of the business school," confessed Anil, who was having a hard time envisioning

Anil's Arjuna Award, India's highest award for a sportsman, 1969.

himself flourishing in corporate America. He was still somewhat active on the squash circuit during the first semester, when he was called to India to receive the Arjuna award, India's highest honor for a sportsman and bestowed upon only the country's very best athletes by India's president. Anil considered returning to India to receive it but, with too many demands in his life to make the trip practical, he asked his parents to accept the award on his behalf instead. "While I didn't go back at that time, the fact I was seriously tempted to return was an indication of my degree of commitment to business school," he said. With a thriving family business in his homeland and his father beckoning him to join it, he ultimately decided to quit business school and, with willingness from Linda, made plans to start his life again in India.

Despite his occasional tough losses during his college years in America, Anil left the U.S. on a high note. He had won every intercollegiate championship since arriving at Harvard, where he quickly rose to the number one spot on the varsity team and stayed there until he graduated, ending his last year as captain of the team. In addition to winning innumerable club and regional tournaments, he had also won one Mexican, two Canadian, and two U.S. men's national championship tournaments as well as every major men's amateur tournament in the U.S. for two years in a row. Most important, he had gained a stellar collection of lifelong friends, who valued him for his gentlemanliness and sportsmanship as much as for his abilities. And in addition to being honored with the Bingham award, Harvard's highest honor for an athlete, he had also received India's Arjuna award, the country's highest honor for sportsmen of every sport. For this pioneering young man from Bombay, life was about as good as it could get.

* * *

PART FOUR

1972-1981:
Return to India

CHAPTER FOURTEEN

East and West

The years between 1971 and the end of the decade provide some striking parallels between Anil's personal journey and that of his mother country, India. In particular, 1972 was a transformative year for the squash champ as he moved back to his roots in Bombay with his newly wedded American wife, Linda. Back in his home country, there was the acrid smell of war in the air as India, under Indira Gandhi, squared off against Pakistan the year before to protect the sanctity of her territory and borders as millions of refugees, fleeing the genocide of Bengalis under Pakistani military rule, crowded the border areas in India's West Bengal. The saber-rattling would last through the entire summer and monsoon. The tally of refugees, as calculated by the Indians, was not very many short of 10 million and it was a humanitarian crisis. On a broader level, social unrest had been percolating throughout the country in the years just before Anil returned and would continue throughout the early '70s, while Gandhi, who served as India's first and only woman prime minister and asserted an unprecedented centralization of power over the subcontinent, began a campaign to suspend basic civil liberties among broad swaths of the population, including censoring the press and initiating a mass sterilization drive among millions of poor rural men.

Added to the volatile mix of political influences shading the atmosphere was a hostile United States, where Dr. Henry Kissinger, then country's national security adviser (who, incidentally, graduated from Harvard in 1950 and later served as director of its Defense Studies Program between 1958 and 1971), was pleading with a beleaguered president Richard Nixon to lay down a policy towards the subcontinent with a "tilt" towards Pakistan. In the history of diplomatic relations between India and the U.S.A., this was the darkest hour. Of course, Washington was also in the midst of its own quickly diminishing trust of the president in light of Nixon's dirty tricks. Nixon's huge confrontations with *The Washington Post* and *The New York Times* were engaging all those manfully defending the freedom of the press in America. Nonetheless, the media in the U.S.A. was seen in India as unfriendly. For New Delhi, the goodwill and understanding built over the Camelot years when president Kennedy was in office was disintegrating, first under president Johnson, who was indifferent to India, and now through the Nixon administration, which was outright hostile. The American society was also deeply divided down the middle between vocal critics of the Vietnam war and the "patriots."

At the same time, the world's largest democracy was rapidly beginning to cozy up to the U.S.S.R. Those were truly stormy years for India, though Bombay, with its hedonistic living and single-minded pursuit of money, was feeling the effects less than any other part of the country. India's first female prime minister had her hands full as she conferred, in turn, with her senior advisers like P.N. Haksar and D.P. Dhar and legendary soldiers like S.H.F.J. Manekshaw, India's first field marshal, who would fight the midwinter war to help sever the relationship between East and West Pakistan and transform the eastern flank of the country into the new nation of Bangladesh to enable it to flourish under its own elected leadership.

So it was a time when Anil and Linda were going from one stifling war-entrenched country to another, and there getting caught up in their own private skirmishes. Since his daily routine revolved mostly around the protected cocoon of the CCI and the posh environs of South Bombay, life for Anil and his family remained largely unfazed by some of the darkest aspects of India's broader sociopolitical picture. Yet, reacclimatizing to India wasn't as easy as he'd imagined it would be. "I was not always strong enough to help bridge the cultural gaps in a tension-free manner," Anil admitted.

The first aspect of this family conflict was the fundamental bias Anil's parents would have against his marriage to a foreigner. Anil does not mince words when he says that if the senior Nayars had known that their children, beginning with Vinod and Asha, would end up with foreign alliances, they might not have encouraged them to go abroad and may have been happy to have stayed back in Amritsar. While it's hardly uncommon that such resistance exists to a degree in any society, the intercultural alliances here occurred well before so-called globalization and the elders' reactions to the breaks with traditions were much more severe than they might be today.

Anil's parents, generous as they were and broad-minded as they had been forced to become, continued for some time to sting with the handicap they felt in not having been been able to choose suitable life partners for any of their four children, a sacred duty, according to social norms of all Indian parents. (Even Vijay, who married an Indian, had aligned with someone their father and mother hadn't chosen.) His parents had skipped Anil's marriage and it had taken many months before olive branches would be offered. And now back in India, a new phase of readjustment would play out for all involved.

Eventually though, in ways not altogether conventional, Anil's parents found the means to connect with their new daughter-in-law and she found common ground with them. As Anil pointed out, "It's often been noted throughout colonial literature that drinks are tastier in India." And his father, whose drink of choice was Scotch, soon learned that Linda enjoyed the drink herself.

"My father-in-law was a very nice man, but very traditional and he had the drawback of being hard of hearing because he worked in a textile factory," Linda said. "But what endeared me most to him was that he'd call every evening around 6:30 or 7 and say, 'Send Linda down for Scotch with me.'" And so, an early evening ritual was soon established whereby the elder Nayar, upon returning from work, would invite his daughter-in-law to join him for a drink before dinner at the flat he shared with Anil's mother on the floor below the younger Nayars' own penthouse home. Of course, this mode of interaction was totally counter to Indian traditions wherein there would be a clear chasm between an elder man, however wealthy and modernized, and his daughter-in-law, whose job was to make life comfortable for the older generation and to reside in shadows. But there was little that was conventional about the Nayar family at this point.

At the same time, Linda began to develop a rapport with Anil's mother by exchanging thoughts on different approaches to food and cooking. "She was an excellent cook and taught me how to make Indian dishes, though she'd use a hell of a lot of pots and pans," said Linda, noting that the cookware was invariably left for the servants to clean up. "But also, because I loved to cook as well, she appreciated some of my American dishes, and we sat together every morning on her little balcony and had tea."

As Anil did his best to thaw tensions with his parents, he simultaneously found another minor battle on his hands. His family and circle of friends, high profile and cosmopolitan though many of them were, often inserted themselves in true Indian fashion with a bit too much familiarity, amounting almost to intrusion. This, from the point of view of an American newlywed wife in India, was unacceptable. And although Anil and Linda had a sprawling apartment on the magnificent Marine Drive with a spectacular view of the Arabian Sea beyond the tetrapods to the west and an undisturbed view of the quaint and historical Rajabai Clock Tower fronting the High Court to the east, cultural differences like these were often left unresolved and certain seeds of discontent were already being sown.

Still, there were good times with some dazzling friends in Bombay—high society, successful individuals from different walks of life, including a prominent businessman Devinder Sahney and his wife, Kanwaldeep, whose lavish parties were legend. Anil and Linda also socialized now and then with his brother Vinod and his wife, Gunna, whose friends Shashi and Jennifer Kapoor (the country's top film star and his wife, a superstar of the English thespian Kendal family) were occasionally part of the social scene they enjoyed. "The Bombay social scene was still evolving even after more than 25 years of independence," said Anil of his perceptions of the atmosphere in India at the time. "Many people of British origin were well-ensconced in their lifestyle in India and it wasn't until the next generation came of age that these citizens would go back to their ancestral land. A few did not leave at all and considered India as much their home as they did their ancestral land—rightly so." While Anil observed that the social scene had become more indigenized, he still saw it as partial to the people from Britain, Europe, and America. "There was an element of cosmopolitan cache for Indians to have them at social events both in public and at home," said Anil. "It often occurred to me that many of the British, American, or European folks in India would likely not have been invited to similar prestigious events in their own countries. Yet for many Indians, socializing with them was a fine way to learn about people from different parts of the world and gradually wean the Indian out of his or her 'colonial' complex." Another couple they interacted with was Sudhir Kilachand, a scion of the renowned industrial Kilachand family, and his wife, Shobhaa De, who would go on to become a popular newspaper columnist and later a TV panelist. The colorful princess Raju Singh was also a friend. And Linda developed relationships with other ex-pats who worked in the American and Israeli consulates, while Anil, of course, spent plenty of time with his top-level squash cronies.

But friends and relatives alike often came and went at will with no prior warning, ringing the doorbell at all times of day. "I loved the casualness of unannounced visits," Anil said. "My mother used to receive guests who stopped by without an invitation with so much grace and ease. I wanted my house to be like that. My father used to come up almost every Sunday after his morning walk, have his fourth or fifth cup of tea with me, and smoke a couple of cigarettes. We often had very good friends show up on short notice on the weekends, too. This casualness was not the western way. It was an area of mutual discomfort between Linda and me as we both grew to adjust in an uneasy kind of way."

And after their two sons, Sanjay and Vivek, were born in 1973 and 1977, the rhythms of the Indian social scene presented another challenge. The typical timing of Indian dinner parties—with guests not expected to arrive until around 9 p.m. and the main meal not served until around midnight—was also something that Linda would simply never get used to. "I had a good time at parties, but because they didn't start until so late and since I enjoy a cocktail or two, I just couldn't last and was usually fast asleep before the end of the party," she said. Anil recalled that Linda would often fall asleep even at their own gatherings not long after a party had begun. Add to these cultural differences, the army of domestic retainers—a cook, a house cleaner, a server, a sweeper, and later a nanny for the kids—that required managing, often in Hindi, which Linda did not speak (though she eventually managed to get by with a limited grasp of the language). And, with a Doberman named Moka eventually rounding off the residents of the penthouse apartment, domestic life—though comfortable—had become complex.

The challenges with domestic help often resulted in a revolving door of new influences, as one disappointing servant would get replaced with another. A particular dinner party hosted by Anil and Linda at their own home one evening provides an example of the kind of mayhem that can ensue when household help turns over. It is widely understood that Punjabis, whether domestic or among the wandering diaspora, are passionate about their food. The *kebabs* and the *chaats*, the elaborate pickles and savories, the tender *naan* and the *chhole bhature* are all part of the folklore of fine dining on either side of the Land of Five Rivers of the Punjab. And on the evening of this particular gathering, alongside businessman Ravi Nathwani, his wife, Neelam, and a couple of other friends, all hell was let loose as a "delicacy" was served up for the guests.

After the usual layers of cocktails and appetizers, a brand new cook produced a special dish with a flourish. The mutton *kebabs* and vegetable *pakoras* had done the rounds, and then came a main course—basmati rice, the ubiquitous *gobi aloo*, and a "round, falafel-like curry," said Anil. Those present each took a bite each and all noted that it tasted like nothing they had sampled before. Queries revealed that the key ingredient was goats' testicles, causing consternation all around. The cook had, in his only partly comprehensible Hindi dialect, tried to explain the preparation, but there was no help for the outcry! As Anil remembers it, the dish, which is called *gurda kapura* in Punjabi and is actually considered a true delicacy in some sections of north India, also made everyone feel sick (though no one actually threw up). And so, the cook was persuaded to make his exit the next day.

There were other instances of the perils of domestic help. Perhaps the temptations are too great, but theft was also always a possibility. In the mid-1970s, a different cook made off with all of Linda's jewelry. Such help, spending many hours in the apartment, would know exactly where all the valuables were stored. Sometimes keys would be duplicated and, at moments of carelessness, trust would be exploited. This particular cook was never apprehended, but Anil expressed relief that there were no assaults, injuries, or personal threats. And it was the person who replaced this light-fingered cook who would feature in the goats' testicles drama.

As is the case with many a cook, there is also a perennial problem of alcohol abuse. This is especially of relevance in well-to-do

Anil with his first wife, Linda, and their son Sanjay, c. 1974.

families where parties are frequent and temptations ever present. And the more wealthy the employers the greater the chance of country liquor, or of what is described as IMFL (Indian made foreign liquor, i.e. locally manufactured whiskey, vodka, and rum, or "hootch," as Anil referred to it) being consumed by cooks in large quantities. In Bombay, this was a trend among the coastal folk, in Delhi the hill people, and in party- and club-dominated Calcutta the kitchen recruits and serving personnel from Bihar and Orissa. As such, the turnover of cooks was large, though with limited supply of good help, there would also be many instances in Bombay of Anil being at a party and being served by the cook he had sacked a month ago.

Despite his own troubles with domestic help, Anil had a unique take on the very touchy issue of behavior with domestic servants, or the household help generally lumped under the categories of "cooks, bearers, and drivers." In other societies, such behavior would be totally unacceptable, but here there was a tendency to be brusque and even abusive towards hired help by masters and mistresses. Children would almost invariably follow suit. *"Idhar aao,"* meaning "You, come here," would be a normal form of address to servants. In restaurants, it was common to observe shouting as a means of catching their attention. Before the days of organized trade unions, such domestics and workers were totally at the mercy of the hire-and-fire principal. And even now, it is only marginally better. In extreme cases, police stations often receive complaints of violence against servants, bearers, cooks, and other service providers.

Whenever he witnessed such rude behavior with servants, night watchmen, lift men, and hawkers, Anil always considered the values of Mahatma Gandhi, who taught about the dignity of labor—the more humble, the more dignified. Driven by this point of view, Gandhi had persuaded his wife, Kasturba, to join him in the task of cleaning toilets like those on the lowest rungs of the social ladder—the sweepers in what is now known in India as the Scheduled caste of people who carried out such tasks and were treated as untouchables. Anil, having spent some years abroad, found this harsh treatment of service providers to be obnoxious—and always made a concerted effort to treat those who helped him with tenderness and consideration.

* * *

CHAPTER FIFTEEN

Family Affairs

By the time Anil returned to India in the early 1970s, his affluent family was undergoing a transition as many of the sons and cousins of Anil's generation had matured into men and now had their own families. Due to internal clashes among Anil's father and his uncles, however, few of the younger Nayars got involved or stayed involved in the family business—instead striking out on their own, often in related businesses. Anil was an exception, though, and was brought in by his father to participate in the textile enterprises, where he played a role for almost a decade.

The Nayar family had among them several operations—Castle Mills in Thane, the Indian Woolen Textile Mills in Chheharta, Eldee Velvet and Silk Mills in Bombay, Doon Valley Combers in Dehra Doon, and Elson Cotton Mills in Ballabhgarh. It was the trend in those days for families with large businesses to "diversify" as a hedge against rapidly changing policies of the central government, which would frequently cause problems for certain enterprises. With a mix of different businesses, a family's focus could switch to an alternative when government-instigated issues arose. So their holdings included a collection of woolen, cotton, velvet, and wholesale businesses along with real estate employing between 3,000 to 4,000 people. Anil's core duty was to study and suggest ways of bringing about modernization to keep pace with competitors. In addition to developing strategies for adapting to the complexities of an evolving business environment, Anil was also engaged in working through labor disputes, which occurred on a regular basis.

While the internal bickering between Anil's father and his uncles invariably added to the din of the textile mill operations, they nonetheless forged enough consensus to develop a collective interest in diversifying into other new areas. With this broader view in mind, the senior Nayar would eventually encourage his youngest son to move beyond the family's textile businesses, as he had with Anil's elder brothers, in part to keep him from getting ensnared in the daily, and sometimes unpleasant, politics among the uncles, many of whom by now had also relocated to Bombay. So with backing from his father, Anil set off to start up a television assembly firm in the mid-1970s near his ancestral home in Amritsar, enlisting as a partner a technocrat who worked for the Punjab Government Technology Development Centre and had a government license to produce televisions. His logic was that television was still an emerging industry in India with ample room for growth. "The TV market was in its infancy, broadcasts were just beginning to materialize, and there was just not enough supply of TV sets in the market," said Anil. While he continued to remain engaged with aspects of the family's textile businesses, he also regularly traveled north to nurture the new television venture, which presented its own set of challenges and barriers to entry.

In Anil's opinion, the primary issue was the lack of consensus with his partner on how to grow the business. "I learned the hard way how difficult it is for a bureaucrat to become a businessman," Anil explained. "My partner was too deliberate and too paranoid to run an efficient, seamless operation." It is part of the reality of startups that they also require hands-on attention, personal nurturing, and, above all, decision making. And while a cousin who lived in Amritsar also worked with Anil as a part-time manager,

Anil was only able to be present for the business part of the time himself, and he was getting fatigued and disoriented by his constant travel between Amritsar and Bombay. "Television manufacturing was licensed by the government to operate only in certain areas, and Punjab was one of them, so Amritsar was an obvious choice as a location for our business as we had relatives there. I should have been present for day-to-day decisions to set the stage for effective interactions and minimize friction among employees, but I was there for only a week each month," said Anil, noting that, with his wife and elder son, Sanjay, rooted in Bombay, he had no intention of relocating to Amritsar. "In retrospect, I would not have gone into this venture unless I could have had the assembly plant near Bombay." Furthermore, Anil himself was on a "learning curve" of running a business—not an easy task in north India from afar.

Ultimately, the boutique startup had little chance of thriving once the government licensing policies changed to permit the mega-corporations, such as Videocon, Weston, Beltek, and Phillips, with their huge finances, their research and development teams, and their capacity to tolerate losses for long stretches, into the TV sector. Anil had launched the business as India was moving into the era of economies of scale—and the corporate giants regularly pushed out small boutique outfits as the Indian government relaxed its protection for the small-scale sector and the jungle law of survival of the fittest played itself out in industry after industry. Though ahead of his time with the right idea at the right moment, the business was launched in the wrong place with the wrong collaborator. At constant loggerheads with his partner, Anil would eventually fire him after two years—and finally shut down the business altogether after three years—before returning to work full-time once again in the family's textile business.

While he was working with Castle Mills, the family's flagship manufacturing plant and the mainstay of the extended Nayar clan's wealth, Anil saw firsthand the perils and frustrations of running a business in an industry at the peak of the union movement in the country, when the political clout of the unions and lockouts by management often resulted in prolonged strikes by the workers. "The main architect of the profitable working of the plant was my father," said Anil. "He was a master cost cutter and an alchemist. He would effectively mix various kinds of woolen waste material, including sweepings from the spinning department, to make higher-end products, such as blankets for Air India, or products within spec for Indian Army clothing. It was an equation of very low material costs and high-margin sales. He was amazing at running the business with his brothers Daulatram and Jagdish until competitors got wise to his blends and competition in all forms of textiles became severe."

In contrast to the positive insight Anil gained into his father's business acumen, however, he also got a ringside view of the kind of violent and uncompromising labor disputes that were not only devastating his family's business but also paralyzing the entire country. Workers around the country had become habituated to asking for lump-sum bonus money during festivals like Diwali, Durga Puja, and other religious holidays and their demands would cause friction. Anil would also personally experience alongside his father, the inhumanity of a *"gherao,"* a supposed contribution to corporate history by communist West Bengal, whereby workers would forcibly surround members of management or ownership in their offices for hours, sometimes days. While the workers would take turns at going in and out, the movement of those surrounded was forcibly restrained. For some of the victims of these takeovers, there were cases of acute suffering, heart attacks, and other traumatic incidents. As they mastered this technique over time, the workers began to allow regularized toilet breaks and humane exceptions when members of the surrounded party became unwell. And in the large jute and tea enterprises in West Bengal, often the unions would field their own doctors. Even *gheraos* were becoming institutionalized.

In the Castle Mills standoff in which Anil was involved, there was a dispute between two unions, one Communist and the other Congress (alongside the country's ruling party). And the fight resulted in a *gherao* of Anil and his father. "About 150 of the 1,100 workers surrounded my and my father's offices, demanding pay raises, ad hoc benefits, and changes in the definition of contract work," Anil remembered. "My father and I did not incite or argue, but kept as calm as we could and talked about how to jointly decide getting beyond the impasse with both unions." Anil also noted that similar *gheraos* at other factories had resulted in managers and owners being beaten and sometimes killed. "But the Congress union was in no mood to collaborate with the Communist union—so we were held captive in our offices for about four or five hours before the police rescued us," he said. "Once we left the factory and all the workers had gone home, we shut the gates and locked them."

Over the next month and a half, both unions pulled hard in conflicting directions. "For 40 days we kept talking to the Communist union, and eventually invited them for tea and biscuits at my apartment so that we could make a deal," said Anil. "As the lockout continued with closed doors, the labor commissioner also got involved as did certain Delhi leaders." The Congress union, better funded and, in that era, more arrogant, was reluctant to settle even after 40 days, but the other union was ready to negotiate. As often happens, a deal was made away from the Congress as the Communists had decided enough was enough, and their ranks stirred action in picket lines after the leaders chose to break the strike to enable the workers to go back to work.

As the Communist-led strike break commenced the next day, their women members were the first to push through and stood inside the gates, while Congress workers shouted anti-owner slogans, even as some were going in to join the other workers. According to Anil, the Communist women stood strong and shouted back in Marathi, "We will cut your balls off if you try to keep us from work!" The capitulation of the union had a lot to do with the fact that food had to be put on the table at home and this brinksmanship had lasted long enough. So in this case, the aggressive turnaround was led by the women, who would rely on their hard-earned pay to keep the home fires burning, unlike many of the men, who would often hit the bottle with money in their hands.

With the resolution—arrived at over cups of tea with the owners—it was back to status quo as the industrial action ended with lessons learned by both sides. The old days of the *mai-baap* culture (wherein the poor or the less powerful bend over backwards to please political leaders, hoping that the latter would throw some crumbs their way) had gone and union workers would be ever ready for eyeball-to-eyeball interactions. At the same time, the owners had a new addition to their vocabulary: Lockout—the word dreaded by all workers and owners in a country without the safety net of unemployment benefits.

Anil also learned some lessons about the changing face of business development and management in industry. Businesses at this time required modern marketing techniques, sales strategies, and market surveys in what was rapidly developing into a battle for survival due to increased competition. Gone were the pre-competitive days of supply-driven markets and the tall order of the day was the need for professional management. The giant textile mills in Bombay, in fact all industrial businesses, were now head-hunting for managers with MBAs and alumni of the IIMs and IITs around the country. The Nayars had yet to tap professional management personnel for their operations. But their competitor Raymond exemplified an enterprise that had embraced a more progressive approach to running a business. Castle Mills was bigger than the Singhania family-owned Raymond in the mid-1970s. "But as a family, the Singhanias were busy professionalizing their management so much so that our family could not understand why they were paying such high salaries to outsiders," said Anil. "They went from a hands-on to a hands-off management style, and they recruited the best talent that was available." As Raymond strengthened its operations along with other competitors, Castle Mills was put out of business.

During these uncertain times—with constant quarrels and plenty of tense moments within the family as a few other cousins of Anil's generation gradually got involved—Anil noted that there was also little direction. Monetary disputes were legion, as is so common in many large and wealthy families, and they often centered around who was taking how much money and why. "There was no agreed-upon system in place to compensate those who made the money for the family," said Anil. "My father and his six brothers were operating under the idea that all would share the profits equally, but a culture of contentiousness was deeply embedded in the Nayar brothers' DNA and there were often quarrels caused by suspicion that the working brothers were keeping more than their share of 1/7th of the proceeds and more than their 1/7th share of the real estate assets, especially the buildings on Marine Drive."

Precipitated by what is commonly referred to as the "License Raj," or an environment of rampant corruption and bribery due to the control of government officials who held the power to issue licenses for various forms of commerce and often demanded payment in exchange for a businessman's legitimate right to a license to import tin or wool or other raw materials, many Indian businesspeople sold fractions of their commerce licenses on the black open market and monetized their values at significant premiums of up to 150 to 200 percent. And some of Anil's uncles who were not involved in the family business suspected their brothers who were running the operations, including Anil's father, were exploiting this environment without redistributing the proceeds equally, though there was no record of such activities on the account books. "The unease among the elders and their inability to resolve situations meant that the brothers would stop talking to each other and unofficial intermediaries would get involved as conduits in an attempt to enable one party to understand the grievances or thoughts of another," Anil said. But, because there was so much distrust among the brothers, even these indirect efforts to broker paths beyond the impasses often failed.

And so the culture of suspicion and quarreling continued. In all this, some gained, some lost, but Anil hung in there as the tensions began to take their toll on his father, whose growing stresses eventually led to harmful tobacco excess and high blood pressure.

* * *

CHAPTER SIXTEEN

Homegrown Champ

While varied pressures had become standard fare on both the work and home fronts for Anil, squash remained an uplifting recreational constant. At the same time, Linda found an escape from the challenges of running a household and raising children through horseback riding at the Amateur Riders Club at the racecourse nearby and amid the hospitable social scene at the Breach Candy Club, which had long catered to the norms of Brits, Europeans, and Americans and was still predisposed toward foreigners, though it had recently begun to accept Indians as members. While he occasionally accompanied her to the Riders Club, Anil's genuine relief from the daily grind of work and travel was in the camaraderie and fulfillment he found on the squash courts.

Whenever he could, he'd play friendly matches at the CCI with fellow peers, like Naval Pandole and Fali Madon, or with older players like Ali Ispahani, who had moved back to India from England and often boasted of winning tournaments and gaining rankings there that his fellow players questioned. An oft-quoted crack from India's squash secretary Ahmed Peermohamed whenever Ispahani would show up at the courts underscored the general feeling about the older player's accounts of his overseas exploits: "Peeru often said, 'Ali was all fart and no shit,'" recalled Noshir Kanga, another of Anil's squash-playing peers and a current member of the CCI. Anil would also regularly play with an emerging group of younger players, such as Ferez Nallaseth, a Parsi player about five years his junior who played competitively on the regional level, Raju Chainani, a passionate and strong player also about five years Anil's junior who eventually translated his love of squash into a career as a squash writer, and Ananth Nayak, a player about a dozen years younger than Anil who became one of India's leading lights in Indian squash in the late '70s and early '80s. With Anil back on the squash scene in India, the awe factor that had enveloped him before he left for America was amplified, especially in Bombay, where regulars on the squash circuit had duly noted the expanded list of international accomplishments that enhanced his luster as a player. Nallaseth, for example, who went on to become a genetic scientist and later moved to the U.S., said he remembered coming up against a psychological block whenever he played Anil during friendly matches at the CCI in the 1970s. Even though Anil had to once again make a transition with his form of play, this time from hardball back to a softball game, he swiftly eased back into the Indian squash circuit, which he would go on to dominate for most of the decade to come.

While the younger players were no match for the champ at this point in his amateur career, Anil enjoyed playing with them as much as they relished playing with him—and many became friends. Among them, Soli Colah, a former international player about 12 years Anil's junior who represented India in the inaugural 1976 world open in Karachi and who offered thoughts just before he died in 2019 on Anil's style of play, remembered observing Anil and the other top Indian players of the time at clubs and tournaments. "Sanjit Roy was in a very high category—his game was silky smooth and filled with controlled aggression," recalled Colah, a hard hitter and creative stroke player who was known as "Soli the Goli" by the Indian squash fraternity. But Colah put Anil in another league. "Anil was different, a born winner who played a balanced game with attacking shots and varied stroke making—he had so much assurance as he covered the court with great speed," said Colah, who had retired to the Nilgari Hills in Coonoor before he passed away.

Ananth Nayak remembered meeting Anil for the first time in 1972 after he had returned to India. "I knew him and interacted with him but did not actually play him—Lucky was too high up on the scale," he admitted. But from the gallery, he said, he carefully observed Anil's sportsmanship and intelligence. "Anil rarely asked for lets," said Nayak, adding that the champion player always left a clear view of the ball for his opponents, in contrast to other players of his day, such as Captain V.K. Paul, whom Nayak said was known for his blocking tactics on court even though he didn't appear to have an aggressive personality off the court. Key among Anil's strengths, said Nayak, was his ability to evaluate and analyze his opponent's game. "And like any great sportsman, he played to his strengths," added Nayak, who would later join Anil and the younger player Nikhil Senapati on the team of squash players who represented India in the world open tournament in Australia in 1979. "I used to be amazed at the rotation of his shoulders and the flexibility of his wrists, but Anil's greatest attributes were his speed and determination," he concluded.

While Anil also sometimes played fellow squash player and sports writer Raju Chainani, one of many of Anil's devoted fans, he had another dedicated admirer in Chainani's younger brother, Sunil, who watched Anil play, but never actually met him in a match. "Lucky is and was a great gentleman on and off the court, a fair competitor and a winner, a speedy and aggressive strategist," Chainani stated emphatically, comparing Anil to some of the players in those days who resorted to unfair tactics. "Often there was too much cheating, picking up balls after double bounces, whacking the opponents, and blocking. But Anil was the ultimate clean player," said Chainani, adding that this did not mean that Anil would take such play by someone else lying down. "He was a true

Anil on the courts at the Willingdon Club, c. 1974. (Photograph by Jimmy Tata)

amateur, someone who had a career, an education, and played the sport for recreation, but that did not exclude him from having a fiercely winning attitude." He also looked at Anil's game in relation to the way squash is played in India in current times. "Today there are great squash players in India—Ritwik Bhattacharya and Saurav Ghosal among them—and others like Dipika Pallikal and Joshna Chinappa—but it is difficult to think of them as true amateurs," Chainani said. "The era was different in Anil's time. Players had to struggle with limited availability of equipment, restraints over foreign travel, and restrictions over prize money. It was a time when you had to work hard to reach the top and even harder to stay there." Reverting to sheer talent, however, Chainani believed that "there was no one even close to Lucky when he was at his best—Anil Nayar was an artist with a brain who overcame the absence of unending stamina."

Elder statesmen of the sport were also keen observers of Anil's game and invariably held him in high regard. Madhav Apte, who was not only an excellent competitive squash player but also a Test cricketer, described Anil as "a stroke player, superbly fit, a great competitor, and a perfect gentleman on and off the court with a deep intelligence to read the game and respond." A celebrated sportsman and octogenarian who lived in princely style on Pedder Road in Bombay before he died in 2019, Apte saw Anil's squash accomplishments within the context of his long view of the history of the sport, particularly in India. "On the one hand, it was a game of kings, princes, and the elite," said Apte, whose penthouse in Woodlands was constructed on family property that is as opulent as it is historical. "Narpat Singh, a Raj Kumar of Jodhpur, was one of the fountainheads of Indian squash in its embryonic stages—to the cognoscenti, he was Raja Narpat Singh," Apte said of the champion player who reigned in the 1940s and '50s.

In those early days through to the late 1980s, squash was seen as a "minority game" and, like Apte, players were often aristocrats, such as Bhuvaneswari Kumari, a 16-time national female champion and Padma Shri awardee who played during part of the era when Anil was at his peak. "On the other hand, there were the 'outsider' pros, including Hindus, local Muslims, and Pathans like Abdul Bari and the great Hashim Khan," noted Apte of the other players who stood out in his own time, when courts were incredibly basic with no roofs and cement flooring. Like Anil, he refused to call the Pathan pros markers, insisting instead that they were mentors and coaches. In Calcutta, since the earliest days of Indian squash, the upper middle class corporate executives also featured prominently as players of the sport. With their expense accounts, these Indian players had access to the exclusive Calcutta Racket Club, the first racquet club on the subcontinent founded by the British in 1793 and one of the oldest clubs in the world. Other players came from the military ranks, mostly from the National Defense Academy in Khadakvasla or the Indian Military Academy in Dehra Dun. Yet most players, whether from Delhi, Madras, or Bombay during the vibrant era of squash in India in the 1960s and '70s, came from wealthy families as Anil did. "Anil played first for fitness, then for pride, and, when he realized he was superstar material, he played to win tournaments on the amateur circuit," said Apte.

Among his peers, even his archrivals held Anil in high regard. Raj Manchanda, perhaps Anil's toughest competitor who had honed his skills in the military cantonments and also ranks as one of India's greatest players, said he appreciated Anil "not just for what he brought to Indian squash, which was no mean contribution, but also for his charismatic dynamism, perfect sportsmanship, total fairness in the game and dealings with people, and zest for life, which created a happy and exciting environment around him wherever he went."

Of all of his fellow Indian players, Raju Chainani, bête noire of many an Indian player, was perhaps Anil's most ardent supporter and fan. Chainani, who had won the western India junior tournament in 1970, had become something of a contender in Indian squash circles before heading to London for a few years to finish his education and start earning a living. "He was an astute, crafty player who had honed his natural talent for cat-and-mouse real-life behavior and was able to put it to good use in the squash court," said Anil of the colorful and often controversial figure, who returned to India in the mid-1970s and parlayed his love of squash into a career writing about it. Chainani, who for years followed Anil on the court, spent quite a bit of of time socializing with him off the court, too. Having met him in New York in the late 1990s and knowing of his propensity to tipple a little more than he should, I wasn't surprised when Anil told me about an incident that occurred in the mid-1970s following a victory celebration after a local match.

"Raju and I were invited to an Otters Club squash party, and Sanjay, who was about 4 or 5 years old at the time, came along," recalled Anil of this particular episode. "Raju had too much to drink so we decided to leave and on our way out I heard a lot of commotion behind me and turned around to find that Raju had wound up in the pool." Sanjay recalled the event well, too. "Raju was taunting me as we were leaving, so one of my dad's friends stepped in and pushed him into the pool," Sanjay said. "He was floating on top of the water with his clothes fanning out and creating a kind of parachute around him." The fracas ended when Anil helped Chainani out of the water and packed him—sauced and soggy—into the back of his car aside Sanjay and shuttled him home. According to Anil, this was but one of many spirited and alcohol-inflected adventures with fellow roisterers during this phase of his life, for as he continued to excel as an amateur, winning numerous Indian national and regional competitions, he also attracted a growing collection of ardent fans, including passionate followers of the game and sportswriters like Chainani, who enjoyed reveling in well-lubricated post-match victory celebrations and kept his spirits bright and his leisure time lively.

"Controversy notwithstanding, Raju was the ultimate follower of squash and writer about the game," said Anil, who was often a star subject of many of the stories Chainani wrote. *Simply Squash*, the magazine he later founded in 1990 and published until he died at the relatively young age of 49 in 2001, not only covered the sport on five continents, especially Asia, but it also included contributions and articles written by some of the Who's Who of squash, including the great Australian player Geoff Hunt, who wrote a regular column, and H.R.H. Tunku Imran, who contributed a piece in

Anil with his son Sanjay at the CCI, c. 1978.

the publication's tenth anniversary issue. "No one has been able to follow, write about, and spice up the game with the professional reporting, intrigue, and conspiracy theories like Raju did," said Anil. "He made interesting reading of the sport of squash, except perhaps to those who were the objects of his wrath or had crossed his path." Anil also noted that Chainani had good relationships with the press, especially the Indian press, and later became instrumental in putting squash on the media radar by calling attention to everything from the good play of the sportsmen to the bad behavior of referees or, especially, administrators. "He loved the game and found a way to cobble a living, though a modest one, through squash as so many of the lovers of the game still do," Anil said.

In addition to the friendly matches he played with people like Chainani, Nallaseth, and Nayak at the CCI, Anil also consistently participated in regional, national, and international tournaments during the '70s, when he continued to play at his peak and competed against many of the same top players he had battled as a junior, such as Fali Madon, Sanjit Roy, and Raj Manchanda. Aside from winning the Indian national championships in both 1964 and 1966, he went on to win every Indian national tournament between 1971-1976. Keeping his play mostly to one side of the subcontinent, he also won virtually every western India regional tournament from 1972 until 1980, more than any other player in the history of the sport in India—before or since that time.

Throughout this period, Chainani remained a friend and committed supporter. And a section of a piece he later wrote about squash at the CCI during Anil's prime aptly sums up the opinion of many in the Indian squash community about Anil's place in the country's squash firmament. He started by quoting the veteran sports scribe Dicky Rutnagur, an honorary member of the CCI, who migrated to the U.K., worked as a cricket correspondent for *The Telegraph* for many years, and wrote a book entitled *Khans Unlimited* about the legendary Pakistani players. According to Rutnagur, wrote Chainani, "Anil Nayar was the only homegrown player of true class India ever produced." Chainani then goes on to offer his own description of Anil:

> Indeed, Nayar was something out of the ordinary. His blinding speed and racket skills remain etched in memory and the general consensus is that he is the greatest player India has seen. Comparisons are often difficult, more so when one looks at the record and ability of Major K.S. Jain, Sanjit Roy, Ali Ispahani, Raj Manchanda, Ananth Nayak, Meherwan Darvuvala and Adrian Ezra. But at the end of the day Nayar stands out with his achievements at home and abroad.

Given Anil's strength as a sportsman and squash player, he is often asked why he opted not to play the touring circuit as a professional. Without regret, his response is clear, especially when he reflects on this particular period in his squash career. "I felt I had won plenty on the American scene and subsequently every major amateur tournament on the Indian scene for several years," he said. "My inner voice since the very beginning had convinced me that this was as far I would go or should go. I had won all I had set out to do and had, from the very early stages of my career, never entertained playing professional squash. It was as if an inner switch had been turned off to prevent me from more advanced professional play. The professional tournaments were just not for me. I simply could not get my mind around the fact that as a professional I would be playing for money, playing to make a living off a sport I enjoyed and loved so much. Would I stop enjoying squash if I turned professional? I'm not sure, but I knew I loved the process of playing and, even more, winning. I also loved the lifelong friends and acquaintances I made through squash and I feared that if the sport became a money-making burden I would lose the love of it."

Furthermore, within the social and cultural context of India when he was playing at his peak, playing as a pro also simply would not have been an option. During his era, professional squash players in India mostly functioned in coaching positions as markers at clubs and these posts were usually filled by players from humble backgrounds like the Khans, who were driven to excel as a means to survive. Squash during the 1960s through 1980s was also an elite sport played among the privileged in Ivy League universities along the East Coast of the U.S. or in private clubs in America and commonwealth countries. So competing for prize money in tournaments would not be top of mind as a means to earning an income among people like Anil, whose education and background had prepared them for careers in business, banking, science, law, or medicine. And in those days, the prize money awarded on the pro circuit in national tournaments or a world open tournament in, say, the U.S. or England, might have been a maximum of a few thousand dollars annually. So it's hardly surprising that Anil, who never played in any tournament for money, along with most of his peers would play as amateurs rather than pursue the sport as a professional career that would yield limited financial returns. Ultimately, his match play as a world-class sportsman was driven by his love of the sport and the simple thrill of excelling for its own sake.

* * *

CHAPTER SEVENTEEN

Ennui

Until the late 1970s, Anil easily continued to play at the top of his game. But with the complications at work and the growing distractions in his family life, particularly after his second son, Vivek, was born, it's hardly surprising that his game would begin to fray as other aspects of his life started to unravel. A positive byproduct of the rebalancing act Anil was playing out at that time, however, was the skill he gained in rather easily transferring his finesse as a sportsman to his evolving role as a father.

"While our loyal nanny, Cecilia, was great with both Sanjay and Vivek, I wasn't good with infants, so I was happy as they grew old enough to spend time with me at the CCI courts in the evenings," Anil said. "I wanted them to feel about me as I did about my father—to see me as their 'rock.' But I also wanted to befriend them as early as possible, I was not going wait until they were 20 or 22 to create a bond with them. And so it was on the friendship side that our relationships developed, as I was certainly no rock in the way my father had been to me and I was prone to share my vulnerabilities with them as they became even older, perhaps a little too often," he conceded.

After playing at a peak for so many years, Anil admitted, too, to a certain complacency that had begun to chip away at the quality of his match play during the late-1970s. And as Anil's popularity had blossomed while his star continued to rise on the squash circuit in India, so too, to some degree, did his hubris. "I was disciplined still, but not enough," he said. The fire in his belly just wasn't there as it once was. And not unlike one of his role models Mohibullah, a lover of women and gin, his attention began to wander. An incident in Calcutta (now known as Kolkata) at the Rackets Club highlights his occasional interaction with the "groupies" who often followed sportsmen of his caliber around. While practicing there at the only permanent gallery court in India at the time, he noticed an attractive woman in a *saree* watching him with great interest. A few minutes later he "accidentally" threw the ball up to her. "She caught the ball and threw it back at me, thereby, without words, completing our introduction," recalled Anil. Over the next several days, whenever she was at the court they chatted briefly and developed a friendship.

Her name was Belle and she was "slim, tall, fair, and very pretty," as Anil remembered her. She was also of mixed parentage with a Hindu father and a Christian mother and she was a good conversationalist and fun to be with at the courts. After returning to Bombay following the tournament, Anil was later surprised to learn that her father would be transferred to Bombay where the two reconnected for a while. But he sees this period as the beginning, in some ways, of his unmaking as a champion. "With this and other distractions, in retrospect, I had begun to lose focus," he said candidly. "I had learned from Mo in the late 1960s to party and drink, go to bed late at night, shrug off a likely morning hangover, and still do well in tournaments. But as with Mo, so with me—it was just a matter of time before self-hurt and opponents caught up."

Further reminiscing on squash in India during the 1970s, Anil remembered an evolving yet somewhat diminishing pool of top-class players, especially after the departure of the great coach Yusuf Khan, who had left for Seattle in 1967 with support from Anil while he was at Harvard. Sanjit Roy, who was affectionately known as "Bunker" Roy and could have been stiff opposition in that decade, played only sporadically as he was now busy with his Barefoot College, an NGO and social work and research center he founded in the village of Tilonia in Rajasthan that offers education and opportunities to uplift rural people. Fali Madon, was playing serious squash, but had a bit of complex relating to Anil. The rivalry between the American tennis player Chris Evert and her Czech competitor Martina Navratilova serves as a point of comparison. Evert admitted to being a bit negative ahead of any confrontation with Navratilova and would never feel confident about her ability to beat her. Observers believe that something similar happened with Madon whenever he was up against Anil.

In the past, the fit young men from National Defense Academy and the Indian Military Academy beat the competition at all levels. But now civilians were challenging with superb fitness levels, too, so their advantage had been lost. Still, there were a couple of younger players of consequence—Nikhil Senapati and Soli Colah—both of whom Anil occasionally played. In those days, though, Anil managed to beat the younger players, recalling in particular a match in the late 1970s against Colah at the Maharashtra state open, when the quick and deceptive younger player, with his wide range of shots, succumbed to errors under the pressure of Anil's all-round game.

Yet Raj Manchanda stayed the course, perhaps better than others. Anil had always had a positive mindset, that of a winner. But when he recalled what was happening in the squash courts around the closing years of that decade with respect to this player, it was tinged with a sense of resignation. Manchanda was one of the outstanding players who had really "bothered" him over the years. Although he had beaten Manchanda several times in the early years and also toppled him in successive western India finals between 1977 and 1980, Anil could not get the better of the elder player in the nationals during the same years. In 1977, shortly after his second son, Vivek, was born, Anil lost to Manchanda in the national final for the first time at his favorite CCI courts, and he remained at a loss to unravel this mystery. Rewinding the match, Anil found himself digging for the ball at the back of the court—Manchanda's deft volley drops and lobs worked well in keeping his opponent away from his traditional attack game. Anil started out well enough but ended up on the losing side.

He still has some of the same searching questions about how it happened as he did then. Was he not mentally prepared? Was he being dragged down by the events around him? Was it over confidence, under-preparedness, or complacency? Or was this the beginning of the decline? Did he handicap himself with the use of

Anil's sons Sanjay and Vivek at St. James Court, c. 1978.

too much wrist on his back hand, which had been an effective style in hardball American squash? Anil also admitted that the shorter, wristier swing with the wooden racquets back then did not lend itself to a deep parallel left wall shot. It was either a short shot or a ball that hit the side wall and popped up in the center that enabled Manchanda to control the rally. Surely, Manchanda had realized that Anil had lost his earlier speed, and now could not reach the ball quickly enough to counterattack. Anil felt that his racquet preparation had gotten quite "sloppy." He also admitted he was trying to be "too cute" by attempting to be deceptive too often, in effect not playing solid squash, which requires at least 70 percent of the balls going to the back corners to set one up for volleys and deceptive front court shots.

More than any slips in his strategy or skill, though, Anil believed this particular loss had more to do with his personal and professional distractions at the time. Again he referred to the great tennis player Chris Evert when she met Martina Navratilova at Wimbledon in 1978, as a point of comparison, this time to his own fate, and quoted a recent article in *The New York Times* in which Evert described a particular moment, when, after a 4-2 lead in the third set, she let the match slip away to Navratilova and lost 12 of the last 13 points. "I have to laugh, but that was the Wimbledon I fell in love with John Lloyd," Evert wrote about her first husband, a British player whom she married in 1979 and divorced in 1987. "I was love struck, we were dating and we went out every night. I was really distracted and I wasn't fully engaged or focused on winning Wimbledon. Sorry, Martina." Evert's personal preoccupations, though of a completely different nature, had a similar effect on Anil at about the same point in his career.

While Anil's issues were multifaceted and revolved around family and work and their accompanying complications—they amplified what he describes as "an ennui of winning." Not only were the complexities of his life eroding his passion, his will to win was simply organically beginning to wane. "The intangible elements in one's life often affect the tangible," he said. "No matter how much physical effort you put in, if you are not a hundred percent committed, it will have an adverse effect." He noted the thinking of another great athlete, the African runner Eliude Kipchoge, as another point of reference in describing his decline. "The training equation and winning formula of Kipchoge, the best marathoner in the world, is a relevant consideration in this context: Motivation +discipline=consistency," he explained. "I had followed that formula myself for nearly two decades, but at that time it was lost on me. Both motivation and discipline levels were in decline for me and so then was the consistency of winning."

He also admitted to becoming more cavalier about his health and fitness and often overdid the celebrating after winning a match. "After a night of celebration that sometimes verged on bacchanalia, the next day would be a blur," he confessed. "In just one night I may have undone months of fitness training and practice—what a waste! The victory celebrations of youth had to give way, as there was too much collateral damage to the body and mind."

Among his peers, however, one question still remains unanswered about his match play at this point in time: Why did Anil only lose to Manchanda in the nationals while winning western India tournaments? Naval Pandole, who until recently served as vice president of the CCI and remembered the 1960s and '70s as the "Golden Age" of squash in India, had a clear take on the variance between Anil's performance against Manchanda in the western India championship tournaments, where Anil won the three times he played between 1977 and 1979, and in the nationals, where Manchanda won the tournaments when playing against Anil during the same period. Pandole feels Manchanda had a plan. "Raj was less focused on western India each time and preferred to conserve his big guns for the nationals, so he had enough to spare in the bigger event," he postulated. "His game plan, therefore, was different. This is a very tricky area in sport. No one deliberately loses one kind of tournament to win another. But perhaps the focus was different. It could be like the extra effort that goes into Wimbledon after perhaps a lesser effort in the Queen's."

Since Anil was winning the regional tournaments in the late '70s, Manchanda admitted that luck certainly played a role in his wins against the star player in the nationals in those years. But his military discipline helped, too—he said he worked especially hard on his off-court training. And after closely observing Anil's style of play as he battled him over the years, he also made a concerted effort to devise a few strategies to beat him. "I had lost to Anil several times before I was posted to Mumbai early in 1977, and every time we played it was a one-sided match," said Manchanda. "His power—he could really whack the ball hard—and his speed and focus were too much for me. No way could I match him in any of those regards. But playing him and a few other national-level players in Mumbai improved my game and getting the better of them seemed a possibility, even against Anil, though that was more remote. I was constantly thinking of how to neutralize Anil's strengths and how to play to my strengths, which were drop shots and lobs and consistency. I thought the best way to tackle his speed would be to slow down the game with more soft length shots and lobs, for he was not at ease in attacking the lob shot. This way he would have to generate all the power, which might tire him out quicker. And I had to improve my fitness to be able to last longer at the speed at which he played, only then could the strategy work."

Fortunately for Manchanda, one of the late-'70s national tournaments was held in the center court at the Calcutta Racket Club, which, unlike the CCI courts, was a slower court with a very high ceiling. "My well-practiced lobs turned out to be a perfect foil for Anil's power shots. And my drop shots had him moving up and down the court, which is more tiring than moving side to side, which I was doing most of the time. Suffice it to say that this strategy worked in the Racket Club courts, but just barely—I knew the tables could turn at any stage," explained Manchanda, who said he subsequently thought hard about more ways to outplay Anil in other settings, and managed to succeed in toppling him in one or two later national tournaments, too. Unlike Manchanda, Anil knew that he had developed some bad habits. He also recalled that at these particular matches it mattered to him that his great mentor Yusuf Khan was not by his side.

Despite his setbacks and the void he experienced without the support of a coach, Anil continued to play high-level squash throughout the 1970s. And despite the relative lack of support of sports by the government in India during this period, squash and its infrastructure continued evolve on a global level, bringing the sport to a wider audience both geographically and through more sophisticated media presentations. In 1973, for example, Jonah Barrington, the legendary Irish player five years senior to Anil, created the International Squash Professionals Association, which hosted the men's professional softball tour. Later that year, the European Federation hosted the first European championships in Edinburgh and the West German Squash Rackets Association was founded. In 1976, the first individual world championship tournament for men was played in London and for women in Brisbane—and the legendary Australian players Geoff Hunt and Heather McKay emerged as the winners. And in 1979, when the men's world team championships were hosted in Melbourne, Australia, Anil was asked to join Ananth Nayak, Nikhil Senapati, and Raj Manchanda to represent India in the world tournament.

Although Anil was seeing cracks in his match play at this point in his life, a silver lining of sorts manifested at the world open that year. Thinking back on the tournament, he wonders how "a fossil like me," would be sent to represent his mother country. He was 33 at the time and beginning to feel his age, and Raj Manchanda was a year or two older. Anil believed by then the two of them should have "been put to pasture," but in the absence of bench strength in a game that has a limited following compared to, say, tennis or badminton, they were still among the very best India had. So there he was, down to play at the number one spot against Mike Desaulniers of Canada.

Watching an opponent at practice or in match play can deliver a huge advantage in composing a strategy or spotting shortcomings or even an Achilles heel. When Anil met Desaulniers in Australia, he had not had the opportunity to see him play, but he was impressed with the younger player's achievements at Harvard, which he'd heard about a decade after he'd attended the Ivy League university. Desaulniers had not only won many national championships, including U.S. professional hardball, but he had several years of softball experience as well. He was also about 11 years younger, fitter, and, Anil learned directly, an out and out attacking player in much the same way Jahangir Khan was during his own individual championship matches played at the same time.

So what is a player in Anil's position to do? "Lob and drop, and slow the pace down," he concluded, recalling the memory of a lesson he'd observed in a Yusuf-versus-Mohibullah match a decade earlier, when Yusuf won the match by throwing Mohibullah off his stride. "Use patience and deliberation." In contrast to Anil's measured approach, however, Desaulniers attempted to speed up the game, speed up his stroke making, and wear down his older opponent. Anil remembered working to restrain himself from heated exchanges. He kept lobbing to his opponent's backhand to prolong the rally, realizing that he could win on slow- and medium-paced balls on the backhand. Anil recalled hitting a medium-paced lob to Desaulniers's forehand every now and then, too, in hopes of inducing an error. His plan worked beautifully and Anil came out the winner in four games. It was a surprise upset for both players and both countries but it also proved that planning and persistence in its implementation can often result in victory as one's strengths begin to fade with age.

Anil's close friend Dinny Adams, the former Harvard squash team captain he'd known since his freshman year in college, later told him the Canadian was "one of the best that Harvard had." Indeed, by the time he played Sharif Khan in a world championship tournament in New York a few years later in 1982, Desaulniers was ranked the number one hardball player in the world. Anil recalled with relief that he did not hear this from Adams until after his match against Desaulniers or it might have turned out differently. Anil felt on reflection that in the Australia match, Desaulniers might have studied him a little more, before and during the game, to change his strategy and play to keep those rallies going as long as possible. Doing so might have tired out the older Indian player.

Although Anil managed to dispatch Desaulniers in the earlier round, he was stymied by Phil Kenyon in a middle round. "Phil had amazing quickness and court coverage and was very fit—a student of proper scientific training both off court and on court," Anil said. "I lost to him respectably 3-1 and I thought he might go on to win the tournament. Indeed, Phil went through the rest of the rounds until he met the unbeatable Jahangir Khan, who toppled him in four games, though Phil later went on to become England's number one player in 1982 and did well on the squash circuit, but never won the big ones."

While none of the Indians won the individual events that year, they did relatively well as a team, especially given that two players on the team were over 30 years of age. "It was an indication of the lack of depth in Indian squash—we needed young legs as much as we needed experience," said Anil. "It was a far cry from the progress made in India from 2000 onwards." Still, India placed a respectable fourth out of seven after Pakistan, Australia, and Sweden by beating the U.S.A., Ireland, and Hong Kong. Anil sees the team's modest finish as a byproduct of their psyche at the time, more than any shortcomings in skill. "We had insufficient confidence in our stamina, in our capacity to grind it out," he said. "Our team had the motivation, but we just were not sure of our capacity to play with the players from Australia or England, as we did not have the experience or practice playing with them." In the end, this was a bittersweet finish to the one of the last major tournaments Anil would play while living in India.

* * *

CHAPTER EIGHTEEN

Crossroads

By the end of 1979, it was clear to Anil that his game had begun to slip, yet he had no way of knowing his personal life soon would fall apart, too. "My family was going through continuous battles over profits, business, real estate, and the separation of assets," said Anil of the stressful atmosphere that clouded his daily life. "We spent two years trying to mediate and settle the property matters by trying to monetize them so all family members could take their share and be free of each other." In-house professionals and company lawyers, inadequately equipped or too partisan in their outlook, were brought in for advice, but there were no solutions. Any thoughts of bringing in professional arbitrators or mediators of a high caliber to decide on the fates of the Nayars were considered either too expensive or too much of a risk. "No one was prepared to give an irrevocable power of attorney to an outside-of-the-family decision maker," said Anil. "In hindsight, everyone lost, lost big. Assets and businesses that could have been sold or held or developed for high values were sold at a quarter on the dollar."

A high point during this period, however, was the deepening relationship between Anil and his father. "We were always close and had gotten closer to the point that I would be one of the few people he would really listen to," said Anil. "My connection with my father started off as a traditional Indian father-son relationship but, over a ten-year period, developed into a profound friendship." Yet Anil's life changed abruptly when his father experienced a heart attack in 1981. Anil had spent the night at the Breach Candy hospital where his father had been admitted to the ICU. The next morning he had a brief and reassuring chat with his father before leaving his room to go home to shower and planned to return later in the day. "I told him he would be fine and wasn't going away," said Anil. Within moments of departing, however, he witnessed a group of medical personnel rush into the ICU and, by the time Anil returned to find out what was happening, the doctor turned to him and pronounced his father dead.

"I had lost my father, my friend, and my anchor," said Anil. "I was devastated and grieved for months and months on end. My father and I had become very close. He didn't have much of a relationship with any of his brothers or his father. Yet, no matter what the difficulties with work, family, or finances he may have had, there was never a day when he ever made us feel vulnerable from lack of resources to do what we wanted. He had begun to take interest and pride in me, my squash career, and he enjoyed the fame it brought the family name. I remember him softly cheering me on with a "Come on, Anil" from the gallery while I was playing a match. We were together almost every working day for five years. He needed a trustworthy figure with whom he could relax and not feel threatened. The finality of his departure is still so vivid and traumatic—his body on a burning pyre with my brother Vinod, the eldest, doing his duty as destroyer of his skull to release my father's spirit to universe."

At the time of his death, Anil's father had lost most of his hearing due to exposure to the loud machinery in the textile mills, and as a result didn't socialize as he much as had in the past. He also feared the demise of the family businesses. "The new mills in Dehra Dun and in Ballabhgarh outside Delhi were not contributing to the family coffers, and instead were a drain," said Anil. "The velvet and corduroy mill in the Bombay suburbs was also flailing. He was convinced his brothers had lost the fire in their bellies. I'm sure he saw, helplessly, the writing on the wall in Castle Mills, too—and the unravelling of the business empire of which he was one of the two main architects. Too many in the family were against him."

The total chaos and growing disenchantment with the family businesses along with the passing of his father contributed not only to Anil's losses on the squash court, but also to his disintegrating marriage, leaving the champion sportsman at a crossroads with concurrent declines in every facet of his life. With his father gone, Anil again attempted to work with his uncles to sort through the business issues to no avail. "In the end there was no solution and when my father died the business remained as it was—in a mess," remembered Anil. "Subsequently, the Castle Mills land, which would be worth over a couple of hundred million dollars today, was sold off at a fraction of its value."

His father's death, in a sense, was the beginning of an untimely end to what Anil believed might have been an amazing business empire. "The family businesses had solid assets and no debt, and although they were pioneers in their time, the family was not capable of growth that required collaboration. My paternal grandfather, Lala Lachmandas Nayar, was said to have had a 'golden hand.' Whatever venture he took on made a lot of money," said Anil. However, he had not fostered open channels of communication among his sons, most of whom had turned volatile and challenging when he planned on marrying Anil's step-grandmother, Pushpa, a woman more than a decade younger than his grandfather, following his grandmother's death. His grandfather's eldest son reportedly threatened to commit suicide if Anil's grandfather even contemplated the thought of remarrying. Although the marriage took place without the loss of life, Anil's grandfather eventually retreated into self-exile with Pushpa to Bradford, England, and later to Victoria, Canada, to escape the ensuing bickering among his offspring. (Anil remembered visiting him in Canada during his college years and found that, despite his wealth, he had been living in a one-room apartment with Pushpa, though he later returned to India, where he died in October, 1968). For a time, Daulatram took over as head of the business, but after his death in 1976, Anil's father, the second son, had taken over the reins as next in line.

"My father and uncles had grown the business to a point at which the pioneering Amritsari mindset had become a detriment," he said, noting that things might have turned out differently had his grandfather crafted an equitable system of distribution of profits or a progressive succession plan based on merit for direct involvement in the business. "Although they were forward-thinking and inclusive with respect to embracing other cultures, neither my father nor my uncles had mastered the essential business tools of internal collaboration and mutual trust. Instead they each turned to their own consiglieri for advice, resulting in indirect and often misguided communication and strained relationships all around."

Within a year, Anil knew he needed to put his family on a new footing in order to give them the lives they deserved—and with the help of an American squash friend Tom Poor, he secured a position at the Bank of Boston through another squash colleague, Skip Vonx. "My marriage at that stage had become unhinged, things personally were not going well and I was ready to go back to America," acknowledged Anil. "I felt I was deserting my mother, but I was so unhappy there that I figured for my marriage and family to survive I needed to go back to the U.S." And so, with a corporate job lined up at the Bank of Boston, he headed back to America to start his life anew.

* * *

PART FIVE

1982-1996: The Unmaking of a Champion

CHAPTER NINETEEN

America, Again

Upon returning to the U.S. after nearly a decade in India, there was no question that squash would take a back seat to the more pressing matters for Anil of resettling his family and recalibrating the working pattern of his life in Boston with a completely new career in banking. Back in the environs of his alma mater, much about the new turf was familiar to him and to Linda. Yet, the context was completely different than the post-collegiate atmosphere in which they'd met, and they needed to create a foundation for their two sons, who initially remained back in India with Anil's mother until they could find suitable housing for the entire family and establish a new routine.

Within three months, however, even before their sons would join them, Anil came up against another detour for which he was hardly prepared. The bank's management advised that they would be relocating him once again, this time to Singapore—and this new twist was simply not part of his plan. Without other options at the bank, he pursued alternatives that would soon alter his path in a completely different direction.

It was the start of the '80s—a decade of prosperity in America with Wall Street booming, the drain of the Vietnam war now a fading memory, and the cold war winding down. Ronald Reagan had defeated Jimmy Carter in his bid for president—and a new era of opulence and excess was about to unfold. Looking at the economics of the new decade, the hawkish newly elected president was determined to put pressure on the "Evil Empire" of the U.S.S.R. by increasing military spending in an attempt to expose its weaknesses and proceeding to ratchet up the provocative tone right up to the end of the decade, when the world would witness the symbolically vital destruction of the Berlin Wall after George H.W. Bush assumed the presidency.

It was also a time of innovation in investment banking and finance, when new terms like Zero-Coupon Bonds, Collateralized Mortgage Obligations, and Asset-Backed Securities were introduced into the finance lexicon and investment banking suddenly became a stylish profession, as bankers made money hand over fist and flaunted it, fueling the indulgences of the decade, including a growing craze for designer clothing, with performing icons like Material Girl Madonna, David Bowie, and David Byrne and models and royalty like Brooke Shields and Princess Diana setting a bold new tone with big hair, broad-shouldered silhouettes, bright colors, and pleated pants. Another fashion phenomenon of the era was designer jeans, which became the second skin of high-living disco denizens and sold for twice the price of the down-to-earth denim produced by Levis, yielding roughly half a billion dollars for their makers in 1979. Leading the pack at the time was the all-American socialite Gloria Vanderbilt. Her company was run by a fellow Indian, Mohan Murjani, who tapped Anil to join the firm in its New Jersey office as a vice president of operations. "Soon after I started at the bank, I got a call from Murjani," said Anil. "He offered to pay me twice my salary at the bank."

And so, Anil made yet another move back into an industry he knew well and relocated his family to Montclair, New Jersey. There he resumed his life and regularly commuted to offices in Secaucus, New Jersey, and in New York City, where many of his squash cohorts had also started their careers and settled. But fashion is fickle and, as competitors like Valente, Jordache, and Sasson started nibbling away at the market share, the company Anil had joined started hemorrhaging cash. "There were money issues due to too much inventory," explained Anil. "And a lot of the discussions revolved around whether the company should be selling to discount retailers to augment cash flow or keep their designer brand image and get an outside infusion of capital." The slide in business swiftly accelerated after Calvin Klein launched his own brand of jeans with 15-year-old Brooke Shields appearing in his sultry television ads, wagging her dungaree-clad derrière and purring, "You know what comes between me and my Calvins? Nothing."

Outdoing Vanderbilt's business approach by relying on sex rather than social status to sell his goods, Klein literally leveled all his competitors. By the early- to mid-1980s most were attempting to offload their excess inventory to discounters and the disconnect was not lost on the consumers. Seeing the inevitable downward

Linda at a horse stable in New Jersey, c. 1984.

trajectory of the company, Anil was forced again to reinvent his career, this time setting off on his own. With some essential experience in the American garment industry under his belt, he developed a business as a clothing wholesaler—aligning for a time with his brother Vinod to produce clothing at the manufacturing facilities he worked with in India, Nepal, Sri Lanka, and Pakistan. But instead of relying on volatile fashion-driven product to sustain his business, Anil made the pragmatic choice to produce men's basics like button-down shirts and khaki trousers under his own labels, including Malabar Hill and Redbank, and he sold the products to large retailers like Macy's, Walmart, Sam's Club, and Costco.

During the 1980s, the working pattern of Anil's life in business and at home gradually stabilized. "There were fewer distractions, the day-to-day rigor of living was no longer such an issue for Linda," he said. But, reliant as he was on suppliers overseas to support his business, he regularly travelled throughout the year, generally spending two weeks every 45 days away from home to visit the manufacturing facilities of his vendors and oversee the production of his orders. And eventually his constant business trips became a detriment to his marriage.

Yet, his business would not have survived without his hands-on involvement in the operations, so traveling regularly was mandatory. In the process, Anil's abilities to deal with a wide range of working scenarios across different cultures were tested on every front. And several business encounters ended badly. One of these involved an emerging relationship he had developed early on with a supplier in Sri Lanka in 1983. "It was expensive to manufacture in India due to the stringent quota allotted by the U.S. government," said Anil, who had to continually look for alternative sourcing in other countries. "At the time, Sri Lanka, with its good, educated, hard-working workforce, was a viable option and my brother Vinod had connections there."

Affectionately known as Ratna Dweepa, which means Island of Jewels in Sanskrit, Sri Lanka resembles a pear-shaped gem. "The name is a reflection of its natural wealth in gem stones, but just as amazing is its unparalleled natural beauty and quaint architecture left over from Dutch and English colonials," said Anil. "The people, too, are very warm and hospitable. The humidity and warm midday rains, so typical of the tropics, accentuated the sensualness of this beautiful island. Unfortunately, the politics of the country contrasted with its beauty, and the tensions between the dominant Buddhist Sinhalese and the Tamil Hindus were raging at this time."

Though the partnership required him to take 20-hour flights from New York to Columbo via Amsterdam on KLM, business was good for a couple of years before the relationship came to an abrupt end. "I had a very strong Sinhalese agent named Prasanna Goonetilleke, who had good relationships with the suppliers there. However, he was also very politically involved," said Anil. "On one of my trips, as usual, I arrived on the KLM flight at around 11 p.m. Prasanna was kind enough to pick me up at the airport, but, while driving to the hotel, he was quick to point out the damage the Buddhists had caused in their riots against the Tamil Hindus," Anil stated, noting that the Buddhists were relying on arson and murder as tactics in their fight to drive the Hindus out of the country. "Prasanna, with some glee, pointed to a Hindu-owned liquor shop, which had been leveled to rubble. Although he knew of my background, I looked him in the eye and told him I was a Hindu, too, and left it at that." Despite Anil's admonishment, the agent carried on with his tour, continuing to point out the destruction in similar fashion until he delivered Anil at the hotel around midnight. "Soon after arriving, I booked the next flight out to Bombay at 6 a.m. the following morning," Anil said. "I was relieved to get on the plane and upon landing in Bombay, I sent Prasanna a telex explaining that it was too difficult for me to operate in Sri Lanka and that I planned to wind down my business there."

Another country with fewer quota-driven restrictions in which Anil did business was Mauritius, which was also a 20-hour plane trip away from New York. "My brother Vijay knew the well-regarded

Currimjee family—some of whom he'd known from Cathedral—and they were well-established in Mauritius, so it made sense for me to contact them and use him as a very credible reference point. I made the connections and the factories I contracted with were humming away with my orders," Anil said of the business he was doing there in 1985.

Before long, Anil's brother Vinod began to lean on Anil's Mauritius connections, when he decided it would be useful to set up an office in Port Louis to assist with their businesses. "Vinod made a connection with a young lady whose husband participated in the Mauritian legislature and, like almost everyone on the small island, they both were friendly with the country's prime minister," Anil remembered. Though she lacked experience in the textile industry, Vinod thought her relationships in the country would compensate for her shortcomings in business and he hired her as a manager. But soon this relationship would also be doomed. "It didn't take long for Vinod to lose his wicked temper with our new manager, and his sharp remarks about her terrible decision-making skills brought the office to a halt. Within a few days, when I was back in New York and Vinod was in Bombay, we received a call from Abbas Currimjee, who told us categorically that we were personae non gratae in Mauritius and that we should never come back as we had been blacklisted," said Anil, who later learned that after the two Nayar brothers had left the country, the manager had complained about Vinod's treatment to her husband. He, in turn complained to the prime minister, who quickly banned them both from entering Mauritius again. "It felt peculiar being banned from a country—we just weren't that threatening or powerful—but I did not feel a sense of loss," Anil said. "It was way too far for me to travel to on a regular basis—and fate had made the decision to end these trips for me."

Whenever Anil was near the subcontinent during his business trips, he would invariably carve out a window of time to spend with his mother and other family members in Bombay. As in America in the early 1980s, there was some stability in the Indian polity as well. The Congress Party had been reinstated after a hiatus during the Emergency, the 21-month period in the mid-1970s when Indira Gandhi had declared a state of emergency across the country, and relations with Pakistan were on an even keel. The only blot on these happy times in India was the violent Khalistan movement, which was taking place in Anil's birthplace, the Punjab. In 1984, the Land of the Five Rivers, a mystical northern nexus in India where a confluence of cultures—Hindus, Muslims, and Sikhs—had historically joined together in life, death, and the afterlife, was experiencing a bitter battle for independence launched by a sect of the Sikhs who followed Guru Nanak, as did Anil's part-Sikh-part-Hindu mother. The fight would lead to the trauma of Operation Blue Star, an Indian military operation ordered by Prime Minister Indira Gandhi to remove the militant religious leader Jarnail Singh Bhindranwale and his armed followers from the buildings of the Harmandir Sahib complex, which includes the Sikhs' holiest shrine—the Golden Temple of Amritsar (now called Sri Darbar Sahib among other names by the Sikhs at the direction of Akal Takht, the supreme religious body of the community). That attack would in turn lead to the assassination of the prime minister, Mrs. Indira Gandhi, by her own Sikh body guards on a warm and still October 31st morning the same year. After her assassination, her son Rajiv Gandhi took office to become the youngest prime minister of India at the age of 40.

At the same time, Anil witnessed the continued unraveling of his family's businesses. "I knew after my father's death the extended family was going to disintegrate, it would put everyone in centrifugal mode," said Anil. "There would be apartment grabs, money grabs, and sales of assets without proper documents. My father had been the *'karta'* in our family, a special designation given in Hindu families to the eldest male who is thus empowered to make the important decisions affecting the family as a whole. He ruled with a heavy hand and most times fairly compared to the implosion that took place after his death." Sadly, according to Anil, the next brother in line was a weak *karta* and the poor communication among the remaining brothers continued through the 1980s.

"It is quite likely the scenario became a free for all with each brother—except the two who stayed in Amritsar—milking where they could amid a scenario of ever growing mutual suspicion and dislike for each other," said Anil. "In reality, none of the brothers wanted to give up control and since the family flagship firm was a partnership, it was a chronic problem to get a consensus to make major decisions on changes of structure to take advantage of newer tax rules and plan for long-term posterity. Movement from partnership to a limited company would have taken away their veto powers. The factories started to lose business. It was no longer a time when they could rely on the cost-cut path that had been so rigidly followed for profitability. The intangible concepts that were driving businesses at that time—merchandising, advertising, promotion, and relationships with wholesalers as necessary conduits to learn from and sell through—were all very alien to our group of pioneers and conventional entrepreneurs. Gradually, one after another of the factories slowed down and were shut down. In some cases, to pay the labor liabilities associated with shutdowns, land had to be sold."

So during the years when he was launching his own business in America, Anil was still stinging not only from the loss of his father, but also from the failures of the family to sustain its own businesses as well as his own failure to get the television business off the ground in Amritsar. And this string of blows was still affecting him psychologically. "From early on, since I was a pre-teen, I made sure I didn't rush to judgments of people, incidents, and debatable issues," said Anil. "On many issues I was often uncertain and couldn't express a strong opinion or take a side unequivocally. I usually gave the underdog the benefit of doubt and hoped he would come out the right way up in an incident. This constant weighing of both sides sometimes led to personal doubt."

This innate trait also sometimes translated into indecision on business matters. And when things were not going well in certain areas of his life, Anil occasionally found himself gripped by a sense of apprehension, which had burdened him to some degree after he'd returned to India. "A feeling of uncertainty crept into my psyche and this only got accentuated in the mid-'70s with the TV factory shut down," Anil said. "How could I have done so well in intense competition and not excel in business? Success in one, I assumed, meant success in other endeavors. It was an invincible kind of feeling! But with one poor performance after another—at work, at home with Linda, and the accompanying amiss behavior—feelings of vulnerability and doubt sometimes got the better of me."

Back in the U.S.A. in the 1980s, Anil often found himself enmeshed in a similar mindset. "Going into textiles and starting a business was a natural progression for me," he said. "But my Punjabi *Kshatrya* background, my affluent upbringing, and my champion pride also played very dominant roles in how I behaved, how I addressed issues, and whom I wanted to connect with. And in the real world of textiles, the buyers, assistant buyers, and their lackeys were just not the kind of people I was accustomed to. I disliked doing what I thought was unfair. I disliked their single-sidedness in addressing issues and I disliked their arrogance and ruthlessness when they didn't meet their short-term objectives or margins."

He was also irritated by the general lack of manners and the sense of entitlement assumed by the retailers' representatives he dealt with in America. "I was used to winning and with winning came respect," said Anil. "That was not the case in my business as a supplier of apparel and home textiles to retailers. Our retail clients expected small businesses such as mine to prostrate themselves to their demands no matter how well you serviced their orders. I was used to respect and this was a humiliating experience." A merchandise manager from Steinmart, a medium-size department store, was a particularly annoying example of the kind of people he was coping with. "He would come in with his buyers, take over an office, put his legs up on the table, and start making loud, bossy phone calls without so much as greeting or a request for permission to sit down," Anil said. There was also a Sam's Club buyer who would take charge of an office, shut the door behind her, and use the telephone for long periods during her appointment time. "I didn't feel as badly towards her, however," said Anil. "Perhaps she had a lover in her life!"

* * *

CHAPTER TWENTY

Front Right Nick

To alleviate his dissatisfaction with other aspects of his life, Anil found an escape hatch in squash just as he had when he returned to India. During the 1980s and '90s he continued to play in age-related national championships as well as state and local tournaments. "But I wasn't as hungry," he admitted. "And I was traveling a lot, so squash took a back seat. As a result, I was playing erratically and in a distracted fashion."

Furthermore, the squash scene in America had changed dramatically while Anil was overseas in India—and, upon his return, continued to transform significantly in the decades ahead. As in India, the roots of squash in the U.S. were entrenched in the courts of private clubs of the social elite and, for decades, had remained the exclusive domain of the upper crust helmed by a blue-blood directorate who kept it out of the reach of the masses. But as new forces emerged within squash's governing bodies and the sport spread beyond the Eastern seaboard into the heartland all the way west and across the whole of North America, the traditions of the old guard eventually gave way to a new commercialized approach to squash that ushered in a new wave of players and with them larger purses of prize money and corporate sponsors.

Among the most significant of developments that altered the sport was the erosion of what had once been the clear line that divided amateur players and pros. While the first U.S. Open tournament in 1954 was a start toward bridging the chasm that had long separated the amateurs from the pros, who at that time continued to enter the private clubs through back doors and were excluded from their inner sanctums and social affairs, squash retained its purebred aura for two more decades as the old guard staunchly resisted the pressure to commercialize. But toward the end of the 1970s, the signs of change in the air were palpable. "Squash, that sport of elitists, is going public," wrote Jim Kaplan in *Sports Illustrated* in 1976. "Out of the private clubs and into the beer halls. The proletariato is invading the boardroom. How do you know? All you had to do was listen at the U.S. Nationals last week, where such talk was flying about as thick and fast as the green balls on the University of Pennsylvania's Ringe Courts. There was just one problem: it wasn't quite accurate. Squash may not be as exclusive as fox hunting anymore, but it isn't played by dead-end kids, either. The tournament was dominated by Ivies and observed by a mink-coated, tassel-shoed crowd."

By the 1980s, according to author and squash expert James Zug, the squash racquet, a social status symbol once seen as an essential preppy accessory, was now a stylish accoutrement for a new breed of players as public courts began opening up across the country and film, media, arts, and sports celebrities like Kris Kristofferson, Tom Brokaw, Frank Stella, Mick Jagger, and Kareem Abdul-Jabbar began to embrace the sport. Women, who had always participated in the sport under its own governing bodies with limited access to the clubs, also entered into the collective fold. As squash stretched out into new territory, the social structures that once controlled it began to crumble, and what had long been a rich white man's sport now began to truly diversify as the number of players quadrupled in 1985 to 300,000 over the prior decade.

While at this point Anil stepped only intermittently back into the American fray, he nonetheless managed to gain the top prize in several tournaments over the next couple of decades, including numerous American national masters titles in 1987, 1988, 1989, twice in 1990, 1992, 1993, 1994, 1997, and 1999. He also continued to gain honors, including being inducted into the Harvard Varsity Club's Hall of Fame in 1991 and the National Intercollegiate Squash Racquets Hall of Fame in 1992 and earning the Willis L.M. Reese Sportsmanship award in 1993. And one of his most memorable matches during this period was against his college nemesis Scott Ryan in 1987 at the Harry L. Cowles tournament, named for Harvard's first and greatest squash coach, which American player and author Rob Dinerman recalled in his book *A History of Harvard Squash 1922-2010*:

> In January, 1987, 20 years after their meeting at the No. 1 position in the '67 Harvard-Navy meet, Nayar and Ryan had a long-awaited rematch in the final round of the Barnaby draw of the Cowles weekend. A disproportionate number of Nayar's college teammates, some of whom had long since stopped playing squash even recreationally, nevertheless made a point of securing seats in the Harvard Club gallery to witness Nayar's decisive victory, as did Barnaby himself, who presented Nayar with the trophy and made a brief speech lauding Nayar and congratulating him on his glittering career. One of Nayar's teammates even said after the' 87 final ended (on a backhand three-wall that dead-rolled out the front-right nick) that, with Nayar's win, that torturous afternoon at Annapolis two decades earlier had in his mind at long last been redeemed.

By then, Anil was in his early-forties, a time for any sportsman to reflect and regroup—and for a champion of a physically demanding sport like squash, more emphatically so. So during this time, his perspective on squash began to expand as he not only looked back at the careers of the top players from his part of the world as they made their way to America and evolved on the international scene, but also as he looked to the future in his observations of younger players from America, India, and other countries around the world who had mastered a sport that continued to evolve.

Recalling a professional tournament during the 1970s when he was sitting with Hashim Khan, the legend of all times, and watching his son Sharif play Mohibullah Khan, a relative and archrival on the U.S. circuit, Anil remembered commenting on Mo's quickness and asked Hashim if he was as fast. "Hashim, in his modest way, looked around, saw no one else within earshot, and then whispered in my ear with his Pashto accent, 'Twice as fast, twice as fast,'" said Anil, marveling that "the bandy-legged, pot-bellied man was so fast on the court, even as a middle-aged man, that he could practically volley a drop shot." Anil's experiences with Hashim, as well as the other stellar squash-playing Khans (including Yusuf, Mohibullah, Sharif, Jansher, and Jahangir, all of whom dominated the international professional squash scene before, during, and after Anil's era on the court) contributed to shaping his views on the elements that produced champions like these. "With the exceptions of Hashim, Roshan, and Azam, few players can come from humble backgrounds and do well, but, in the 1950s, '60s, and '70s, squash was their *terroir*," Anil observed, noting that, especially during this time period, certain countries produced more significant players than others because of an infrastructural support system that fostered excellence. The players that rose to the forefront then, as they do now, were ones who practiced and played tournaments full-time in the U.K., Australia, New Zealand, Pakistan, Egypt, and the U.S.A. While infrastructural support is critical to the success of a sportsman, Anil believed hunger and talent are also essential ingredients in becoming a top world player.

"In Hashim, there was a hunger that translated into excellence on the world stage," Anil said. "The British in Peshawar facilitated his travel and international play. His brothers Azam and Roshan followed in the path laid down by Hashim. Another British officer gave a gift to Yusuf, another Khan who hailed from Nowshera and was distantly related to the Peshawar clan, to pay for his competition abroad. For the Peshawar Khans that followed, there was a continuing hunger to let neither the country nor the Khan name down and we later saw Sharif, Jahangir, and Jansher excel, too. But that hunger gets diluted and, by the time the fourth generation comes into the picture, this passion for excellence can become a peripheral activity and by the fifth or sixth generation, the domination can become a dim memory." Rahmat Khan, the son of the late Nasrullah Khan, a member of the same Pathan tribe who taught the remarkable Irish player Jonah Barrington, played a significant role in his cousin Jahangir's success and shared Anil's thoughts on the elements that contribute to the making of a top player. According to a post on the website of the Indian Squash Professionals organization, Khan noted that among the qualities that made Jahangir special was the fact that he lived and trained like a monk and that he played with a single-minded goal: to be the best.

From Anil's perspective, the players who succeed at the highest levels also come from rich, nurtured squash *terroirs* with sufficient courts, good teachers, and grassroots programs with coaches who understand the science of winning. "Egypt has been exceptionally successful in going this route and has fostered excellence amongst many different people, rather than keeping it concentrated in a clan or a family," Anil said. "Dynasties don't last, but systems do. And the Egyptians have created the depth and breadth of players that have enabled them to be a global powerhouse for a long time."

During Anil's time in India, however, such resources or support were wholly inadequate to produce top champions. "It's amazing that the government allowed the Squash Federation of India to exist at all given the myriad demands for its strained resources," Anil said of the context in which he evolved as a player. "As Indians, we weren't fit enough, we weren't used to the pace, and we weren't used to the intensity of playing in an international arena—we could have done a lot better with training and foreign play experience. India could have been a powerhouse from the 1960s onwards. It had the nucleus of players in Bombay who were in close proximity and could compete to make each other better. India also had a similar nucleus at the Indian Military Academy in Dehra Dun and the National Defense Academy in Pune. I strongly believe that if we could have pooled the players of Bombay and Pune, imported Sanjit Roy from Delhi, kept Yusuf from going to Seattle, and had the long-term backing of the Indian government and the Indian Squash Federation and private benefactors, India could have produced some very serious world contenders. India then had some very talented players who could have made a difference."

Yet given the context, it was perhaps inevitable that few Indian players would rise to the level of world-class play. And in many ways, the very fact that he was able to excel at the top as an amateur for as long as he did is a testament to Anil's innate talent and sheer dint of will considering the forces working against high-level accomplishments in sports in India. Despite the shortcomings of the Indian support system for its sportsmen, Anil had excelled in squash as a young player and managed to transition back and forth between the international softball and the American hardball versions of the sport with relative ease throughout the course of his career.

Amplifying the adverse conditions for sportsmen in India, Anil's fellow player Ananth Nayak points out that the psyche of Indian parents with respect to their children was oriented toward occupations that would provide security, so a career in sports, and especially squash, was never really an option among those who excelled as sportsmen at the time. "They weren't ready to have their kids go out on a limb," Nayak said. His own experience at the Singapore open in 1979 exemplifies this attitude, which continued to prevail through the 1980s and '90s. According to Nayak, the Pakistani coach Umar Daraz, who was nicknamed Ustaad—which, in Urdu, means Master—by the Pakistani players, had seen him play a match and told him and the press that Nayak could become a really fine player in six months, but to do so he would need to come to Pakistan and the U.K. to train. Nayak's father noticed the article in the paper, and when he subsequently met with his son and the Pakistani coach, he categorically told them both that squash would not be a likely route for Ananth and that he should pursue academics instead.

On a broader level, however, the game continued to significantly evolve during the 1980s and 1990s. Hardball squash had been largely the only form of the game played in North America until the 1980s. By then, though, squash had expanded on an international level on both the professional and amateur circuits, with courts and players now emerging from across Europe and other parts of the world where the international softball game was played. This growing exposure to the international version of the game resulted in many clubs in North America building 21-foot-wide courts (6.4 m), and the soft ball was now being used more often on both wide and narrow courts in the U.S.

As in tennis, equipment was changing, too. The old wooden racquets had been completely replaced by metal racquets, first made from steel and aluminum and later with graphite composite. Courts, too, had begun to evolve with transparent back and side walls being installed to allow for wider viewing audiences. To further aid in viewing at the French open in 1984, instead of wooden floors and black balls, a blue floor and white ball were introduced. And later that year, when the American player Mark Talbott beat Jahangir Khan 18-16 in the fifth at the finals of the Boston Open, he did so on America's first portable glass court (Anil also played on such a court during the 1980s in a tournament at the Winter Garden in the World Trade Center in New York after professional tours started springing up to present the sport in dramatic locales to wider audiences). And by the mid-1990s, the softball game had become the world standard with the hardball game being largely phased out in North America. As the sport evolved, coaching techniques and strategy changed, too. But by this time Anil was no longer as attuned to keeping up with the nuances of the current forms of play, nor was he as driven or as fit as he'd been in the past.

Still, with a new generation of talented players coming up in India, many of them would look to Anil for guidance, inspiration, and support—whether he was ready for them or not. Anil's influence in America had been helpful in getting his own coach Yusuf Khan to the states while Anil was still at Harvard, when Khan sought his assistance in easing his entree into Seattle (there Khan would become a coach at the Seattle Tennis Club, and later at the College Club of Seattle and the Seattle Tennis Club, where he would remain a powerful influence on young players for the next several decades, producing champions like his daughters Shabana and Latasha Khan, Mark Alger, and numerous others). And younger Indian players, such as Darius Pandole and Adrian Ezra, saw Anil as a role model, fashioning their path toward higher education in America via excellence in sport on the template he had set.

"Unwittingly, I had started a squash movement to the U.S.A. after my move to Harvard in 1965," Anil said. "First the players came from India and, in time, from the world over. Soon after I left, my peer Anil Kapur and later "Deputy" Dinesh Nayak, Ananth Nayak's elder brother, left for the University of Penn and played for its team in the late 1960s and early '70s. After that, it was like a whole world of sourcing opened up. Later came Darius Pandole, the Indian junior national champion in 1981 who went to Harvard and was ranked number one in the intercollegiate and U.S. men's amateur championships in 1988. Farokh Pandole followed his brother to Harvard and was also on its team for several years. Adrian Ezra, who was Indian national champion in 1988 and 1989, also went to Harvard and won three intercollegiate titles in 1991, 1993, and 1994 as well as the Bingham award. His brother Dan Ezra followed him to Harvard and won the 1996 intercollegiate championship. During this time and later, Diniar Ali Khan from Calcutta and other young Pandoles from my schoolmate Naval Pandole's family and many other juniors from different parts of India also left for the U.S. to various colleges." And among the many younger Indian female players later following the same path and ascending to the international stage, Supriya Balsekar stands out. Coached in America by Satinder Bajwa, she rose to become captain of the Harvard team in 2008 and her high-minded sportsmanship was celebrated among teammates in a rallying cry that became known as the "Spirit of Supi." A few years later, Alisha Mushruwala followed Balsekar to become Harvard team captain in 2010 under coach Bajwa as well.

Anil had also served as a catalyst for the coaches of colleges of the Northeast. After he played squash at Harvard, they realized that there were good student players to tap from other parts of the world and gradually adapted their approaches to building teams as they began looking farther afield to find top players like Anil and proactively recruited them. Ultimately, the world began to open up to squash and squash opened up to the world. According to Anil's son Vivek, "Today many American colleges, not just Ivy League universities, across the country have teams made up largely of foreign students from places like Pakistan, Egypt, Europe, Australia, New Zealand, and Southeast Asia." And just as the line between amateurs and pros had blurred and enabled what was once a sport that was played only in a limited collection of commonwealth countries and mostly in private clubs to now expand across continental Europe and other parts of the world and regularly take place in facilities with broad access to the general public, the college recruitment process began to professionalize, too. "It was like opening a spigot," said Anil. "Now teams have three or four or five foreign students. That whole dynamic became commonplace."

While democratization, without doubt, elevated squash to a new level, the professionalization of the recruitment process at the college and high-school levels elicited mixed reactions, especially as the approach blossomed in the 1990s. In a piece on the professionalization of Ivy League sports in a 1997 issue of *Harvard* magazine, Craig Lambert, after noting the oft-repeated story on Anil's surprise entrance onto the Hemenway courts in 1965, wrote:

> The days of such surprises are over. Today, squash coaches would spot an athlete of Nayar's caliber years before he applied to college and all American schools with varsity squash programs, including Harvard, would vigorously recruit him. College sports in general, including the Ivy League, have changed radically since 1965. Long-established amateur traditions, guided by patrician rules and played out on pastoral fields, have given way to a complex, highly competitive, multibillion-dollar enterprise, shaped by the values of business and professional athletics.
>
> In this rapidly evolving context, the mainstream of American college athletics has moved away from the Ivy League's classic ideals about the proper role of sports in higher education. And within the Ivy League, Harvard represents the staunchest holdout for amateur values that are under increasing attack, from sources both within the league and beyond it. The recruitment of athletes, their development before college and their training and competition once enrolled, their character, and their distribution among sports—are all in flux.

Lambert went on to describe the experience of two Harvard coaches:

> Maura Costin Scalise '80, who coached women's swimming at Harvard from 1984 until this year, says, "In the sport of swimming, I'm only as good as the athletes I bring in; 95 percent of my success is due to recruiting." It was not always thus. Until the mid-1970s, institutional policies and gentlemen's agreements minimized recruiting within the Ivy League. Harvard

had especially stringent guidelines against it: "We didn't recruit, period," says [Jack] Barnaby. The policy forbade coaches to talk with prospective students unless the student had first contacted Harvard. "I always felt that someone should be grateful to attend the College and that it was a privilege to play for Harvard," Barnaby recalls. "I wasn't going to get down on my knees and beg anyone to come here, no matter how good he was." [Dave] Fish, who was Barnaby's protégé, explains that, "to Jack, recruiting was a dirty word. When I was in college, to recruit implied that you were lazy: the assumption was that if you recruited, you didn't coach." In those days, "recruiting" often meant persuading undergraduates to take up a new sport.

At the same time the phenomenon produced an exodus of college-age players that contributed to a player vacuum in India, as so many of the talented juniors were no longer present there to create the depth and excitement in the sport.

Keenly aware of the void, Anil attempted to leverage his experience and offer strategies to those running the Indian Squash Federation on how to tap India's vast sports potential. Just as there had been an exodus of players from India, coaches, too, were leaving the country for more hospitable shores. Knowing how heavily he had relied on his own coaches for the support he needed to elevate his play to international caliber, Anil urged those manning the Federation in India to support a higher level approach to coaching as a starting point for improving the turnout of top players for the country. Fresh off a win in the finals against the Englishman Bryan Patterson at a U.S. nationals tournament, where his old coach Yusuf Khan was in attendance to support him, Anil wrote an article for "The Sunday Observer" section of *The Times of India* in 1992, part of which described the match and highlighted his thoughts on the state of the sport in India at the time and how it could be improved:

During the break between games [Yusuf] came down, said a few things and it all came good in the decider, which I won. It was like wanting to win for the master. It's important to have a good coach whom you respect. It helps if he can be with you over the long run so that there is continuity. In India there is an acute shortage of coaches. There has been a drought since Yusuf left.

To remedy the problem, Anil went on to suggest tapping India's top players, such as Ananth Nayak, then 33, who had given up competitive play, and providing them with long-term contracts. He also urged the development of sponsorship programs that would ensure a financial commitment to continuity in training and facilities. As it turned out, Nayak was later enlisted by the Squash Racket Federation of India to coach the Indian junior team for the world junior championships in 1992 and 1994, and for the Asian junior championship tournament in Singapore in 1995, when the Indian team won its first silver medal in the team event. "Unfortunately, Ananth was not retained as a coach after 1995 for internal reasons, known perhaps only to Raju Chainani and K.S. Mehra, the president of the Squash Rackets Federation of India at the time," said Anil. However, Mahendra Agarwal, a prominent squash supporter in Bombay, saw the dearth of coaches and founded the Indian Squash Professional Association, which encouraged professional training, in 1993 (by then pros were no longer referred to as markers). Since then, his association has benefited squash by not only increasing the number of coaches, but also the quality of coaching.

At about the same time, Anil also envisioned developing a program to nurture and support Indian juniors, which was driven in many ways by his observations of and experiences with the Khans. He initiated the effort with Raju Chainani, whom he had reconnected with in the mid-'70s, after Chainani returned to India and launched a publication called *Simply Squash*. The aim of their plan was to train juniors from the CCI along with outsiders, particularly less privileged athletes whom they hoped to groom into champions. "Both of us thought then, and I still do, that from this lot in India, we could produce champions from backgrounds that might have been similar to those of the Khans," said Anil, who noted that the program was later continued by other sponsors and, while it lasted, did exceedingly well, ultimately enriching U.S. squash with the numerous boys and girls who trained in the program and later were accepted into colleges in the U.S., where coaches like Paul Assaiante at Trinity particularly appreciated the foreign talent it produced, as did Satinder Bajwa, an Indian player who served for a time as a coach at Harvard, and Ned Edwards, who was the coach of Anil's son Sanjay at Penn.

Among the American colleges, Trinity benefited most. "Paul Assaiante evolved into an outstanding coach on and off court," said Anil. "He is a very effective communicator, he treats his players as though they are part of an extended family, and this made the Indian players feel safe, secure, and comfortable. Each year he would get the best of the crop of young players from India and all over the world." Assaiante would eventually lead Trinity to 13 consecutive intercollegiate championships starting in 1999 and a total of 17 championships as of 2018. And though it took a while for the admissions offices and coaches of the other colleges to catch on, colleges from all over the country are now recruiting foreign players, too.

Anil's consistent interest in the evolution of squash on the subcontinent during the 1980s and '90s did not go unnoticed by the younger generation of players there, especially in Bombay. "What do Anil Nayar's younger counterparts remember most about him?" asked Chainani's brother, Sunil. "That he always had time for them, to play with them, and to chat with them. This, in the early stages, is so valuable for an aspiring youngster." Among some of these

At the Chatham Club in New Jersey, c. 1994: From left: Coach Geoff Mitchell, Anil, Jansher Khan, Ahmed Barada (then the world junior champion), and Satinder Bajwa.

younger players was Adrian Ezra, who, some two decades younger than Anil, looked up to the senior sportsman with some adulation, spent time with him when permissible, and was delighted to be compared to the elder player when he played at the CCI.

"When you entered the CCI courts and heard the sound of the ball making contact with the racquet and the wall, you *knew* it was Anil on the court. Those who observed me said the dynamics of my game were somewhat similar to Anil's," said Ezra with pride, noting that both players underwent the transition from softball to hardball after their moves overseas. Ezra recalled that even after moving to the U.S.A., he would talk frequently on the phone to Anil for advice. "He was always there," Ezra remembered, noting that his coaches at Harvard were Steve Piltch and later Bill Doyle, who filled the void after Jack Barnaby retired.

While Anil was supporting juniors in India, he also nurtured an emerging appreciation for squash among younger American players, including his sons Sanjay and Vivek, when both were young teens and played at the courts at the Chatham Club not far from their home in Montclair. Notably though, both sons pointed out that he did so only when they were ready. "My father never pressed a squash racquet into my hands," said Sanjay. "He just said, 'Go play sports.' So we played a lot of sports. I started out playing tennis, so I got into squash late and didn't make varsity until I was a sophomore in college at Penn, but my father was always supportive."

"He never pushed a racquet in my hands, but I wouldn't have enjoyed it if he had," echoed Anil's son Vivek, who eventually went on to start on his college varsity team at Vassar. "I didn't start playing in earnest until I was a freshman in high school. I was a tennis player. At one point Dad said, 'I know you haven't been interested in squash, but if you worked on your volleys in the court it would make you a better player.' So I did, and we had a great time. My first year I didn't win a single match. I remember playing and losing to someone who had been playing since he was 5. But my dad was as cool as the other side of a pillow. He let me deal with it. He never made me feel bad about things. He cared enough to never compound the tension. In hindsight, I see this with a lot of appreciation."

When Anil wasn't playing at the Harvard Club in New York during these years, he often played recreational matches and in club tournaments with other members at the Chatham Club as well as with Geoff Mitchell, a Canada native and the club's professional coach who continues in this capacity today. Mitchell remembered the joy of playing with Anil at this time, remarking, like all of his fellow Harvard teammates, on his superb sportsmanship. "When you're in competition, you have no choice about who you would play, but at a certain point when you're really not competing anymore, then you can choose who you train with and who you would have fun with on the court—and I would often play with Anil," said Mitchell, who also coached Sanjay and Vivek as they were growing up. "Anil was always extremely graceful on and off the court, and if I had to go back in time and play someone who was at their peak or if I could play someone when I was at my peak, Anil would be one of those people."

Like Anil's sons, Mitchell also commended him on his sagacity as a father during this time, especially with respect to his approach to his sons' attitudes and approach to sports. "Unlike other families I've dealt with, Anil, as a parent, was so not pushy—and that was so unusual for a really good player," said Mitchell. "He didn't put any pressure on them to do well. And I think that is one of the reasons why they still love the sport. That's quite rare for someone who's the son of a prodigy like Anil. You have to be a very good parent and put yourself in a different spot to have that happen with your child. I also remember people saying, 'Oh my God, you teach Anil's kids, you must feel so much pressure.' But I never felt any pressure. It was obvious from the beginning that the main goal was that they learned a lifelong sport. And that they were happy on and off the court. It was never about what ranking they got or how good they got."

Both Sanjay and Vivek agreed that squash not only reinforced their collective bonds but also contributed to their approaches to life. "Squash improved my relationship with my dad," said Sanjay. "Certainly one lesson that comes to mind is the lesson of patience. You wait for an opportunity, but when you have it you take it. You can apply it even in real life. Squash is like a chess game on the court, and life is a chess game if you're at all political or interact with people. But it includes movement, the physical along with the mental. It builds perseverance to move forward to a new level of mental progress. It's very similar to life and gives you the ability not to give up." Vivek offered a similar take. "You can make an argument that how you play squash is how you approach life," he said. "My dad was a tremendously fast, gifted player, but just as important was his sportsmanship and he was fun to be around. He instilled in us the right way to play, competing in an intense environment. And underlying his approach was being a gentleman. He taught us to be humble, play fair, not give up, and recognize the value of teamwork."

While he remained intensely interested in squash and the emerging players at the time, including his sons, Anil helped Mitchell organize an exhibition match in the mid 1990s at the Chatham Club between Jansher Khan, who was then the world champion, and Ahmed Barada, an up-and-coming Egyptian junior champion, to expose top-level play to younger American players in New Jersey. "Anil was bringing people over and paving the way" for more exposure to foreign players, said Mitchell, who noted that

Anil (center) with Raju Chainani (left), Jahangir Khan (right), and Indian juniors (far right) at the Downtown Athletic Club in New York in 1998.

increasing financial rewards and endorsements during 1980s and '90s also contributed to an uptick in foreign professional players coming to the U.S. to play. "Jahangir Khan came over because it was very easy to make money in the U.S.—there was substantial money in the U.S. hardball tour on the pro circuit," Mitchell said. "Jahangir came over and was the only one to beat the number one U.S. player, Mark Talbott, who owned the singles circuit. And the talk at the time was that Jahangir was also the first squash player to earn a million dollars in a year. Usually 70 percent of an athlete's income comes from endorsements, so that means he maybe made $300,000 in prize money." And while the financial rewards for a professional squash player are significantly lower than for higher-profile sports like tennis or soccer, they started to become substantial enough to induce more strong players from all over the world to compete on a professional level.

As structural elements of squash continued to evolve throughout this period, which in effect forced players to change their approach to the game, Mitchell believed the techniques and methods deployed by the top players to adapt to the conditions of each era, like Anil did in his day or Jahangir Khan in the 1980s, also pushed the game forward. "There are some basic techniques that survive throughout that you might call archetypes of the game, rudimentary elements that haven't changed. But so much has changed because a group of players discovered something, whether it's a new shot or a new way to play a shot or a new way to move the ball," Mitchell explained. "It's almost like survival in the evolution of the game. It's very Darwinian. It evolves to survive. Because it's a competitive game and the best players rise to the top, new things are discovered by those players whether it's footwork, stroke work, strategy, or training."

Mitchell pointed to Jonah Barrington, the stellar Irish player who was known for training and being exceptionally fit, as an example. "He was the fittest out there and that's why he won, but then softball changed and it became less of a fitness game, especially as the scoring changed," Mitchell said. "Instead of being a 9-point game and you had to be serving to win when Anil and I played, squash was changed to a 15-point game for a while, then to an 11-point game, and the tin was brought down from 19 inches to 17 inches, the same height as for hardball, and that changed the strategy because it makes attacking the ball so much easier." The question that continues to be debated, said Mitchell, is, who is really making the changes in the game? If the stroke and foot work are changing, is it the coaches or the players? "It's an interesting discussion because you get a group of players who will excel and do something different and do it really well. Look at players using an open stance on the forehand, we would get yelled at for doing that by our coaches and in that respect our coaches were holding us back," said Mitchell, who added that players now use this approach all the time. "Now, some of us just wouldn't listen and we would do it the way we thought was best and there was a whole group of players who came out of each era that did things their own way, and then you get the good coaches who change with them and no longer teach the same way."

Since a lot of American players during this time were making the transition from hardball to softball they were learning the importance of shot making and attacking over containment, which is what a lot of the softball game had been about, Mitchell added. "Hardball and softball are completely different games, played on different courts, and the strategy and shots are completely different," said Mitchell. "The things that really drove softball squash into becoming more of an attacking game were players like Anil and Jahangir coming here to play hardball and learning some different shots, and in many ways they drove more attacking into the softball game." Mitchell also believed that Anil, like other top players, stretched conventional wisdom on the courts to contribute to its evolution. "He had to break rules," said Mitchell of Anil's approach to squash at his peak. "He was ahead of his time as a deceptive player. He was also known for his 'wristy' form of play. The transition from softball to hardball is a much easier transition than the other way around, especially if you have great hands. And Anil was a magician at the front of the court. It was difficult to tell where he was hitting the ball. He was definitely one of the first players I played with who had that wrist that could do whatever he wanted to with the ball and surprise the heck out of you in the middle of a rally. He was great to train with for that reason."

* * *

CHAPTER TWENTY ONE

Weekend Warrior

As Anil embraced the younger generation of players entering into the squash firmament, he also witnessed the community's elder statesmen gradually fade from the scene. Among them was Mohibullah Khan, who collapsed and died outside a court at the Harvard Club in Boston after giving a lesson in 1994. His demise, Anil was told by Khan's occasional doubles partner, Ed Mank, had been accelerated by the failure of his liver and his fast-paced life. Anil attended Khan's funeral in Boston, where many of his high-profile supporters were in attendance, among them Ted Kennedy, then the only surviving member of the Camelot era who had played a considerable part in the squash pro's life. The youngest Kennedy brother had also been responsible for getting Khan naturalized, quite an event in those days, and he spoke about Khan as having left an indelible mark on America. Anil also had his brief moment to convey his appreciation from the podium for the squash star's influence before the end of the service. "The world lost the most magnetic racquet player I had ever seen," said Anil.

This was also a time when Anil was facing greater challenges on the work front, as pressures from big-box retailers were squeezing margins and elevating their quality control measures. To ease his frustrations and buffer his direct contact with his retail counterparts, he had hired a female business partner, Marsha Cutler, a young Jewish woman from Long Island, who was better equipped to serve as a client interface while he focused on operations and management. Instinctively an equal opportunity employer, Anil also hired other staff from various backgrounds—including an Indian salesperson and partner, Pavan Uttam, a Puerto Rican-American salesperson, Carlos Lamourt, and a Muslim Indian support person, Ahmed Pabani, a slow moving fellow who eventually became known to his fellow workers as Flash after Anil spied him quickly picking up his pace whenever he or Marsha came into the office or met him on the street. With a dedicated team in place to field some of the day-to-day stresses, Anil could more readily see the humor and charm in some of his business interactions while managing the sometimes surprising and often aggravating logistics.

One amusing incident involved a tough buyer who represented the behemoth retailer Walmart. As such, he conducted himself like a big shot and forced Anil's team to adapt to Walmart's painful cost control measures, including requiring its vendors to place the calls to its employees or reversing the charges to its vendors when its employees made long-distance calls to them. "Our Walmart shirt buyer was known on the subcontinent as the 'King of Bangladesh' due to the large orders he placed there," said Anil. "He wore tight fitting suits and bought from us at razor sharp prices and, over the course of three or four years, made our buying and supply chain very efficient and helped us make good money on his orders. Some years later, during a visit to him in Bentonville, my sales manager, Carlos, accidentally entered his new office, which was a small shared cubbyhole housing two desks. When we learned of his humble workspace we had to chuckle. Even the King of Bangladesh had been downsized by a firm that relied on cost cutting in every facet of its business."

Other incidents overseas reminded Anil of the tenderer sides of his foreign business encounters. One occurred in Mauritius (before he and Vinod had been kicked out of the country), where the car Anil had rented failed to start after a dinner at the home of a prominent couple, Abbas and Gita Currimjee. "The temperature had cooled late at night and it was wet," remembered Anil. "My hosts were one of the very few Hindu-Muslim couples I had known. The Hindu wife was quite religious and would often go to India on pilgrimage, while the Muslim husband had a secular, inclusive view of what world order should be. Upon seeing the stalled car, the Hindu wife believed she could will the car to start with prayer and warmth and proceeded to lay belly down on the bonnet of the car and offer blessings. Soon, with her unseen powers, she was able to get the car to behave and start—it was a totally delightful scene under a mixture of clouds and stars by the seashore."

Another memorable business trip overseas took place in Oman, another country with a lenient quota allocation in which Anil did business after his eviction from Mauritius. While visiting a pair of brothers who owned an Omani garment-making firm outside Muscat, Anil noticed that they looked nothing alike. "One was dark, stern, and sharp nosed with a straying eye, the other was tall, well built, fair, and more attuned to connecting with us," said Anil. "My partner Marsha and I just couldn't believe these two were brothers." Detecting their doubt, the fairer brother explained the relationship. "We take decisions together, we have one heartbeat," Anil recalled him saying. To further press his point he invited Anil and his partner to their home outside Muscat for a Friday meal. "We sat on the floor in a gazebo outside their residence in the compound as a fresh, warm breeze filtered through," Anil said. "With both brothers present, lunch was served communal style and the brothers pulled the food off the serving plates by hand, chewed the chicken and mutton meat off the bones, and spat out the bones in every direction. It was a like a scene from a Fellini film."

Despite the occasional bright spots in his business and his relative success as a small businessman, Anil found this period of his life to be mostly frustrating. "There was a part of me that wanted to grow my business and there was another part of me that was just tired of work and ready for my business to be bought out in the mid 1990s," he said. "During the 1970s and later in the '80s, when I moved back to the U.S. and began building my business, I could see the extreme financial success of a few of my school and college friends, both in India and America, and there was a part of me that regretted not finishing business school, as I considered how I might have worked in the corporate world and achieved the same kind of success if I had gained a Masters degree. But there was another part of me that knew that at heart I wasn't meant for the corporate world, or for working long hours during the week or on weekends." He also believed his habit of escaping from the office and heading to the Harvard Club to play squash as a relief from the day-to-day pressures of his business dampened the possibilities of further growth of his business. "My business partner handled all the backend problems and dealt with the buyers, and this allowed me the free time I wanted to enjoy with my squash friends and kids, yet I didn't have the ambition or the mindset to use that extra time to canvas with suppliers and clients to grow my business further. The balance I enjoyed in my life was how I weighed my success, it was how I justified my choices," said Anil. Yet, he admitted this "toss up" between extreme financial success and quality of life is a choice he continues to wrestle with today. Nonetheless, his squash game suffered, too. "I practiced less, played fewer tournaments, and had too many distractions to allow me to focus," he said.

Compounding theses problems, a series of injuries dampened his spirit further. "At 45+ as a weekend warrior you're just more likely to get injured," said Anil, recalling a national masters tournament he played in Baltimore in the early '90s. "I was going through the routine of defeating my opponent, but in response to one of his lobs, I got cute and jumped up to hit a cross-court volley nick, landed slightly off the center of my foot, and collapsed to the floor. I had torn the ACL in my left knee." Three years later he was operated on to get a meniscus cleanup in one knee, then the other. "I was tired of being operated upon," Anil said, adding that the sum total of his disappointments led him into a downward spiral. "The constant 'beating up' by retailers at work, my injuries, and my poor squash play was psyching me out. In addition, an unhappy marriage did not help. I felt myself becoming a loser. I needed some victories somewhere. My reflective time was spent focusing on losses on several fronts. I had to find a way to break out of this malaise and regain some of my currencies so I could start to enjoy life again."

When Sanjay and Vivek were in college, it became clear to Anil that his marriage to Linda simply wasn't working. "We had tried to regroup, but I believe both Linda and I had both fallen out of love," said Anil. "She was also often oblivious to the tussles and struggles of my work, as I may have been to hers. I remember leaving home in a terrible mood before playing a match in Philadelphia and lost because we'd had a fight. Afterwards, I remember thinking, 'I can't live like this.'"

Living in an empty nest in the fall of 1995, Anil presented Linda with the idea of moving to New York, where they could be closer to his work, friends, and the Harvard Club. After getting a somewhat indifferent response, he went ahead and purchased an apartment in Battery Park City and moved in. "I didn't really leave so much as we started living apart," said Anil. "She said she couldn't leave the house and the garden and her flowers. And this was the turning point that marked the end for us. It was a de facto separation, that subsequently led to a divorce." And by the time his son Sanjay graduated from Penn and had found a job at Deloitte & Touche in 1996, Anil was comfortably settled alone in his new home, which was vaguely reminiscent of his childhood flat with its wonderful water view of the Arabian Sea, though in this case the apartment overlooked the mighty Hudson River and the picturesque Statue of Liberty.

* * *

PART SIX

1997-2019: Full Circle

CHAPTER TWENTY TWO

Fresh Start

After Anil moved to New York, he readily readapted to city life again and occasionally ventured out on dates. A couple of years later, he met me at an event at a restaurant in midtown Manhattan. The distant friend who introduced us made a point of letting me know that he was a champion sportsman before moving on to another conversation. Although Anil was good looking at the time in a salt-and-pepper-masala kind of way, he didn't appear to me to be someone who had been—and still was—a superstar athlete. At 5'8", he's not tall by American standards and, not surprisingly for a man at the ripe age of 50, he had a slight paunch. Nevertheless, I was impressed that he was athletic and after an extended and easy conversation, his youthful, sporty personality sufficed for me to forgive him his age and take up his invitation to meet him again the next day for a bike ride.

The following afternoon, we started out at a leisurely clip on a pair of ten-speeds along the esplanade near Battery Park City where Anil lived. Before long I decided it was time to pick up the pace and, quite certain I'd leave him struggling to keep up, I took off like a shot. Within moments he blasted past me, however, and it was I, instead, who was left in the dust. And so I quickly learned that he was indeed a very fit person with the champion spirit still very much alive and kicking within him. And, perfectly healthy though I was, I was also reassured by the fact that while my aerobic capacity paled in comparison to his it wasn't enough of a problem to dampen his interest in me. "History tells me this was the beginning of the best, longest lasting date I ever had," said Anil of our first adventure together.

Still there were plenty of gaps to bridge between us before our relationship would get off the ground. In contrast to Anil's Hindu upbringing on the subcontinent, I had grown up in an all-American Catholic family in the heartland—my father, William Gorman, was of Irish and German descent, my mother, Merriam, Swedish and Dutch. Also, unlike Anil, who had swiftly married just after college and shortly thereafter started a family, I was still holding out for the right person after beginning and eventually ending a few long-term monogamous relationships. Although Anil came from a family with quite traditional parents, like mine, he and his siblings had all broken ranks with certain customs of their heritage and married outside their clan, while my sister, Carol, and my three brothers, Bob, John, and Charlie, had all married their high school sweethearts and had children in their twenties. And unlike the business context in which most of Anil's family members thrived, mine worked mostly in medicine, engineering, or law (my mother graduated from law school the same year I graduated from college). There was also an age difference of almost a dozen years between us.

Furthermore, before I met Anil, squash was simply not on my radar. But art, music, architecture, and literature were. About the time he had returned to America to kickstart his career in business in the early '80s, I had moved to New York, landing in Hell's Kitchen, to start my career as a journalist. It was a heady time in the art world then, and I was hanging out with an arty crowd at East Village galleries and Soho lofts and coming across the hieroglyphic graffiti art that emerging artists like Keith Haring and Jean Michel Basquiat had painted on subway walls or splashed around the interiors of the Limelight, the notorious nightclub built by the club king Peter Gatien in an old Episcopal Church on West 20th Street. At velvet-roped clubs like Limelight or the more intimate lounges of the time, such as Nell's or M.K., nightspots I'd dipped into now and then, the disco and punk music that had pulsed in iconic clubs of the '70s like Studio 54 and CBGB had been displaced in the newer venues by various forms of Euro, hiphop, and house music. And since the internet and cellphones didn't exist on a mass level at this time, news about these clubs was passed around by word of mouth or Xeroxed flyers.

By the time Anil and I became acquainted in the late '90s, I was working as an editor and writer covering architecture and interior design when the reigning postmodern architects of the '80s were

Anil and Jean at the Taj Mahal in 1998.

getting eclipsed by Deconstructivists and other progressive thinkers, who were beginning to see the implications of the fledgling internet on the future of architecture. At the same time, instead of American writers, like Jay McInerney and Tom Wolfe, who had defined the '80s with novels like *Bright Lights, Big City* and *Bonfire of the Vanities*, Indian writers were experiencing a high moment and the short stories of authors like Jhumpa Lahiri and Anita Desai were regularly appearing in *The New Yorker*. Arundhati Roy's *The God of Small Things* was also at the top of many people's reading list, though I was more intrigued by a less-talked-about book by Rohinton Mistry called *A Fine Balance*, which a colleague had loaned me shortly before I met Anil. The story completely opened my eyes to the chaos of India during the time he'd grown up and lived there.

Anil and I both remember attempting to find common ground in a conversation we had after pausing for a while during our first bike ride and I brought up some of the stories I'd been reading by Indian authors. "We stopped at a quiet spot near Chelsea Piers to take in the cool evening breeze and watch the sun as it descended into the horizon," said Anil. "Jean was interested in my Indian background and relayed a story she'd recently read in *The New Yorker* by the Indian author Anita Desai." The story, as I recalled it, revolved around an Indian fellow with an irrational attachment to a dog that constantly ran away. After retrieving the dog several times, the story ended with the dog literally jumping into a dog catcher's vehicle, while its devoted owner tripped over a curb in desperate pursuit of the animal, cracked his head on the street, and died on the spot as the dog was carted away.

Somewhat mystified by the story, Anil was reminded of a commonly told tale in Hindu mythology that also involved a dog and told the alternate narrative to me. This one centered on a family member of Arjuna, the central figure in the Mahabharata, named Yudhisthira, who had renounced his kingdom and was making his ascent up a mountain as part of a journey to eliminate ego-driven desires in his quest for enlightenment. In Anil's telling of the story, along the way Yudhisthira and his loyal dog were met by the god Indra, who'd come down from the sky on a chariot and invited Yudhisthira to join him in heaven, but only if he'd be willing to leave his dog behind. On the brink of heavenly access yet unwilling to part with his devoted pet, Yudhisthira chose to decline the offer and turned to head back down the mountain. At that moment, Indra advised him to wait and revealed to him that he had passed the test of devotion. Then, before his very eyes, his dog transformed itself into the god of Dharma, blessed Yudhisthira, and accompanied him along with Indra into heaven.

Piqued by the possibility that the author had simply subverted a classic Hindu tale, I could see there was much to learn about Anil and his culture. So even though arts and culture weren't top of mind for Anil, we managed to find common touch points, as he learned more about my interests and I learned more about his. And despite our differences we managed to begin to craft a bond from the very start. "Jean and I both preferred the story line of the mythological tale and its emphasis on devotion," said Anil, noting that the storytelling had gotten our relationship off to an offbeat yet enchanting start. And though Anil's squash career may have been coming to an end, this early adventure we shared together also signaled that a new chapter in both of our lives was about to unfold.

One of the chief pleasures—and challenges—of developing a relationship with someone of another culture is the discovery of new ways of seeing the world. So, as Anil and I were getting to know one another, in addition to opening up to his passion for squash, a sport I knew next to nothing about, I also was keen to learn more about the mysteries of his motherland, India. Some of the touch points I had with India as a child came from my father, who had been drafted into the army during World War II and deployed to the China-India-Burma triangle, where he functioned largely in a medical clinic of the barracks in Bombay and got his first taste of dentistry before he returned to the states, attended dental school under the G.I. Bill, and became a dentist. He had mementos and photos from that time of his life that fascinated me as a child and triggered my initial interest in this foreign land. In addition, one of my aunts had joined an order of Catholic nuns known as the Maryknolls and spent her days in a convent in Katmandu, Nepal, and so our home was peppered with Indian and Nepalese curios and objects—enameled dishes, carved wooden elephants, brass tables, camel saddles—which she would bring back with her whenever she returned to America for a visit. Her experiences along with these objects also stoked my curiosity about how people lived on the other side of the world. Later, after reading old-school yoga books I had found in bookstores as a young teen after reading about the Beatles' misadventures with their guru, Maharishi Mahesh Yogi, in Rishikesh, I taught myself yoga by imitating bearded yogis in *dhotis* posed in the various *asanas* illustrated in the black-and-white photographs of the books. Though my family members observed with quiet puzzlement as I stood on my head or twisted myself into pretzel-like poses and likely saw my exotic interest as a passing phase, I continued with the practice throughout my adult life. So shortly after I met Anil, I asked him whether he had any interest in yoga as another way to find shared experiences. To my surprise, he had never practiced it, even though yoga studios were commonplace across the U.S. by then.

By this time, Anil was gradually detaching from playing squash competitively on the national level, keeping up with the sport mostly in local tournaments or friendly matches at the Harvard Club. There he played with other alums like Jay Nelson, who, a few years senior to Anil, would continue to win national masters tournaments into the decades ahead, Tad Friend, an author and writer for *The New Yorker* magazine, Kip Gould, a theater producer and frequent doubles player, John Moon, an investment banker, or Bob Horn, a private equity banker. Since Anil was beginning to suffer from various aches and pains due to his years of top level play on the squash court, I suggested he join me and take up yoga as an alternative form of exercise. While the stretching and twists involved in the *asanas* were incredibly foreign to him, I believe the shift in his point of view with respect to yoga's emphasis on cultivating a sense of detachment from a particular outcome was transforming him in subtle ways.

The course of events of an age-related national tournament he played in at Trinity College in Hartford, Connecticut, in 1999 at the age of 52 seemed to prove this. After joining me at yoga classes about three times a week for several months, Anil opted to compete in the tournament in Connecticut at the urging of a friend. Since he signed up late for the event, all of the slots in the 50+ age category were closed, so he had no choice but to play in the 45+ category. Since he would be competing against younger and presumably fitter players, he had low expectations for a positive outcome and told me he would likely return the same day. Later he called to report that he had fared better than expected and won the first round, but wasn't counting on going far in the next one and said he'd come back the following day. To our mutual surprise and delight, his newfound sense of detachment worked well for him during the next match and he won that one, too, and eventually he came through in a hard-fought semi-finals match against Chris Burrows and then again in the finals against Riaz Arshad to emerge as victor of an age group younger than his own and claim another national masters champion title.

I was quite pleased to be a part of a fresh phase in self discovery for Anil vis à vis his squash game. I also see this victory as something of a turning point when he could actually pull himself away from a kind of obsession with squash and find some pleasure in an alternate form of physical activity. Later that year, Anil's accomplishment at Trinity was recognized again at a dinner hosted by the Jesters at the Racquet and Tennis Club in New York, when its directors singled him out to be the recipient of its Broken Racquet award, a trio of warped and broken racquets given annually to one of its members for "distinguished play in a national championship." Originally created to honor "some old, tired, broken down Jester whose glory days were behind him," the award's earlier purpose had been reinterpreted over the years, possibly by a member too old to remember why it had been created. And although Anil would continue to play squash regularly in the coming years, undertones of its original intent had begun to surface for the champion player and in some ways presaged his experiences in the decade ahead.

By this time, the wear and tear on Anil's body had already resulted in several surgeries on both his knees. A year or so later, experiencing debilitating pain in his right shoulder, he again underwent surgery to repair an impingement problem. "My body was not prepared for the beating it took playing squash," said Anil. "Furthermore, my style of play, using one or two quick steps and a lunge to reach a ball, plus the old non-support canvas shoes I wore when I was young and my early training running on a hard cement road added to the wear on my body. Yet, many of my peers also experienced more or less the same kinds of injuries. Perhaps, our bodies are just not built for long years of high-level squash play." So, while he continued to play sporadically, he simply wasn't able to snap back from his injuries as he had in the past. Several years later, after experiencing pain again in one of his knees and his hip, an orthopedist advised him to consider a hip replacement. Other fellow players like Michel Scheinmann and Tom Poor had followed through with hip or knee replacements, but Anil was unprepared for yet another episode under the knife. Furthermore, he admitted his confidence, drive, and will to win had significantly waned due mostly to his joint injuries.

"I found myself in the late 1990s and thereafter often losing to those I considered weaker players," admitted Anil. "Although I worked hard and won the national tournament in 1999, subsequently, I just could not seem to win. In the early 2000s, I lost a nationals tournament to Gulmast Khan in Denver and subsequently to Gul Khan in Boston in 2005, after I had been up two

Anil (right) at the Tournament of Champions at Grand Central Station in New York with Raju Chainani (left) and Hashim Khan (center) in 2000.

games. In another nationals tournament in 2009, I lost to Ed Scully. In the last singles nationals tournament I participated in, I lost to Bruce Simons-Morton, a 'runner' from Washington D.C., in five games at the University of Virginia in 2014 when I was playing with an injured knee after the first game. These were hugely depressing, ego-crushing losses." Although he continued to play in these nationals tournaments, Anil had all but retired from squash in the early 2000s, so his practice during these years was sporadic at best.

Still, Anil's interest in supporting younger players remained strong, and he continued to press forward with his budding effort to nurture Indian juniors from afar with the squash program he'd developed with Raju Chainani in Bombay in the early 1990s. As the program evolved, Anil also enlisted interest in the venture of other like-minded Indian players, such as Ananth Nayak, who was coaching part time in India and working with the emerging forces in the Indian squash community to advance the sport, and Satinder Bajwa, an Indian squash player widely known as "Baj" who had worked as a coach in England and various parts of the U.S. "I had met Baj at various tournaments, including the Tournament of Champions at Grand Central, when he accompanied the great player Jansher Khan," recalled Anil of his early interactions with Bajwa. Shortly after they met, Anil telephoned the coach in 1994, when Bajwa was 39 years old and working in Baltimore, and asked him whether he would be prepared to go to India on an assignment. Anil's focus at the time was on how they could help the youngsters, particularly the underprivileged youth, to prepare for squash excellence and discipline in life. For his part, Bajwa saw Anil as a "great champion" and readily accepted his invitation to regularly participate in the fledgling training program and did so for several years until he settled in Boston in 1999 after being tapped to serve as a squash coach for Anil's alma mater, Harvard. But eventually the effort would be thwarted, first by getting mired in Indian squash politics, and later by the death of Chainani, whose early demise in 2001 came as a shock to Anil and all in the squash community who knew him.

"Our plan did quite well for a while, and many club members' children in the training camps succeeded in the local tournaments and finally left for college overseas," said Anil. "However, we had not been able to achieve our second and more important objective of recruiting less-privileged kids from the government schools, who turned out to be more interested in getting coaching in cricket, soccer, or kabaddi rather than squash, and eventually the program got lost in politics and posturing, partly because Raju was a master operator. While I was providing the funding for coaches to travel to Bombay to play with the juniors for two-week stints, there was, in typical conspiratorial fashion, talk about who was making how much from the program, and certainly Raju's name came up, but I didn't put any credence into these accusations," added Anil, noting that the funding for the program simply wasn't substantial enough to make this a valid claim.

"Raju was good to me and, despite my concerns about his penchant for drinking and his inclination to concoct conspiracy theories, we had good times together," Anil said. "In late spring of 2001, I remember enjoying a customary get-together with Raju at the CCI bar. When I ordered a beer and lunch for both of us, Raju told me that the doctor had forbidden him to drink alcohol and he was now on a strict diet. He then looked at me straight in the eyes and told me he was not sure how long he had to live even if he followed the strict dietary regimen. I was sure he would beat the diabetes and liver issues if he remained disciplined. But it was not to be. He died a few months later. I lost a *jiggri yaar* that year."

Chainani's death and career was also posthumously covered in the November, 2001, issue of *Squash* magazine a few months later:

> Squash journalist Raju Chainani's death, from heart problems, came completely out of the blue. He was in Hong Kong for the Cathay Pacific Open in August doing his usual wide-embracing delivery to various parts of Asia. He didn't seem in top form but didn't look ready for the ultimate penalty stroke decision. He flew home to Mumbai, suffered acute chest pains at home and died on his way to the hospital....
>
> Chainani was a colorful fixture on the world squash scene, always ready with a quip, an all-inclusive giggling laugh never far from his face. Until this year, a glass of something alcoholic and an evil-smelling cigar were also integral to the picture.... Mischief and squash politics were central features of Chainani's life, but he was pretty serious about the game and an astute observer of the action. Squash in Asia benefitted hugely from his contacts and his ability to raise sponsorship....
>
> There will be some who heave a sigh of relief at the passing of Raju Chainani, but they are not among the best of our game. We will suffer for lack of his detailed and voluminous memory,

his mischievous humor, his love of the battle both on and off the court, and his sheer distinctive commitment to squash.

After Chainani passed away, the junior program Anil had developed with him was continued by different sponsors and promoters for a while. But Anil lamented that they were never able to accomplish their main objective of developing talent from India's vast pool of underprivileged people by exposing them to squash. Yet, the seeds he and Chainani had sown with this early program started to blossom later, when prominent locals in the Indian squash circuit, including Khalid Ansari, the publisher of the Indian newspaper *MidDay* and a former president and currently chairman emeritus of the Squash Racquets Association of Maharashtra, and especially Mahendra Agarwal, the force behind the Indian Squash Professional organization, put forth their own efforts to develop Indian professional and junior champions and built a more substantial infrastructure with coaching camps and videos, including a classic featuring Jahangir Khan when he was at his prime.

At the same time, a concurrent movement to expand squash beyond the sphere of the elite began to take place in America shortly after Anil had initiated his program in India. By the mid-1980s the international squash community had also introduced mobile glass-enclosed courts that would allow a 360-degree view into the court, enabling the number of fans viewing a match to expand from, say, 250 or so to as many as 3,500. By the early 1990s, the International Squash Rackets Federation had changed its name to the World Squash Federation and the pro hardball and pro softball men's associations merged to create the Professional Squash Association and its Tournament of Champions, now part of the PSA World Series, was staged for the first time in New York's Grand Central Terminal in 1995. Later, a dynamic group of Harvard players began to launch their own American squash programs aimed at supporting urban youth, and some of their fundraising efforts occurred at Grand Central Station during subsequent

Tournament of Champions events. Among those spearheading the new programs were Greg Zaff, who launched Squash Busters, the first urban squash program in Boston in 1996, George Polsky, who founded Street Squash in New York City in 1999, Andrew Nehrbas, who co-founded SquashSmarts in Philadelphia in 2001, and Sanford Schwartz and Tim Wyant, who launched City Squash in 2002. These and other groups focused on improving inner cities and the lives of disenfranchised youth by exposing them to squash and supplemental education in a safe environment. "The initiatives triggered similar undertakings in India," said Anil. "And their programs to support and encourage underprivileged kids in the U.S. gave validation to some of the nascent programs that have since emerged in India and encouraged institutions and individuals to give back to squash in precedented and coherent ways."

* * *

CHAPTER TWENTY THREE

A Changed World

On a broader level, anyone who lived through the turn of the millennium was affected by the uncertainty aroused around the globe with concerns of how the digital infrastructure, which by then was on the verge of creating a truly global economy, would impact our daily lives. Google, which had launched in 1998 and would soon become the internet's dominant search engine, was then in its infancy and poised to become a massive information exchange. E-commerce was also beginning to take hold and would later have a profound effect on bricks-and-mortar retail, eventually impacting Anil's business. And it wouldn't be long before digital and social media platforms would forever alter the traditional print and television media landscape in which I had built my career.

The immediate concerns arising around the globe in the weeks and months just before the turn of the 20th century, however, revolved around the idea that the hardware and software that was transforming our lives hadn't been developed to take into account the implications of what was referred to as Y2K, the acronym widely used to refer to the Year 2000. Leaders around the world suddenly focused on how programming deficiencies might affect our daily lives if the computer networks that were critical to the functioning of everything from airline travel to financial records might shut down at midnight on January 1, 2000, and grind our modern world to halt. It was an epic event that elicited irrational fears and anxieties, but in reality the turning point was as anticlimactic as a damp sponge.

Yet, what followed as the decade began to take shape were disturbing ripples that would soon result in the most chaotic political events of the current era and completely transform the lives of everyday citizens around the globe. In America, the start of the orthographically hard-to-define decade—variously referred to as the "Two-Thousands," the "Twenty-Ohs," the "00s," and the "Aughts"—is often associated with the presidential election of 2000, when Al Gore and George W. Bush were vying for the country's top job. The hanging chads of ballots cast in Florida were still being counted more than a month after the election, until the U.S. Supreme Court, in its ruling on Bush v. Gore, declared the election in Bush's favor by a margin of 537 votes and stopped the recount effort that had earlier been initiated upon a ruling by the Florida Supreme Court. Later that month, Gore (incidentally a key proponent of greater public access to the internet and an instrumental figure in developing the "Information Superhighway") eventually conceded the presidency to Bush in the country's fourth election in which a candidate who won the popular vote lost to a candidate with a majority of votes in the Electoral College.

Others look back at the decade's defining moments and recall the following year, when the commercial and political capitals of the U.S.A. and, many would say, the world were devastated by terror. In broad daylight, two commercial airliners were deliberately flown into New York's Twin Towers, while another was flown into the Pentagon in Washington D.C.—symbols of the power, pomp, and hyperbole of the West—and yet another crashed into a field in Pennsylvania, all steered by agents of modern armies of destruction from thousands of miles away. Coincidentally, in India, the new century also started off with a cataclysmic event. In 2002, while there had been communal conflagrations for decades after Independence in 1947, there was a major face-off between Hindus and Muslims in the state of Gujarat, also the hub of the country's commerce. Thousands died, hundreds of thousands were left homeless, and peaceful life in the area was profoundly compromised.

In the U.S., though, the preoccupation would be with 9/11 and its aftermath, including the need for increased security at many sporting events because of the fear of terrorist interruption linked to either the leftovers of the Twin Towers attacks or to Arab-Israeli issues. India had her own problems with even a tennis tournament or a cricket match becoming problematic, especially if there was any connection at all to Pakistan or Kashmir. Of course, the trend had started with the Munich Massacre during the 1972 Summer Olympics, when the Palestinian terrorist group, Black September, took eleven Israeli Olympic team members hostage and killed them along with a West German police officer. And sporting events would also be used as a platform for political protest, such as in 1980, when the United States led a boycott of the Summer Olympic Games in Moscow to protest the late 1979 Soviet invasion of Afghanistan and 65 nations refused to participate in the games, or in 1996, with the domestic terrorist pipe bombing attack during the Summer Olympics in Atlanta. With events like these, and particularly 9/11, it became clear that sport, like other aspects of everyday life, had become damaged by the politics of hate around the world. In the U.S., India and, ultimately, the rest of the world at the turn of the millennium, there was a kind passing of civilized society, an end of innocence.

While the overwhelming catastrophe of 9/11 was the last thing Anil and I would have imagined occurring when we had planned our wedding in Lower Manhattan earlier that spring, the chaos and confusion that permeated the city, and indeed the world, in the aftermath of the attacks would be the backdrop against which we would be married later that very week. As it turned out, Anil's mother had been staying at our home in Battery Park City in advance of the wedding when the planes crashed into the towers just a few blocks to the north. Anil had gone to work earlier that morning and was unaware that the destruction had occurred, but I witnessed the first tower on fire as I left the apartment and I heard the blast of the second plane hitting the other tower as I walked through a parking garage on my way to the subway. The thundering sound of the collision was like a sonic boom and the ground beneath me shook as I walked. Unaware that the explosive noise was caused by an aircraft smashing through the tower and thinking instead that a bomb had gone off, I swiftly headed for the subway along with other stupefied citizens in the streets as dust and debris were falling like confetti from the sky above.

By the time I arrived at my office in midtown, my colleagues and I were told to return home as one of the towers, which was visible from the 42nd floor of our office building, came crashing down. At this time, there was still considerable confusion about whether the destruction had been caused by a bomb or an errant aircraft. Knowing I would be unable to return to our Battery Park City apartment, I attempted to call Anil, but telephone service had been completely interrupted, so I walked to the Chelsea home of our friends, Susan and Andy Carpenter, who at the time were working in the arts and publishing, she as a museum consultant and he as an art director at Random House. Meanwhile, at his office on 29th Street, Anil had received a call from his son Vivek in Boston, who explained that a bombing had occurred near the World Trade Center. About an hour later, Vivek called again and reported that the towers had actually been hit by passenger jets.

Anil then understood that he would need to return to Battery Park City to fetch his mother amid the chaos, but by that time all transportation to Lower Manhattan had been shut down. So he walked several miles, often being diverted by policemen and national guardsmen, and passed from the crystal clear morning light into the thick gray dust that enveloped the whole of Lower Manhattan like a blinding acrid cloud until he reached the apartment. "I saw my mother sitting on the sofa, looking out at the Hudson, wondering what all the dark clouds and smoke were about," remembered Anil. "I quickly packed her vanity case and brought her out to the pier in front of our home, where a police boat ferried us to New Jersey. Once there, we were directed into a tent, where we were given a basic medical check up and a bottle of Gatorade. My mother described the experience as 'five-star Partition,' wanting to infuse some lightness into the devastating occasion, which reminded her of India in 1947, when the Muslims and Hindus were butchering each other in their effort to move to their 'promised lands.' It felt as if my mother had watched this scene before, several decades earlier. She had a numbed look as if she were going through the motions to survive. Not many words were exchanged between us, but I could sense the thoughts going through her mind, and I felt numb in a similar way."

Later that day, after the phone lines had been gradually restored, Anil and I were able to connect—and with arrangements made by Anil's son Sanjay—we eventually moved into quarters at the stately University Club in midtown, where Sanjay was a member. The following day, Anil and I made the decision to go ahead with our planned wedding and, as was later reported in *The New York Times*, so did everyone else who had planned to be married in New York that weekend, with the exception of one couple who were to marry at Trinity Church, just blocks from the devastation in Lower Manhattan. So together the same day, we walked back to Battery Park City to inspect our home and fetch some basic belongings.

Since Anil knew how to navigate through the barriers to entry in the form of police barricades and national guardsmen stationed at key points along the way, he was able to get us close to our home. At the final stop before entering Battery Park City we were asked by the National Guard personnel to show our IDs and were then escorted on foot to our home. But before we set off, we were told we would only be allowed to remove prescription drugs and pets from our homes. No clothing of any sort would be allowed. With that, I explained that Anil and I were to be married later in the week and wondered if an exception might be made to part with our wedding clothing. At that point, the guardsman hesitated for a moment, and then said, "Go ahead and pack a small suitcase with your things, no one will tell you to turn around."

After entering our home and seeing it covered with dust but otherwise undamaged, we proceeded to pack Anil's Nehru suit, my slim wedding dress, and Anil's mother's sari into two small rolling suitcases and trudged back uptown, where, unlike the oppressive gray cloud covering the whole of Lower Manhattan, the sun was shining and the sky was dazzlingly clear and blue. With Lower Manhattan completely closed south of 14th Street, we knew we wouldn't be able to marry at the India House, a lovely historic building near Wall Street where we'd planned to wed. "The place was abandoned and covered with a shroud of fine dust as were most other places in Lower Manhattan," said Anil. But, everyone in New York was brimming with supportive spirit at this time, and Sanjay was able to arrange for the ceremony to be moved to a lovely room at the University Club, where another wedding was taking place and serving virtually the same menu that we had planned for our wedding downtown.

As the week wore on, however, reverberations of the events in New York started spreading to the rest of the country—and the world. And it would soon become clear that most of our family members would not be able to attend our wedding, since flights were grounded across the U.S. and others were being diverted in other parts of the globe. My entire family was planning to fly in the day before the wedding, but air traffic restrictions at the time would not permit them to travel. Meanwhile, Anil's eldest brother Vinod and his then-girlfriend, Joanne, who were en route to New York, were told their flight would be canceled when they arrived to change planes at Delhi airport. "My sister Asha, her daughter, Ulricke, and her 1-year-old granddaughter Lea were diverted to Newfoundland in Canada, where they were housed in a school for a day and then stayed with an incredibly welcoming local family until they were allowed to fly back a few days later," said Anil. So without most of our immediate families able to celebrate with us, we carried on with our marriage with only the dozen or so friends and few members of Anil's family with easy access to the city in attendance.

Bittersweet and downsized as it was, the wedding was still beautiful—and it gave all who were there welcome moments of joy amid the tragic catastrophe that was unfolding all around. Anil and I were incredibly heartened to share our marriage with his sons and mother and our friends in New York. And we were especially grateful for the graciousness of our immediate families in Minnesota and India in supporting our marriage and celebrating with us in the months that followed. Despite its challenging start, marriage was very good for us and our social life was a highlight as the decade began. After he'd moved back to New York, Anil reconnected with old friends, many of them Indian, and met new ones, including my circle of friends in New York, Connecticut and New Jersey. Rather than dwelling so much on sport, Anil joined me in focusing more of our time on arts and culture.

Over time our personal circles of friends began to loosely intersect, too. My friend Kelly Tagore became one of our essential points of connection. An editor at Hearst at the time, she had hired me to work with her on a group of special interest magazines affiliated with the *Good Housekeeping* and *House Beautiful* titles, which she was overseeing. At that time, her husband, Sundaram Tagore, the great-nephew of the Nobel-prize-winning Indian poet Rabindranath Tagore, a contemporary and friend of Gandhi and Nehru, had also just opened his first gallery in Soho. Although Anil and Sundaram did not know each other then, after some extended wrangling on Kelly's part and mine, they eventually met at one of Sundaram's openings. Not surprisingly, they became instant friends and now believe they introduced Kelly and me, rather than the other way around. While our husbands might be fuzzy on the

Anil and Jean (right) with friends Sundaram and Kelly Tagore (left) at the Harvard Club on New Year's Eve, 2017.

details of their introduction, Sundaram Tagore remembers clearly the qualities in Anil that immediately appealed to him after meeting him. "The first time I met Anil I saw him as an individual who was non-judgmental, but what was really attractive about him is that he has a joie de vivre that's really infectious," Tagore said. "He is also compassionate and that came through immediately—and all these are qualities that allow a friendship to be fostered with a sense of celebration, of joyousness, of bonhomie."

Of course, as is typical of the six degrees that separates most of the people in the Indian community in New York, many of the people Kelly and Sundaram were friendly with were people Anil was acquainted with or knew well, too. After meeting the Tagores,

Anil's interest in the visual arts also grew. Sundaram, who was carrying on the artistic lineage of his family and through his gallery in Soho, was representing, as he continues to do, a stellar range of international artists, including Indians Sohan Qadri, Natvar Bhavsar, and Anil Revri as well as many others from around the world—and we both continue to find the work of these artists to be particularly compelling.

Later, yet still early on in our relationship, after Anil and I ran into Anil's old Cathedral School friend Aroon Shivdasani and her husband, Indur, while enjoying a nightcap after a New Year's party at Bar & Books on the Upper East Side, we spent more time taking in Indian movies, dance, music, and literature. Aroon was then the executive director of the Indo-American Arts Council, and was instrumental in bringing a wide cross-section of Indian arts to America for more than 20 years. I distinctly recall the moment when Anil and Aroon reconnected. From out of the blue a high-pitched voice with great gusto called out: "LUCKY!!!!" I turned to Anil and said, "Someone who knows you from way back is trying to catch your attention." Anil looked behind him and saw that the vivacious Indian arts impresario was sitting with her husband at a table nearby. And from that moment, a wonderful friendship was instantly resumed as if the decades that had passed since they'd last seen each other had simply melted away.

Among the first experiences Anil and I shared at Shivdasani's invitation was a viewing of the retro Indian film "Shakespeare Wallah" at the Paris Theater on 57th Street. Since Anil had actually socialized with the film's stars with his brother Vinod, the star-crossed love story reminded him of aspects of his direct experiences in India as a child and young man. It also gave me clearer insight into his world and the tenor of India at the time he was growing up. The film's producer and director, Bombay-born Ismail Merchant and American-born James Merchant, were friends of Aroon and the showing of their early film was just one among many cross-cultural artistic events that Shivdasani would share

After brunch with friends in New York City, 2017. From left: Sundaram Tagore, Anil, Gautam Patwa, and Anil Kapur.

with us and the large contingent of art lovers in New York interested the work of Indian artists.

During this time, Anil also reignited many other relationships with Indians from his childhood who had moved to America and, along with me, started new ones as our global network continued to grow. At the same time, he continued to nurture his relationships in India, with friends like the preeminent newspaper publisher Khalid Ansari and his childhood squash buddy Naval Pandole, who always welcomed Anil and me with classic Indian hospitality. He also developed some new friendships, including with Jaggy and Anita Shivdasani—a common bond between Anil and Jaggy being their champion sportsmen status (Shivdasani remains one of India's premier bridge players—yes, in Asia it's considered a sport—and recently won a Bronze Medal in the 2018 Asian Games).

Shortly after Anil and I met, Anil also became a U.S. citizen, taking the oath at City Hall in 1999, yet he has always maintained that he sees himself more as a citizen of the world with his heart and allegiance firmly attached to both America and India. "It took me a couple of decades to decide to become American," said Anil. "But I always had this underlying fear that, one fine day, I would arrive at JFK after a long trip from India and one of the immigration officers, whose behavior I often found to be surly and erratic, might randomly deny me entry. Furthermore, my children and many of my friends were American. Most important, though, in my decision-making was that I had finally passed the point of ambivalence—I could, with ease, belong to both the countries I cherished, the U.S.A. and India." And his enduring connection to Indian culture and friends in both his mother country and in the U.S. reinforced the bridges he has built between the two countries since he was a young man.

As we continued to get to know each other, more of our friendships started crossing over, and, in turn, I got to know Anil's wonderful circle of squash friends, some of whom enlightened me about the nuances of the game. Among theses friends are Geoff Mitchell, the pro at the Chatham Club in New Jersey, and his wife, Bernadette, as well as the stellar Indian squash player Ananth Nayak and his wife, Urmila. Through them, not only did I gradually begin to see what an extraordinarily complex and difficult sport squash really is, but I also came to know the exceptional community of high-quality people who participate in it. They, along with Anil's sons, Sanjay and Vivek, also clued me in to how much the training and politics of the game had changed over the years since Anil started playing, as have the structures that control how it's played and who plays it.

* * *

CHAPTER TWENTY FOUR

Passages Through India

Before and after Anil and I married, travel, too, brought a thrilling sense of adventure to our lives, as it continues to do. Among the more inspiring journeys we took were several trips to various parts of India, including Rajasthan, Rishikesh, Goa, Kerala, Delhi, Kolkata, and Chennai, all of which have enabled me to appreciate the vast country and culture that has shaped Anil in so many ways. Oddly enough, these trips have also shone a light on just how much Anil has changed since he rerooted himself in America, and how his countrymen now perceive him.

Among our many eye-opening experiences in India, a few stand out. One of them was my first trip to the legendary state of Rajasthan in 1998. After landing in Delhi, we were driven to Udaipur, one of the region's celebrated cities known for its stunning Lake Palace Hotel, which is carved of pure white marble and seems to float like a jewel in the middle of a beautiful lake ringed by mountains. Upon arriving at the banks of the lake in the quiet of the night amid total darkness except for the beaming light of a full moon, we stepped into a row boat, the only way to reach the palace, and, as the oarsman gently rowed us to the doorstep of our destination, the atmosphere was magical.

After a quiet night's sleep, we awoke the following morning to the hauntingly melancholic sound of a Muslim *muezzin*'s voice, wailing out the day's first call to prayer, which to my ears was otherworldly and beautiful. Our first foray out of the hotel was across the lake to the nearby City Palace and home of Maharajah Arvind Singh Mewar, who, incidentally, had married Princess Vijayraj of Kutch, AKA Princess Booty, whom Anil had met as a child when she was friendly with his brother Vijay. After spending some time on his terrace enjoying a leisurely cup of Darjeeling tea with the Maharajah, as his massive Great Dane sat dutifully at his feet, we set off on foot to see the sights and swiftly encountered the madness of the town center the moment we stepped outside the palace walls. Literally hundreds of townspeople approached us with entreaties to visit their shops filled with ruby and emerald jewelry, hand-painted parchments, inlaid boxes, finely embroidered *sarees* and *kurtas*, hand-tooled *chappals* and belts, hand-printed linens, pretty pashminas and now-banned *shahtush* shawls. A little boy approached Anil and offered to polish his shoes. Though Anil declined, he offered him a few rupees without the shoe shine, but the boy refused to take it, preferring instead to earn his compensation. Several other men and women gathered round us with beaded necklaces, colorful bracelets, or strands of flowers on their arms, pressing us to make a purchase, while many others simply held out their hands, hoping for coins. Dizzied by the throngs, we ducked into a temple for a while, where a prayer ceremony was going on and I was given my first *bindi*, the red dot of pigment positioned by *pandits* on the foreheads of both men and women at the location of their "third eye" just above and between the eyebrows. After we'd had a chance to calm down, Anil quickly realized he was no longer up for the craziness of India and we hopped into a *patputti*, a three-wheeled open-air vehicle driven by a local guide, who took us around to see the sights of the town, many of which had the dubious distinction of serving as settings for a James Bond film called "Octopussy."

Later visits on this trip to the beautiful pink city of Jaipur, with its chaotic streets brimming with elephants, camels, bicycles, festooned trucks, and bullock carts, Agra, the home of the glorious Taj Mahal, and the Samode Palace, a beautiful 475-year-old structure built by India's noble feudatory in a regal Indo-Saracenic style in the rural outskirts of Jaipur, gave me a rich sense of the magnificent state of Rajasthan on India's northwest border. Most striking to me, however, was the sharp contrast between the opulence and beauty of many of the region's historic structures and the abject poverty all around.

I immediately got a bittersweet taste of the conditions and spirit of India's multitudes of shockingly poor upon our arrival in Delhi. After venturing out to walk around amid the Parliament buildings, my first encounter was with an impoverished yet surprisingly happy little boy on an adult-size bike. Since the bottom of his small body came nowhere near the seat of the large bike, he rode it standing up entangled amid the frame as he pedaled around on the oversize two-wheeler with ease. He whizzed up from out of nowhere, stopped next to me and asked Anil to take a photograph of the two of us. After Anil obliged, he whizzed off as swiftly as he arrived. Later, as we walked near a slum not far from the Oberoi Hotel, where we stayed, a beautiful young woman about my age, standing amid the squalor that was her home, looked straight at me and softly smiled. I smiled back, thinking the only real difference between us was the simple fate of our births. A few days later, when we flew to Jaipur, I stepped out onto the terrace of our hotel room and noticed a poor family sitting together atop a blanket on the dirt of a vacant lot below and waving vigorously to catch my attention. When I waved back, they collectively cheered. And later still, in Agra, as Anil and I waited for a train in the crowded station, I could hear the sound of something heavy and large, like a sack of cement, being dragged along the platform toward me with a slow, rhythmic, swish, swish, swish. When the sound suddenly stopped, I could see that it had come from a little boy with a massive leg afflicted by elephantiasis. He had chosen to pause directly in front of me and quietly looked into my eyes. By then, Anil and I had been confronted with so many beggars—many with severe deformities, some with naked babies, and others on roller boards without limbs—that, had we given to all of them, our pockets would have been empty. But for this little boy there was simply no choice, and I handed him a 100 rupee note just before Anil and I boarded the train.

The sensory overload of this first experience in India—with its rags and riches, high and low extremes of human experiences and emotions—was not only overwhelming for me, but also for Anil, who was accustomed to experiencing India mostly within the sheltered confines of his home on Marine Drive or amid the comfortable clubs to which he belonged in the well-developed neighborhoods of South Bombay. Contributing to his feeling of estrangement in his own country on this particular trip was the fact that, while speaking Hindi to a hotel attendant in Jaipur, he was asked to pay the foreign rate for our hotel room. Though Anil sternly objected and made clear his Indian descent with proof of his Overseas Citizen of India card, the man continued to hesitate, then pointed toward me, and asked, "What about her?" Anil took umbrage at the question. "That's what happens when you're accompanied by a white American wife," he said. I'm sure my presence contributed to the foreign air that was was shading Anil's experience of India at the time, yet I had explicitly noticed that, by this point in his life, Anil dressed and walked and talked in a distinctly different way than his fellow countrymen.

"The locals also notice the disconnect and leave me to convey to them through my *'shuddh'* Hindi or Punjabi that I am still a son of the soil," said Anil. "Usually, it's no big deal except when I have to bargain down prices that are quoted to me as a foreigner!" Though Anil eventually succeeded in getting the room at the promised rate, we didn't find it acceptable, and ultimately moved on to another hotel, where we encountered a more hospitable reception. This first trip served up just a taste of the complexity and diversity and chaos of India, yet the psychological impact on both Anil and me was profound. And the humility and quiet grace with which so many of its poor accepted their fate was both humbling and heartbreaking.

Another early tour of Anil's home city of Bombay shed light on its gradual evolution into a sprawling megalopolis and on the history behind the change of its name to Mumbai. Like other prominent global cities once known by different names, such as Istanbul, formerly dubbed Constantinople when it was the Eastern capital of the Roman Empire, or New York, which was called New Amsterdam in 1624 by the Dutch settlers who founded it until it was surrendered to the British who later named it after the Duke of York, Bombay had also been called many other names before it was renamed Mumbai in the late 20th century. The origins of the name of India's largest metropolis and home to more than 12 million people, are as layered and fuzzy as its complex history. Although by the time I first visited the country in 1998 the government of India had already officially changed the name to Mumbai some two years earlier, its new designation was not in common use—and Anil's family members and everyone he knew continued to refer to it as Bombay, as they still generally do—and it seemed to me that it took more than a decade before the new appellation really became part of the common parlance.

I wasn't aware of its various historical eponyms until after Anil and I were married and we opted to take a local tour of the city in 2003, when we visited several of its notable sites, including the *Dhobi Ghat*, where the city's *dhobis*, the people who do laundry as a profession, wash linens on open-air flogging stones, the lush Hanging Gardens perched at the top of Malabar Hill, and the grand landmark Taj Mahal Palace hotel, where we looked onto the Arabian Sea brimming with wooden fishing boats beyond the Gateway of India. At that point, our charming guide, a young Maharashtrian woman, filled us in on strands of legend that contributed to its many different names over the centuries. She began by reminding us that the bustling metropolis is built on what was once an archipelago of seven islands. Inhabited since the Stone Age and home to the native Koli fishing community, the archipelago city was under the control of successive indigenous empires for centuries before it was ceded to the Portuguese Empire and some sources attribute the origins of the name Bombay to the Portuguese.

Our guide went on to explain that the name might have sprung from a Galician-Portuguese phrase *"bom baim,"* or *"bom baía"* meaning "good bay." Yet, numerous other variations of this name, such as Mombaym, Mombaim, Bambaye, Bombeye, Boon Bay, and Bon Bahia, were also recorded throughout the 16th and 17th centuries, though after the English took possession of the city in the 17th century, the Portuguese name was anglicized as Bombay. She also told us that the new name Mumbai is thought by many to have derived from *Mumbā* or *Mahā-Ambā*—the name of the patron goddess of the city's native Koli community.

And so, by the late 20th century, at the insistence of the Marathi nationalist Shiv Sena party, the city started to be referred to as Mumbai. Still often interchangeably referred to by residents as either Bombay or Mumbai, especially among the generations of people who were born before the turn of the millennium, calling the capital of Maharashtra by a name other than Mumbai can occasionally produce politically charged outbursts. So while Anil and I are still inclined to call his home city Bombay, we try to call it Mumbai while we're there, though doing so is often challenging in much the same way it might be if a friend or brother you'd known for 50 years as, say, Ted or Mike, were to suddenly ask you to start calling him Theodore or Michael. It has nothing to do with politics for either of us or anyone we know, and according Anil, "the name Bombay, to me and many other inhabitants, connotes secularism, cosmopolitanism, inclusiveness, while Mumbai denotes regionalism, so for many of us 'Bombay' more accurately represents the place where we grew up and went to school, and is more in tune with our experience."

Other memorable trips were to the very north and south of the subcontinent. In Rishikesh at the foothills of the Himalayas, we spent time at a yoga retreat called Ananda, where we were treated to the freshest food, most amazing Ayurvedic massages, and enlightening yoga lessons by masters. We also had a chance to dip our toes into the cleanest part of the Ganges after listening to an *aarti*, an a cappella spiritual recital performed a group of orphan boys of different ages, many in a trancelike state, who live in the ashrams and regularly gather to chant beautiful religious songs for the townspeople on the riverbanks. Rishikesh is a place where young Europeans love to visit because of the many ashrams in the area, and we found the environs to be filled with a heavenly air befitting its reputation as the land of the gods—the river valleys themselves, as legend has it, are said to have been formed by the footprints of the Hindu god Vishnu.

Another trip to the Kumarakam Lake Resort in the South Indian state of Kerala was also in many ways an extraordinarily relaxing adventure, though our journey to the resort exemplifies the craziness that is typical of India. After landing in Cochin in the late afternoon we were to be taken by a driver to a jetty from which the speedboat to our resort cottage would depart. In this part of India, the single-lane dirt roads brim with colorfully painted trucks, bullock carts, and elephants as well as small cars like the one shuttling us. Despite the treachery of passing slower moving vehicles along these roads, most drivers take their cars at maximum speed as they barrel toward the oncoming traffic only to dart to the side just moments before colliding head-on with oncoming traffic.

Our particular driver was racing along just a little too speedily for both Anil's comfort and mine, so Anil asked him to slow down. In the north, he often speaks Hindi to his fellow Indians. But there are more than 20 languages, along with hundreds of dialects, spoken in India, and, in Kerala, Malayalam is the spoken language, which bears no resemblance to Hindi and is written in a completely different script, so Anil was as out of his element as I was and had no choice but to speak to the driver in English. With his limited grasp of the language, the driver responded, "Can't slow down, can't slow down." Anil asked, "Why not?" He abruptly answered, "No headlight." As dusk was beginning to fall by this time, he continued at his rapid pace until our vehicle was about to run out of gas just as we arrived at the nearest village. When he stopped at a station to fill his tank, it started to rain. After replenishing the vehicle with fuel, he repeatedly tried to start the engine, which refused to turn over and we missed the last boat to the resort. Resourceful as Indians must invariably be, the driver asked us to step out of the car, pulled out an umbrella, and walked us over to a tiny structure housing an operator at a small desk containing a dial phone. After collecting a fee for his service and upon Anil's instruction, the operator called the resort and requested that someone be sent to take us the rest of the way to our destination by car.

After riding in the rain in our new vehicle for about 20 minutes, the driver finally stopped at a small wooden footbridge, where we realized our passage by automobile had come to an end. Again we were asked to get out of the car and were guided beneath a large umbrella up to the bridge. At its base, I could see that it was only about a foot and a half wide, was missing some slats, and had no railings. But the rickety arch was the only path over the swollen body of water rushing beneath it to the islet where our resort was situated. With no choice but to trek across it, we soldiered on amid the downpour in the middle of the night. Of course, at this time of night women are nowhere to be found in the streets of the villages of India, so when I came face to face with a man on a motorcycle at the top of the bridge, the look of shock on his face made it perfectly clear that the question whirling through his mind was, "What's a girl like you doing in a place like this?" Determined to press on, I gingerly stepped around his motorcycle as he watched me, frozen in his tracks, carefully continue on my way while I did my best to keep from slipping into the surging torrent below with Anil following behind me along with the driver, who brought up the rear with our suitcases perched upon his shoulders. When we reached the gooey red earth on the other side, I turned to Anil and quietly said, "You're so lucky I'm not high-maintenance." He agreed, and soon we were shown our comfortable villa, a wonderful little bungalow built in a historic South Indian style with a steep terra-cotta tiled roof, timber ceilings, and a private courtyard. By then, though, we were so exhausted that our thoughts swiftly drifted off into the distant darkness like the gray heavy rains that passed through the night and the day's tribulations seemed as remote as our immediate surroundings were from our customary environs. An ornate motif carved in the dark wooden beam over our bed was the last thing I remembered as I listened to my husband softly purring, already asleep like a baby.

The next day, we embarked on an overnight boat trip on Kerala's legendary back waters, a chain of brackish lagoons and lakes on the Malabar Coast. Shortly after we set off in a *kettuvallam*, one of the many traditional South Indian rice barges with thatched roofs and wooden hulls that have since been converted into houseboats for tourists, we quickly observed how the locals lived along the lotus-strewn waterways, often in huts or small concrete-block homes without running water. For these people, all bathing, dish washing, and laundry are done directly in the lagoons and rivulets. The men stood in the water in *dhotis* and lathered up their bodies in the warm sunshine, but the women stepped into the water fully clad in their pretty *sarees* and bathed beneath the water's surface while wrapped in their petticoats and swaths of colorful cotton, giving their clothing a good scrubbing at the same time. Goats and cows stood roped on the dirt yards surrounding some of the larger houses and queues of uniformed barefoot children skipped along on the paths near the waterways to school.

With little or no electricity along the backwaters, night began to fall early. So our captain and his mate prepared our spicy meal at the back of the boat around 7 p.m. When Anil and I walked out to the deck following the meal we saw them washing the pans and cookware in the murky backwaters and hoped for the best for our stomachs the next morning. Some of the larger boats chartered for such excursions were equipped with air conditioning and operable windows. But ours was a smaller private boat, large enough to accommodate only two passengers, so the window openings not only lacked glass panes, but were also devoid of screens. As a result the many large and plentiful insects—about 57,000 different species!—that thrive along the waters here were free to flow in and out of our cabin at will. Thankfully, our bed was topped with a mosquito net, so we knew we'd be unbothered by bug bites when we retired to sleep. But as the peaceful atmosphere of the daytime shifted into night we quickly learned we'd be falling asleep amid what sounded like a war zone as all of the area's nocturnal creatures—armies of amphibians and insects, battalions of birds and monkeys—suddenly joined in a pounding cacophony that permeated the cool night air like thousands of machine guns. Complementing the wildlife chorus were a variety of primal drumbeats as locals celebrated a religious holiday around bonfires lighting up in the distance throughout the night.

Out of sync with the din, however, were the guttural vibrations emanating from the husky throat of our captain, who was snoring like a wild boar as he lay sleeping in front of our cabin door. Despite the deafening decibel level, the sounds of nature were tolerable—like an amplified variation of the country crickets and cicadas I listened to as a child growing up in the American heartland. But the sound of our snoring captain was unbearable, so I asked Anil if he'd kindly ask the fellow to tone it down. With that, Anil awoke the gentle man and asked him in English to stop the snoring. Not quite catching his meaning, both the captain and his mate shrugged and shook their heads. Anil resorted to imitating the captain's nighttime breathing technique with a loud snort followed by a sharply stated "No!" and got the message across. With a polite apology from our guide, he kept quiet on deck for the remainder of the evening. It wasn't long, though, before I awoke again to the thud, thud, thud of Anil's feet stomping around our cabin in his shoes. I asked him what the shoes were about, and, without a satisfactory explanation, urged him to quiet down and come to sleep.

The following morning, after taking in sights of the wildlife—cormorants, kingfishers, mudskippers, otters, frogs—amid the leafy green plants and shrubs along the waterways, our floating journey came to an end. When we stepped off the boat, I again asked Anil about the shoe stomping episode during the night. By then he was comfortable enough to express his relief when he heard no screams from me in the morning upon entering the loo, where he'd encountered a scorpion during the night. Fraught as our trip to Kerala was with chaos and no shortage of surprising twists and turns, it was also among our favorite journeys in this incredible country and reminded us that expecting predictability anywhere in India, even at a luxe resort, is an exercise in futility.

Other memorable visits in India highlight the extraordinary hospitality of her people and the mysteries of her spirt. One was to the home in Delhi of I.K. Gujral, India's former prime minister. His son, Vishal, a distant friend, invited Anil and me to meet the aging ex-leader for lunch and afternoon tea at his compound, where we quietly spoke of days gone by and watched peacocks roam the grounds for the better part of an afternoon. Before we left, the former prime minister signed a copy of his autobiography, *Matters of Discretion*, as a parting gift. And a recent trip to Calcutta brought back memories of an episode we'd shared about a dozen years earlier with our friends Kelly and Sundaram Tagore at our home in Battery Park City. Shortly before my father died, he loaned Anil and me an album of the photographs he'd taken while stationed in India during the war. As we leafed through the photographs after enjoying dinner one evening with Kelly and Sundaram at home, Anil noticed a photograph of St. James Court, his childhood home on Marine Drive. A few pages later, Sundaram noticed a photograph of the Metropolitan building, his childhood home in Calcutta. At that point, I asked: "What are the chances that my future father would take a photograph of my future husband's home and my future friend's home halfway around the world before any of us were born?" We all sat silently for a moment, stunned by the coincidence and I saw it as a sign from the cosmos that our collective relationships were meant to be. "It was as if Jean's father had already accepted me as a son-in-law in a futuristic kind of way," said Anil. "It seemed that Bill had cast the die for my spouse, his daughter, and who would end up being our friends!"

Our friend Sundaram Tagore offered a similar perspective as he remembered the sentiments the image of his home elicited in him upon seeing it, and again when he learned that Anil and I had seen it in person many years later. "When I see the Metropolitan building, I become full of intense nostalgia that pulls at my heart strings—it's an iconic building in Calcutta and there were so many people from different backgrounds living there—families from Canada, England, people who were Sikhs, Maharajas, Biharis, Jews, Armenians," he explained. "We were the only Bengali family there, which shows how cosmopolitan it was before the Naxalites, the far left Communists, started holding sway in West Bengal—and, although the Naxalites were a highly intellectual and idealistic group who wanted to improve conditions for the disadvantaged, their actions added to the devitalization of the city in the economic and cultural sense as the intelligentsia, commerce, and powerful business people left. Yet the Metropolitan building still stands as an icon of those days when Calcutta was at the forefront as one of the great cities of the world, and it brings back a tremendous amount of memories. The fact that Jean's father photographed it at its height and we all saw his photograph together years later was very powerful. It is like a big circle that draws you in, like a river flowing and coursing back and forth to the same point. In the villages of India, people used to create alters at the base of trees by painting them and ringing them with garlands to create a spiritual vibration that attracts other like-minded people. In a way, whether it is the place I lived in while I was growing up, or a structure that Jean's father photographed 75 years ago, or a building Jean and Anil stopped to visit on a recent trip, it brought us all together in some way, it's as if we're drawn to people and places with the same vibration, it's in our DNA. And this visual gave us the concrete sense that we share a common past across cultures."

* * *

CHAPTER TWENTY FIVE

Giving Back

Although Anil's busy personal life and professional career were eclipsing his involvement in sport at this point, squash still remained a vibrant constant. Indeed, a high point occurred shortly after he and I married, when Anil received word of plans for a significant recognition of his squash career in Bombay. A great supporter of sports and the then-president of the CCI, Raj Singh Dungarpur, contacted Anil by phone while we were belatedly celebrating our marriage with my family in St. Paul and told him the club intended to memorialize Anil's achievements and contributions to the sport of squash by commemorating its courts in his name. "I was totally thrilled that the CCI courts, my second home while I was growing up, were going to be named after me—I couldn't have asked for a better recognition," said Anil. According to fellow player Ananth Nayak, there had been some debate among some members of the squash committee about who to name the courts after, but the consensus and prevailing sentiment among the overwhelming majority, and especially Raj Singh Dungarpur, was that naming them after Anil was the only choice. "Everyone saw him as a son of the soil who grew up playing at the CCI courts," said Nayak. "Anil is seen not only as India's greatest amateur squash player, but also India's greatest amateur sportsman." And so, as his competitive squash career was coming to an end, this new acclaim for his prodigious accomplishments as a sportsman would be preserved for generations of Indians to come with his name now cast in stone and crowning the CCI's courts.

To commemorate the distinction, the executive committee of the CCI planned to hold a ceremony at the club on December 4, 2001, and asked Anil to attend as the honored guest. Elevating the proceedings would be the presence of Digvijay Singh, the chief minister of Madhya Pradesh, whom Anil had met many decades ago on a squash court during his first central India squash tournament. So, at the request of CCI president Raj Singh Dungarpur, Anil flew to Bombay to join the festivities and recalled the celebration with fondness and appreciation. "Digvijay and I played the finals at the tournament, which was held at the Daly College in Indore in 1963 or '64," Anil remembered. "It was a delight to be honored with him as the leading dignitary at the event."

"I cannot express in words the joy I felt when the Cricket Club of India's then-president Raj Singh Dungarpur, a committed sportsman and overall sports enthusiast, whose magnificent obsession, especially, was cricket, told me the club's managing committee had agreed to his proposal to name the then-nameless courts of the club after our own squash legend, Anil Nayar," said Khalid Ansari, the newspaper publisher who would later go on to serve as the president of the Squash Racquets Association of Maharashtra and who, the same year, was awarded the Padma Shri, India's fourth highest civilian award, for his excellence in journalism and literature in service to the country. "'What do you think of the decision?'" Ansari recalled Singh Dungarpur asking him at the time. "My spontaneous reply: 'If 'Little Master' Gavaskar can have a stand at the Wankhede Stadium named after him, why shouldn't we name our squash complex after our own Squash Master, Anil Nayar?' I'm an unabashed admirer of Lucky, the sports champion and exemplary human being, but his gracious, cultured speech of thanks to the club, where he mastered his art and craft, his humility

At the ceremony to dedicate the CCI courts in Anil's name, CCI president Raj Singh Dungarpur (left) and Chief Minister of Madhya Pradesh Digvijay Singh (right) with Anil and his mother (center), 2001.

and soft-spoken, self-effacing deportment won the hearts of the distinguished audience that afternoon. Heads were held high and chests puffed as we left the C.K. Nayudu Hall. It felt wonderful to be Indian!" he exclaimed, as he fondly remembered the ceremony that he and many other Indian sports fans attended that day.

About this time, the profile of squash as a sport was also beginning to rise in India as the reins of the Squash Rackets Federation of India (SRFI) had been taken over by a dynamic and somewhat controversial South Indian by the name of Narayana Ramachandran, who was serving as the organization's secretary general. According to squash player Ananth Nayak, the lack of depth among Indian players started to change when Ramachandran, both a patron of the Squash Rackets Federation and the ex-president of the World Squash Federation, developed the Indian Squash Academy in

Chennai in 2001. "The academy aimed to offer lodging and facilities and top-class coaching—an ideal setup for talented players from India's middle class and less-well-off families to gain skills as squash players," said Anil. "The depth now is phenomenal by Indian standards—nine or more players are world-ranked, including two superb women players, Joshna Chinappa and Dipika Pallikal. We have a long way to go to get to the Egyptian gold standard but it is a step in the right direction," he said, acknowledging the concrete results accomplished since the academy was launched.

While Anil applauded the progress made under the helm of Ramachandran, other Indians deeply involved in the sport and closer to the action, such as Ansari, maintained that more can be done to elevate squash on a more collaborative level. "It cannot be denied that the squash academy Ramachandran has set up in his native Chennai in South India has done a degree of creditable work, but, on the flip side, his focus has been rather limited to players of a certain high standard and from his own state, especially to the detriment of budding aspirants from other parts of the country," said Ansari. "This preferential treatment, exacerbated by his predilection to ride roughshod over dissent and an aversion to give state squash bodies even a modicum of autonomy, has caused serious friction, especially in the state of Maharashtra and with the Indian Squash Professionals."

More concerning at this point to current top Indian players is the shortage of sufficient coaching. In a story on the website Rediff, Dipika Pallikal, the first Indian to break into the top ten, recently slammed the national SRFI for failing to appoint a new full-time coach since Egyptian Achraf Karargui left on a bitter note ahead of the Commonwealth Games in April of 2018. "If you want to try and take squash forward in this country, the first rule is to have a coach," Pallikal said. "It's just bizarre to head to the Commonwealth Games and the Asian Games without a coach. It's disheartening to see what is happening to Indian squash. There has to be a structured program, to become world champions a lot of

Anil Nayar Courts plaque at the CCI, 2001.

planning has to be done." Pallikal, like other top players, such as Joshna Chinappa and Saurav Ghosal, now must travel abroad to get the training they need to stay at the top of the game.

Recognizing the views of Ansari, Pallikal, and other Indian squash players who have similar outlooks, Anil acknowledged that "Mr. Ramachandran has the infrastructure and sufficient resources to build a public-private partnership, but without a more collaborative approach it will not have the ingredients to become the center of excellence that Indian squash so direly needs. In addition, the 2018 regulations relating to sanctioned and unsanctioned events are so restrictive and draconian that they are going to discourage players, supporters, and state organizations from grassroots development of the game. Especially in the state of Maharashtra, where I grew up, I've heard firsthand of disillusionment among

Anil Nayar Courts from across the pool at the CCI.

strong followers, supporters, and sponsors of the game for many years, including Mahendra Agarwal, Ranjan and Arun Sanghi, M.K, Sanghi, and Khalid Ansari to name a few."

After the turn of the century, like some of his American counterparts, Anil would continue to focus his attention on aiding young players in India, especially the poor, to either excel in squash or use it as a platform to enhance their lives. Before he would turn his attention to this interest, however, he was drawn into another opportunity to help underprivileged Indians in his mother's hometown of Batala, where he had spent many good times as a child. Though he hadn't returned there for many years, his maternal grandfather's legacy lived on after his mother donated her parents' sizable home to the community to convert into a school for less-well-off children. Now known as Dr. M.R.S.

Outside the Dr. M.R.S. Bhalla D.A.V. School in Batala, Anil (far right) and Jean (center) are celebrated by the school's faculty and principal, Rajni Salhotra (left of Jean at center), and Anil's relative Ashwin Marwah (far left). (Photograph by Sunil Badyal)

Bhalla D.A.V. High School, it has functioned relatively successfully as both a grade school and high school for local children for several decades. Though Anil and his family had lost track of the fate of the school over time, the school's principal never lost sight of the gift bestowed upon them and, after she and several board members managed to track down Anil, they invited him to visit the school and re-engage him in its evolution.

Intrigued by the prospect of seeing what had become of his mother's childhood home, Anil asked me to join him on a pilgrimage to the land where his parents were raised and he had been born. In 2006, when we made the journey to Amritsar and Batala, this agricultural and brick-making hub was bustling with energy, but still largely undeveloped with mud roads, open sewers, and random bullock carts roving over the main thoroughfare. Upon our arrival, we were driven first by car, which rocked us back and forth like pendulums as we traveled over the zigzagging grooves randomly cleaved into the squishy roads by the wheels of bullock carts hauling mounds of bricks and logs. Bobbing and weaving among the carts and occasional four-wheeled vehicles were bicycles steered by elders carrying wire-enclosed platforms of baby chicks or bags of coconuts and mobs of small scooters transporting carefully balanced families of five on a single seat, all breathing in the pervasive smell of burning dung, just as we were. Just before we arrived at the school, when the roads narrowed too much for our vehicle to pass, we were transferred to a bicycle rickshaw powered by a young man who, huffing and puffing with a smile, diligently got us to the top of the hill where the school building was perched. We were welcomed as honored guests and shown the various classrooms and the outdated computers the children relied on as tools toward a higher education. After getting a thorough tour, we were brought to a courtyard, where our photographs were snapped for a local newspaper, before making our way back to Bombay.

Anil was hooked. From that point forward his relationship with Batala was reignited and he committed to continuing to help support the school and collaborated with his brother Vijay to provide the funding it needed to embark on an expansion program. With their financial help, the school was able to purchase and renovate a neighboring building, which was completed in 2019 and commemorated in the names of their parents.

Visiting both Amritsar and Batala was also nostalgic for Anil. "The journey brought back memories of growing up amongst the dust and the smells of the scrappy frontier city of Amritsar, which is now slowly being gentrified as the roads have been dug up to accommodate water and sewage pipes," he said. "There is still dust all around though, as it is in most Punjab towns with their roads edged in raw earth. Batala has also cleaned up with fewer open sewers and invasive smells—and the flies may have migrated elsewhere with these gradual improvements, which now include running water in some homes interspersed with those that still rely on well water pulled up by a manual lever."

All of this was a far cry from the fanfare going on at the time around Bombay, where, upon our return from the journey and stuck amid the beeps and honks of standstill traffic on Pedder Road, we were struck by large billboards and the covers of latest issues of India's lifestyle magazines. Shuffled before us and pressed against our car windows by the homeless children who were hawking them in the streets, the publications, like the billboards, featured images of Anil's oldest nephew, Arun, fancily attired with his then-fiancée, Elizabeth Hurley, the well-known British model and actress, whose wedding was to take place the following spring. Somewhat stunned by the magnificence, I welcomed the quieter form of renown Anil enjoyed both in the far reaches of northern India and amid the social scene of the CCI, where everyone who knows him brightens up and smiles at the mere sight of him.

These early efforts in fulfilling his wish to support underprivileged children in some ways laid the groundwork for a later venture he was asked to support founded by Satinder Bajwa, who, after collaborating briefly with Anil on the squash program he had initiated for juniors in India in the mid-1990s, had launched a squash academy of his own in North India in 2009. Anil and Baj had loosely maintained a relationship over the years since they'd met on the American squash circuit, and occasionally connected while he was coaching at Harvard for almost a dozen years until 2010, when his career there came to a complex and politically fraught end.

"When Baj started as a Harvard squash coach I thought that he would understand both the emotions and psyches of the foreign players and the Americans due to his international experience and background," said Anil. At the outset, Bajwa was faced with the daunting job of building both the men's and women's teams after several of the best team players had graduated the previous year. "It was an especially formidable task since Trinity had displaced Harvard and other colleges as champions due to what many saw as its carte blanche admission policy," said Anil. "While this, indeed, may have been the case, as years went by, most concluded Trinity's strength could actually be attributed to Paul Assaiante, the college's squash coach, who had brought to the table a winning combination of smart coaching, a family-like relationship with his team players—past and present—and his strong connections with Trinity alumni. He understood clearly the importance of each of these requirements."

Though he had had high hopes for Bajwa, Anil learned through various locker room conversations at the Harvard Club in New York that he was receiving conflicting reviews. "Both critics and supporters assumed that I would have a sympathetic ear," said Anil. "John Thorndike, a fellow player of my era, was very complimentary of the work Baj had done with his two daughters. Another alumni said Baj was preferential to the men's team and others said he really didn't care for those lower in the team ranks. In contrast, my coach, Jack Barnaby, had a completely different coaching strategy, and had always made clear to us very early on that my win at a number one counted only as much as my teammate's win at number nine. Every team member was equally important. Off-court complaints regarding Baj were those of not giving sufficient respect to alumni and not communicating with them in an effective way."

Concerned about what he was hearing all around, Anil, without revealing the sources, reported what he'd heard, good and bad, to Bajwa, including rumors of the coach's possible discrimination suit against Harvard. "Awful," Anil remembered thinking. "Harvard was not discriminatory to me, so why him 30 years later?" The imbroglio surrounding the coach near the end of his contract eventually went public with reports of the controversy appearing in local newspapers and the *Harvard Crimson*. A 2010 edition of the *Crimson* reported: "An individual familiar with Harvard squash who asked for anonymity said that 'internal politics' played a larger role in the lack of renewal and expressed uncertainty regarding the alleged racial motive. 'I think that it was mainly internal politics that caused this. Whether or not race is something that affected those internal politics is hard to say,' the individual said. 'I'd say it's people butting heads based on cultural or other sorts of clashes.'"

With no breakthrough to resolve the matter in sight, Anil urged Bajwa to consider a positive path beyond the impasse. "I'm sure Baj learned from these reports, but the situation with the athletics association and the alumni was beyond repair. Working lunches to improve the communications and deal with complaints were to no avail," Anil said. "So I suggested to Baj that he should move on—he had had a good long innings and both Harvard and he were no longer comfortable with each other. I urged a move to India where his services were much needed."

And Bajwa eventually did just that in 2010, when he relocated to his hometown of Chandigarh to commit full-time to running Khelshala, the squash academy he had launched the prior year, and dedicate himself to improving the lives of underprivileged children in northern India.

* * *

CHAPTER TWENTY SIX

Loss

While his modest extra-curricular philanthropic efforts had provided some uplifting diversion for Anil during the mid-2000s, his business was sapping his energy and, in many ways, crushing his spirit. A recurring drumbeat of personal and professional losses would slowly transform Anil's attitude over the coming decade. Property matters still remained an issue in India, and Anil's business in America was becoming more stressful. And while he never talked about his disappointments on the squash court, I could clearly see that a part of him was mourning the loss of the champion sportsman that had once shone like sunshine from within as an important aspect of his identity—and his silence on this subject was breaking my heart. At the same time, changes in the media industry presented more challenges for me. I was working for the French publishing giant Hachette Filipacchi Media as an editor of various special interest publications on decorating and remodeling. While the digital revolution was unfolding, the print media business was falling apart as the internet changed the overall media dynamic and consolidations in my company, as in others, resulted in mass layoffs over the course of several years. Though I had managed to survive the restructurings in my company early on and was promoted to editor in chief of a pared-back group of publications, I was burdened with heavier workloads. At the same time, Anil was working through the issues of restructuring his own business, transitioning from the manufacture of apparel into soft home furnishings like decorative pillows, bedding, and table linens. Simultaneously, the declining health of our parents emerged as a dominant issue—with my father dying in 2006 and Anil's mother later suffering a severe shingles setback that would effectively mark the beginning of her slow decline.

Later, the financial crisis would hit the world hard and, as with many industries, Anil's business began to quickly unravel. Another blow was the 2008 attacks—often referred to as 26/11—in Mumbai, when ten members of Lashkar-e-Taiba, an Islamic terrorist organization based in Pakistan, carried out a series of coordinated shooting and bombing attacks lasting four days. During the attacks, which drew widespread global condemnation, the terrorists stormed high-profile locations throughout the city, including the Trident Oberoi Hotel, where Ashok Kapur, then the chairman of Yes Bank and the older brother of Anil's childhood friend Anil Kapur, was among the victims who were shot and killed in the sieges. Anil and I both remember being in constant contact with Kapur over the course of two days, until we finally received confirmation by phone from him of the worst imaginable news of his brother's murder, a tragic echo of 9/11, while we were hosting a dinner at our home on Thanksgiving day. "As we reach our 60s, poignant harbingers like these remind you of the reality of impermanence," Anil said.

Another devastating loss was the demise of Arif Sarfraz, a dear friend, top squash player, and successful investment banker in New York and later London, whose brother-in-law, Wasim Shajjad, had served as the acting president of Pakistan for two non-consecutive terms in late '80s and 1990s. "He hadn't told his friends he was sick, though Jean and I suspected he was not well," said Anil. Sarfraz and his wife, Anne Johnston, had recently purchased a home in Coconut Grove, a Miami suburb, and Anil and I were looking forward to spending more time with them in the states, when Anil received a call from Johnston in London in May, 2014, informing him of Sarfraz's passing after a prolonged illness. "Arif was my best Pakistani and Punjabi friend," said Anil, who often was greeted by Sarfraz with the phrase, *"Meri Jaan,"* an endearment that literally translates to My Life. "Proud of Pakistan, he stoically tolerated my comments about his country behaving like a stepchild on the subcontinent."

In contrast to the losses of many friends Anil was experiencing at this time, the marriage in 2011 at the University Club of his son Sanjay to Amy Nicole Grudzinski, a young woman from Michigan who had spent her career in the pharmaceutical industry and was working as an executive at Pfizer, was a highlight for both of us after the decade had drawn to a close. But the honeymoon period of our life was clearly over. Shortly after being promoted to editor in chief of a group of magazines at Hachette, which was spinning off and selling its U.S. publications to other companies or closing them down, I and most of my colleagues were downsized out of our jobs. Soon Anil would also sell his own business and shutter its doors. But he saw this crisis phase as an opportunity to move back to India and spend time with his mother as she neared the end of her life and convinced me, though not without some hesitation, that we should make the move together.

The Land of Ten Thousand Lakes, where I grew up, is about as different from the Land of Five Rivers, where Anil was born, as the sun from the moon. And while I had always seen Bombay, with its melting pot of cultures and cosmopolitan air, as the New York of India, day-to-day living in India's largest city presented stark contrasts to the urban experience that came so naturally to me in America. Among the most challenging prospects facing the can-do spirit of a heartlander like me was the idea of enlisting and managing a crew of domestic help that is an integral part of any Bombay household in Anil's sphere. But I wanted Anil to be happy and opted to indulge him in his dream and the next time we went to India we worked to renovate and prepare his flat as a full-time dwelling.

The renovation process opened a wider window into the worlds of the people who worked in service to Anil's mother and brother Vinod and who regularly walked into and out of our home, often without so much as a knock on the door, as they went about their daily business. One sunny afternoon, after I'd moved a chair against a wall to stand upon as I attempted to remove a work of art from the wall, Vinod's lead support man, Ajay, walked in and frantically shouted out "*Memsahib*, no! I'll do that. Please!" Another morning, after I'd made some *burji*, Indian-style scrambled eggs spiced with onions, tomatoes, turmeric, cilantro, and chilis, Sitaram, my mother-in-law's cook, entered our home after announcing himself by clearing his throat and, upon seeing the food on the table, was mystified as to why I hadn't ask him to make our morning meal, especially when he knew how much I loved the way he prepared my favorite breakfast dish. And later that day, as we climbed a back staircase adjoining the elevator to the roof, which we'd enlisted a contractor to shore up after it had begun to deteriorate with the pounding monsoons year after year, I discovered the personal quarters allotted to Vinod's driver, Bhan Singh, a kind, tristful man with a deep, plaintive voice like a softly lowing cow, who regularly transported us around the city whenever we came for a visit. A narrow strip of padding topped with a neat, colorful quilt and crowned along one wall with a drawing of a Hindu saint was squeezed into a slim section of flooring near the greasy elevator gears, which clanged like a bell as they moved the cables up and down along the shaft. "Why is this bedding laid out here?" I asked Anil as we stepped past the mat. "It's Bhan Singh's sleeping place," he replied. My heart sank as I imagined Bhan Singh occasionally waking throughout the night as the gears turned round and a peppy rendition of "Jingle Bells" rang out every time the elevator doors opened with the comings and goings of late-night reveling residents. "I can't believe this is where he sleeps," I whispered. Anil explained that this setup was better than a room in the decrepit, unsanitary *chawls*, or shanties, in the distant slums outside the city, where many a neighbor's driver would spend the night.

As we worked to regroup and smooth the way for a life in India, Anil's younger son, Vivek, announced his engagement to Jaclyn Rudolph, a young woman he'd met in law school and eventually married 2012. Their wedding in Lower Manhattan at the India House, where Anil and I had originally planned to marry, was another peak experience during this time. But less than a year later, as Anil and I continued to collaborate to update Anil's flat to prepare for the move, Anil was socked with another blow: The death of his mother in June 2011.

"It was a shock like no other, a grief like no other," remembered Anil of his feelings after learning his mother quietly passed away at the age of 92 on a hot, rainy Bombay morning. "My beautiful mother had been disfigured due to a debilitating bout of shingles in her 80s. She had also become immobile and weak but remained quite clear in her head. She so wanted the family to stay together and continually stressed the importance of 'unity.' She had lived for her children but in my mind some of her children never really grew up. There were so many grabs of her property, jewelry, saris, and precious objects. Such was the ethos in my family. As I launched her casket with the help of my brothers into the electric furnace, I was heartbroken."

His last journey with his mother was with his three siblings, who brought her ashes in an urn to Haridwar, where they set them off into the polluted waters of the Ganges River in the final rites. "It was an awkward time for the four of us. We had not often been together as a group in adulthood and here we were trying our best to follow our mother's wish of 'unity' knowing full well that this would only be short lived. Our four-hour journey with the brass urn containing my mother's ashes in Vijay's SUV from Delhi to Haridwar was largely uneventful except for Vinod's frequent fixes with his *bidis,* which smelled up the whole vehicle just as they did when we ate together at my mother's lunch table," said Anil, knowing that the *bidis*—small hand-rolled cigarettes made of tobacco and wrapped in *tendu* or *temburni* leaves—also contributed to the lung cancer that eventually led to Vinod's own death in 2019.

"Upon arriving in Haridwar, amid the rain and *kichad* and dung with flies in over-active mode, we started to look for our family *pandit*, whom none of us had ever met," Anil explained of their efforts to properly bid their mother a final adieu. "He and his forefathers had supposedly kept our family history over many years. After several false leads, a slim young man appeared and, astonishingly, identified himself as our *pandit* by telling us the names of our father and grandfathers and where they were from. Relieved that our mother would be given the final rites in accordance with our custom, we followed our *pandit* to the river, where he offered a prayer and we emptied the contents of the urn into the river. Had I known how dirty the river and its banks were, I would never have agreed to send off my mother's ashes there." Anil believed a more fitting resting place would have been the Arabian Sea right in front of the apartment in which he and his siblings had all grown up and experienced the dramas of life.

Later the siblings followed the *pandit* to his office to update their family history. "Up the narrow winding stairs we went to his small work space, where we saw 20 or more bulky manuscripts containing our family history," remembered Anil. "After he started reading the history from as far back as a 100 years ago, I had to cut him short as the discomfort of sitting on the floor amid the swarms of flies and mosquitoes became unbearable. Before concluding, the *pandit* asked for updates on the current status of our family, and Vinod, who really did not care much for one our uncles, commanded him to delete some of this uncle's recent history! As our *pandit* updated the records in Hindi and made note of my mother's death, I also asked him to update my family's history, including my marriage to my first wife, Linda, the birth of my sons, Sanjay and Vivek, and my marriage to my second wife, Jean." After the record-keeping was completed, Anil and his siblings set off to return to Bombay.

With his two sons married, his mother gone, his business sold, and his squash career over, Anil was adrift. Meanwhile, I had rebuilt my career as a freelance writer, authoring a few more books and taking up real estate for additional income and broader experience in a completely different yet related field. The pull to India had been diffused after the loss of his mother, so Anil and I opted to remain in America while Anil turned his attention to his property matters in Bombay. And, after ultimately deciding to sell his flat on Marine Drive to his nephew Niki rather than move into it, Anil began to fantasize about a Bombay substitute. Eventually, he homed in on Miami, where he and I had often escaped the New York winters for long weekends over the past decade or so. With its multiple Art Deco buildings (so much like the one he grew up in on Marine Drive), subtropical climate, turquoise waters, and profusion of palm trees, the city beckoned like a long lost American twin to India's Mumbai.

Now that his business was in the hands of a Chinese purchaser, Anil was ready to make a move. Seeing clearly that my husband was due for a change of scene that would boost his spirits, I provisionally agreed to give it a try for a couple of years on the condition we would move back to New York if the fit wasn't good. After searching for a week for a place to live, we found and purchased an apartment on Miami Beach and within weeks of resettling Anil knew he was in his element. My freelance career also quickly expanded as I began to contribute to magazines in both New York and south Florida. And with the regular trips we took to New York for business and family, we ultimately opted to purchase a pied-à-terre in Manhattan and now live in a way that offers us the best of both worlds.

* * *

CHAPTER TWENTY SEVEN

Reinvention

While the preceding decade brought with it plenty of heartache, Anil looked back with appreciation for its many uplifting moments of beauty and happiness. "Squash play notwithstanding, marriage and family life was exciting. I didn't know it then but, after a couple of years of dating, Jean casually told me that everything would get better if we were to get married," Anil said, now looking back over the 22 years that have passed since he and I met. "*A bait*, I thought, and I took it. Now, I often wake up and think, *I just don't know why I got so lucky!*" And shortly after Anil and I recalibrated the working patterns of our lives between two cities, Anil's extended family life gradually began to unfold in not necessarily surprising yet wonderful ways with the introduction of three granddaughters—Victoria, Aili, and Oona—and a grandson, Hudson. "Two daughters-in-law and now four grandkids, what better gifts could I have to make up for the losses of others?" he asked.

After kick-starting his life between two cities, Anil also reinvented his approach to business, developing a stream of activity as a consultant, advising on joint ventures between small- and medium-size companies in India and the U.S., and occasionally raising capital for new startups. With a nudge from me, he also got a real estate license in Florida, and began to get involved in commercial transactions as he developed a network in Miami and other parts of the country. Yet, just as he was settling into his new routine, Anil's attention would again be drawn back to India after he received a call from his squash compatriot Satinder Bajwa in 2013.

Bajwa, who had managed and mentored eight-time Pakistani world champion Jansher Khan and coached a string of top players at Harvard, had witnessed the success of the sustainable nonprofit models established by the urban squash programs that had emerged around the turn of the millennium in the U.S. After leaving his position as squash coach at Harvard and moving to India a few years earlier to replicate such a program in India, Bajwa had managed to make early progress on his NGO, Khelshala, but he needed assistance in getting it to the next level. Knowing of Anil's interest in supporting the poorest of India's children through sport, Bajwa tapped him to participate in the nascent enterprise as a member of its advisory board.

"Baj revealed to me that he had always wanted to give back to India and he knew I had wanted to do the same for many years, though I was not able to make headway since I was no longer rooted in Bombay," Anil said. "When he talked to me about his progress with Khelshala and asked me to be on its advisory board I gladly accepted the invitation." Anil was also pleased to collaborate with Darius Pandole, another Harvard alumni living in Bombay whom he'd seen growing up at the CCI and who was also a member of the board. "Darius was an Indian national junior champion, a number one ranked intercollegiate U.S. player, a U.S. national softball champion in 1986, and has so much to offer," said Anil.

According to Khelshala's founder, Anil has much to bring to the organization as well. "Anil has contributed both inspirational and financial support that has made Khelshala a success and Chandigarh is the richer for it," Bajwa said. "Unlike team sports, individual sports like squash, tennis, or badminton develop responsibility

Thanksgiving in Chicago, 2017. Clockwise from left: son Sanjay, grandson Hudson, Anil, Jean, son Vivek, granddaughter Oona, Vivek's wife, Jackie, granddaughter Aili, granddaughter Victoria, Sanjay's father-in-law, Tony, Sanjay's wife, Amy Nicole.

and accountability in a person that result in building a strong character in those who participate or compete in them." Since Bajwa's aim with Khelshala has always been to leverage sport for better health and education among the poorest of the poor in India and give them the tools they need to break out of the cycle of poverty and participate as functional members of society, he sees the character-building aspects of his program as essential ingredients in his students' development.

A year after he joined the board, Anil and I made a trip to visit Khelshala's facilities. "Chandigarh, which is known for its phased planned development and partially designed by Le Corbusier, was and still is a city like no other in India with its grid structure, wide boulevards, and a level of cleanliness unique to itself," said Anil. "Nehru said it should be 'a new town, symbolic of the freedom of India, unfettered by the past.' And in many ways it is a model city." Chandigarh, which means "city of silver," is the capital of both the states of Punjab and Haryana. It was conceived as an egalitarian city in which the living quarters, open spaces, and public facilities were designed in consistent fashion from sector to sector. Though much of the city continues to exist in this format, migrants from the agrarian sector have filtered in over the decades looking for new employment opportunities, as is the case in most emerging cities, and their influx has resulted in surrounding slums. "One Khelshala center is situated in one of these slums known as Attawa," said Anil, and this is the facility he and I visited on our tour in 2013. "The center includes squash courts, a fitness area, and a roofed space for learning. Sixty girls and boys, from 4-16 years of age and raised by parents who are garbage pickers or cleaners, attend public school, come to Khelshala to participate in its after-school programs to learn sport and yoga, and get additional teaching to supplement their daily school work."

Since Anil joined its advisory board, Khelshala has also developed the Majra Khelshala farm in New Chandigarh, where twenty to thirty young boys and girls—Muslims, Sikhs, and Hindus from farmer and laborer backgrounds—come after school to learn to play tennis and work on strengthening themselves both mentally and physically. Most important is that the program is yielding results with its students now being admitted to private schools or excelling in squash tournaments. Priya Gupta, for example, Khelshala's first female graduate and a recipient of a Young India Fellowship, is now pursuing a post graduate diploma at Asoka University. Manish Kumar, on the other hand, is Khelshala's first graduate with a bachelor's degree in computer engineering, and Sonu Kumar, who is pursing a Bachelor of Arts degree, is the first Khelshala player to receive a sponsorship from the Indian sportswear brand Salming. At the same time, Khelshala is launching new initiatives aimed at even more broadly enhancing the lives of its students, including the Khelshala Achievers Club, which provides additional support for high-achieving students in the form of extra academic classes and advanced coaching, a medical checkup camp aimed at providing children with information on health, hygiene, and nutrition, and seminars on self-care and empowerment for women, which enable both Khelshala girls and their mothers to prepare for the challenges of the future. "Those are important benchmarks for a program," Anil said. "The kids now have a confidence level that tells us of their readiness to self empower. That is the ultimate Khelshala goal. I really noticed this change between the time when Jean and I visited in 2013 and when I returned in 2018."

By the time Anil got involved in Khelshala, the urban squash programs in America had exploded with astonishing success, and many are now part of the Squash and Education Alliance, co-founded by Harvard squash player Tim Wyant, who has collaborated with other leaders in the sport to expand squash's influence among the underprivileged throughout the U.S. and other countries. And Khelshala is a part of this international organization. In a piece he penned in the fall 2018 issue of *U.S. Jesters* magazine, Wyant succinctly summarized the growth in urban squash over the past two decades:

> "It's been 22 years since Greg Zaff and a group of local squash enthusiasts—many of them Jesters—launched SquashBusters in Boston. The after-school program served 28 middle school students and had a budget of $70,000. No one could have guessed that the model would grow into the movement it is today. There are now 19 U.S. member organizations and five international affiliates in the Squash and Education Alliance, and together these organizations enroll more than 2,500 students. Nearly 200 people work full-time for our programs, and over $17 million is invested in the network annually. What has begun as an East Coast phenomenon now has roots in nearly every part of the country. Charleston, Minneapolis, Pittsburgh, San Diego and Santa Barbara are just a few of the cities outside of the squash beltway where programs can be found."

Anil with a group of children at Khelshala, 2015.

Like Khelshala, these groups produce results with some of its participants going on to top colleges or universities, including Ivy League schools, and several have gone on to successful careers, often in business or government, or sometimes as coaches or administrators within the programs. According to Wyant, the programs have also drawn widespread community interest, especially among politicians, including Michael Dukakis, Kirsten Gillibrand, and Michelle Obama.

Given its consistent evolution in the U.S., Anil sees so much potential for similar growth in India and is heartened by the emergence of squash academies like Khelshala in other parts of India. "There are programs sprouting up all over the country led by stellar players—Gaurav Nandrajog has one in Delhi, Ritwik Bhattacharya founded the START program in the Western Ghats an hour

Anil showing Khelshala kids how to serve at the Majra facility in Chandigarh, 2018.

outside Bombay, and Gautam Das at the Calcutta Racket Club has started a similar program," he said. "We have millions of 'potentials' in our midst. The challenging question is: How do we as a country, through our institutions and clubs, progress to the new world standards?" To get it to the next level, he believes a coordinated approach that can overcome political constraints is essential. "To elevate both social impact and the level of play through squash programs in India, the sport would benefit from the development of a unified body that could help the NGOs with funding from the government and corporations, which are currently mandated to contribute an average of 2 percent of their net profits from the past three years toward economic, social, and environmental development," he said. "There's an enormous pool of talent that might be tapped to not only produce future Indian champions but also uplift thousands of young girls and boys to become constructive members of Indian society. We have the human capital in sport just as we do in the world of technology. But we need a credible structure that can appeal to the large pool of donors."

With a strategic approach to the support of committed squash academies like Khelshala, Anil envisions a day when such organizations will provide a transformative effect on India's output of world-class athletes. "It's easy to imagine the trickle-down benefits," said Anil. "Consider Khelshala and other squash 'give back' programs in India. Consider, too, a selection of kids from each of the groups slated for excellence. Let's say a total of twenty girls and boys are handpicked each year for further development at a squash center for advanced competitive training where you have a high-quality committed coach. A homegrown coach would be preferable, but an outside one may also have much to offer on technique and strategy. If twenty kids come to this center every year with the right profile and background, India could readily build a deep bench of high-caliber players and we should get a world champion within a decade."

By maximizing the emerging teaching programs, Anil sees the positive ripple effects extending well beyond the sport itself with social benefits unfolding along multiple levels. "The uplift should have impact across class lines," Anil said. "When the poor have access to improved health and education and the ability to break out of the cycle of poverty and participate in the workforce, the positive effects will expand to their families and future generations. Over time, when a few of these people become heads of corporations, they might also give back and build new squash complexes that may continue to expand programs to other cities where the sport is less known."

Anil (seated at front left) with a group of children at Khelshala along with founder Satinder Bajwa (standing at back right), 2018.

Anil believes that not only India and the U.S., but also other countries engaged in a unified approach to supporting squash and making it accessible to a wider group of people can benefit from tapping the "fortune at the bottom of the pyramid," as it has been described by the Indian author C.K. Prahalad. "The positive effects can extend the world over in a way that has not taken place before in the history of squash," said Anil. "I believe the process now unfolding in India and the U.S. and a few other countries is just the beginning of the democratization of squash." The statistics support this view. A recent survey conducted by the Sports and Fitness Industry Association, for example, found that squash was the 12th fastest-growing activity in the United States, with 1.7 million participants, and participation has grown 32 percent since 2012.

To make the effort complete, Richard Millman, a British squash coach who works with both pros and amateurs at Scenic City Squash in Chattanooga, Tennessee, believes it is equally important to find ways to include the vast middle class, an often forgotten group, into the mix. "We are putting money into urban squash, but it has been well said that the money that used to flow just into blue blood squash, Ivy league squash, private school squash is simply being diverted into urban squash," said Millman, who sees squash as a sport that's still in its infancy. "There's no money going into middle class squash or working class squash. We've either got the very top or the very bottom, but nothing in the middle." And that's huge pool of people who could benefit from squash, and perhaps bring the most to the sport.

On a more exclusive level, Anil envisions the development of elite academies, or centers that cater to excellence as they do for tennis and badminton, which might nurture and develop players who could eventually participate in championships at high levels of play. "These players will become mentors and role models in their communities and will, in turn, provide seeds for new entrants, talent, and champions," Anil said.

The Squash Academy in Chennai is an example of this type of focused sports training facility. As of 2016, the Squash Academy produced 62 national champions in various categories. In addition, it has produced numerous internationally ranked players with good player groups in the secondary and tertiary levels. And Ramachandran, its founder, has stated that his aim with the academy is to produce a world champion. According to Cyrus Poncha, the official coach for the Indian Squash Federation and at the Academy, "It would be a dream to have it happen within the next ten years. But we need to get players playing full time. We're losing people when they're 19 or 20 years old and they go to study in America and then don't come back. Most drop off because of lack of sponsorship. We need to make players believe there is security with corporate backing, so that they realize that once they're 50 years old they can get into another job."

If the Squash Academy in Chennai is serious about producing world champion Indian squash players, Anil suggested they need only look a few hundred miles north to the Pullela Gopichand Badminton Academy in Hyderabad created by its eponymous superstar player-turned-coach-with-a-mission to get great ideas on how to do so. In a piece that appeared in a 2018 issue of *The Indian Express*, Gopichand referred to two of his star pupils, Saina Nehwal and P.V. Sindhu, as "precious diamonds." "That's the kind of relationship administrators, coaches, and players should have rather than the often prevailing attitude in which players and coaches are seen as dispensable commodities, as pawns to the administrators and organizations," said Anil. "With the right attitude and environment, Indian squash will flourish."

In Anil's mind, the cultural changes that have occurred in India since his time will further help to produce world champion squash players. "There has been worldwide success in several sports, including badminton, cricket, chess, and shooting to name a few," he said. "The champions of today aren't burdened by colonial and dominance complexes. Indian athletes like cricketers Virat Kohli and Mahindra Singh Dhoni, fearless in their captaincy and play, have been outstanding role models not just for their own sport but for other sports, too. So, too, have the Indian squash players, such as Ritwik Bhattacharya, Saurav Ghosal, Ramit Tandon, Mahesh Mangaonkar, Joshna Chinappa, and Dipika Pallikal. India will get world champion squash players as the mindset and *terroir* are now

Anil (center back row) with former CCI vice president Naval Pandole (to his left), junior players at the CCI, and coach Abhinav Sinha (far left), 2019.

more conducive to superlative performance. But good, consistent coaching is an essential ingredient of the mix to create champions."

With the introduction of squash academies in India, the opening of courts across continental Europe and around the globe, and the emergence of urban squash programs in the U.S. and internationally, awareness of and access to squash has grown significantly. And as it gains wider recognition, it has also gained more enthusiasts willing to support it with greater prize money and endorsements, which will likely attract a broader pool of professionals. For the 2018-2019 World Championships, for example, the Chicago-based Walter family committed to offering prize money of $1 million, the highest amount ever awarded, and splitting it equally among the men's and women's brackets at the magnificent Union Station in Chicago.

Increased efforts and concerted coordination among the international squash community to expand participation in the sport promise even wider recognition in the future. For example, a substantial contingent of the squash community continues to put forth efforts to bring squash into the Olympic Games. To many squash players and fans, the fact that sports like pistol dueling and tug of war have Olympic status and squash does not defies understanding. Squash is one of the most physically and mentally demanding sports with a history that is generally believed to date back to England in the 1700s. It requires extreme athleticism and skill, is now played in 185 countries, and is governed by a sophisticated global organizational structure. The Olympic Charter indicates that in order to be accepted, a sport must be widely practiced by men in at least 75 countries and on four continents and by women in no fewer than 40 countries and on three continents. The sport must also increase the "value and appeal" of the Olympic Games and retain and reflect its modern traditions. So squash is a natural fit as an Olympic sport. And many of those who are entrenched in the squash community remain hopeful that the sport may finally gain its rightful place in the Olympic Games in Paris in 2024.

As squash continues to evolve globally on social, organizational, and political levels, Anil pointed out its internal changes on both athletic and technical levels as he imagines the future of the sport continuing to shape-shift just as coaches like Geoff Mitchell note that squash must continually evolve to stay relevant. "I don't teach the same footwork that I was taught 20 years ago," Mitchell said, after observing the changes that technology and body types have brought to the game. "I've gone through a half a dozen iterations of the footwork and the stroke work based upon what the top players are doing. The softball game is becoming closer to hardball with the type of rallies and the training you do. The fitness training now is completely different. It's much more explosive, players are much faster. Tennis has gone through similar changes. It's not unusual in a racquet sport to happen." And such changes have influenced how he teaches his program. "I look at what the top 50 or 100 pros are doing out there and not all is appropriate to younger kids, but it is once they're 15 or 16," said Mitchell. "And they can learn bits and pieces that they can develop and they're learning those things at a much earlier age and that's another reason the players just keep getting stronger and stronger."

"The sport has already been revolutionized to a high level of both fitness and artistry," said Anil. "The current 11-point game is a fine melding of the prior 9-point international game with the 15-point American hardball game. The attributes of both the American and international games have come together to make a very fine sport, which has enabled squash to change in a similar way that the 20-twenty rules did for cricket. These changes turned them into sports on steroids, bringing instant gratification to the spectators, thus keeping up with the sports and social psyche of our times."

Anil also sees technology as a key in enabling squash to evolve with even more sophistication in the future, much as it has with tennis. "Simulated altitude training technology that already exists is going to increase the efficiency with which athletes intake oxygen, which will subsequently improve their stamina and strength," he said. "Videos and artificial intelligence reviews now add to the standard of play and will continue to shape it in the future." Anil pointed to a report on thematic investing from Merrill Lynch that highlights the potential of technological advances, including the growth of e-sports, that might be applied to the evolution of squash and sports in general. The Chinese internet giant Tencent, for example, is using AI to help e-sport athletes with data and algorithm-driven training analyses. According to Anil, even a very small percentage of transference from e-squash to actual squash might result in a substantial increase in player standards and spectator interest. "Imagine current top players like the Egyptian Mohamed El Shorbagy using the marginal advantage of a short-swing front-court hard drop that would be more effective at a certain time in a match with, say, Ali Farag, than the hard, low cross-court shot that Farag would usually anticipate," said Anil. "With this slightly more effective approach, he might even win the point, but he would certainly save energy and put his opponent in greater difficulty at the least."

Advances in equipment and gear also continue to optimize the game and how it is played. For example, take improvements in the support elements and non-skid features of the newest squash sneakers, which have helped raise standards by permitting players to take off faster. "The newer generation of squash sneakers will most likely integrate the technologies and design of the Nike Vaporfly 4% running shoe, which is purported to enhance running economy by 4 percent and, if true, would propel squash players to move even faster than they currently do while enabling them to conserve energy," said Anil.

As the sport and athletes continue to evolve, sports enthusiasts invariably look at champions of the past and wonder how they would fare in today's context. "How would the play of Hashim Khan or Azam Khan or Jonah Barrington or Geoff Hunt compare against today's best-in-the-world players?" wondered Anil. "Are the present-day world champions superior to yesteryear's modern players, such as Jahangir, who has the best open record in history, or Jansher, the master cat-and-mouse player? It's a question that can only be answered subjectively driven by gut instinct." Our friend Lesley Visser, an award-winning sports commentator for CBS, has her own theory on the subject, however, and firmly believes that if yesteryear's champions could play at their peaks in today's conditions, they'd still be the champions of today.

To come to a more definitive conclusion, Anil envisions computer simulations that would make adjustments for innumerable variables, including differences in body sizes, racquets and balls, tin heights, sneakers, and career spans of players. "We could simulate a modern day Hashim playing Ramy Ashour or El Shorbagy," he suggested. "I would risk saying they would be equally good. Remember, as folklore has it, Hashim was so fast that he could practically volley a drop shot and Mohibullah Khan could hide his magic wand to hit drop shots in directions that would totally wrong-foot his opponents."

A key question for the future, however, with the potentially large inflow of players, especially from the "bottom of the pyramid," is how much more can a sport played in an area of 32'x21' (9.75m x 6.4m) be made more interesting and stay relevant for both spectators and players? Anil sees the question as especially important as players get taller and quicker and racquets allow for both more power and delicacy. "Perhaps a faster ball would allow for more artistry and winners and make the game more interesting for the viewers. Or the rules may be tweaked for the topmost red-line to be adjusted higher, enabling players to use the height of the court as a significant tactical change to slow the game down and create relief from the non-stop breathtaking rallies for the spectators," said Anil, noting that players are now taller by approximately 4 to 6 inches than they were in the 1950s and will likely get even taller over the years. "As players get bigger, the strategy and effect of the lob game, which allows for that much-awaited suspense pause, is not as effective. What if the front top line were

Jean and Anil at the Tournament of Champions at Grand Central Terminal in New York City, 2018.

raised by a foot and the other side and back wall top lines raised proportionately? Lobs would once again be important in a player's repertoire and different kinds of players may come to the fore. It's worth remembering Gogi Alauddin, the lob and drop specialist and winner of the British Amateur Championships in 1970 and 1971, who thrived on lob-and-drop accuracy. The precision available to players who specialize in a slower game could become important again."

The creative use of technology is also key in enabling the sport to stay relevant in an era of e-sport and ubiquitous mobile app usage to produce the best experience for viewers and attract off-court spectators who have many choices now and will have many more in the future, according to Anil. "To maintain the interest of viewers, significant improvements are needed in camerawork to catch the movement and angles of players and their shots. The colors and designs of players' clothing should also be elevated, as they have for tennis players. In the end, if the viewer experience is not enhanced significantly, squash may stay as it is now—a boutique sport," said Anil. Another way to maintain and expand participation and help enhance what Anil calls "the stickiness factor" might be to make it more appealing to people with varying levels of ability, especially children and beginners. Imagine courts or lines that could be electronically adjusted in length, width, or height, just as tins have over time. These changes might make the sport more inviting to children or elders, who could play on courts scaled and modified to suit their limitations and sustain their interest in the sport for a longer span in their lives. "In short order, squash would change to stay relevant for both players and spectators," said Anil.

* * *

CHAPTER TWENTY EIGHT

Haardik Shukriya

As he looks to the future of the sport, Anil is sometimes stirred by twinges of nostalgia for his glory days, along with frequent pleas by fellow players to get back into the court and play. And if a recent event in Anil's life is any indication, there's a sliver of possibility that he might have another championship title in the stars. After withdrawing almost completely from squash play, except for friendly round robins at the University of Miami, Anil's recent connection to squash has continued mostly on an advisory level to Khelshala. But an invitation from his former Harvard teammate Fritz Hobbs to participate as a partner in a doubles tournament in Philadelphia in February, 2018, stoked his interest in the possibility of competing again and got him mobilized to play. Although Anil and Hobbs lost in the first round to Tom Poor and Molson Robertson, Anil was inspired to work on getting his mojo back and scheduled some one-on-one training to age-adjust his game with Richard Millman, aka the Squash Doctor, in Tennessee. "I keep wanting to get back that magic to win again," said Anil. "When I play in friendly matches these days, I still enjoy hitting the ball with a flick of the wrist or doing a head fake to wrong-foot my opponent. But I get lost in enjoyment and end up losing the game or match. I need time to reset as I feel I may have a few years left

Harvard squash friends. From left: Dinny Adams, Alan Quasha, Anil, Rick Sterne, Jay Nelson, and Craig Stapleton with NYC Harvard Club coach Richard Chin, 2017.

to play despite being a candidate for knee and hip replacements." So in the fall of 2018, Anil and I booked a trip to Millman's squash camp, where he learned some new tricks.

After working with Anil for several hours on the court, Millman observed that he still possessed many of the attributes and skills that had made him a world-class player. "He still loves the ideas behind the game, which is fantastic because it tells me he has an open mind," Millman explained. "He's more interested in the squash he's going to play than in the squash he has played, which is exciting. He is a tremendous exponent of the competitive game of squash and has extra qualities that are rare." Among them, he said, are "his capacity to wrong-foot people, to suddenly strike a very pure ball, to produce a variety of shots from one situation which surprises." Yet one of the abilities that had served him well as a younger player that he's now lost is speed. "Speed is a form of time management," Millman said. "And as far as where he is now, he's become frustrated because he doesn't have the speed he used to have. So we are changing the paradigm so that we are putting him into positions before the opponent can hit his next shot rather than to try to hit shots that his opponent can't get. This is a completely different thought process because he never had to think about where he was going to move before the next situation until after he had played his shot, but I'm teaching him to think about the movement before he hits the shot so that he's already on the way to the next situation before he's struck the ball and before the ball is available to his opponent."

To make this thinking work for Anil, Millman taught him one of the strategies used by top players today, such as Ramy Ashour, Karim Abdul Gawad, and even giants like James Wilstroff, which is to always be moving on his way away from the ball as opposed to stepping into the ball, an approach that was historically taught in the old days. Another was to move with smaller steps rather than lunging to control the timing of the movement so that his effort would be about going to the future. "The good news is that the particular version of physical chess—the cunning spinning of the spider's web to catch the fly in your evil cocoon—is very available to Anil," said Millman.

In explaining his approach to understanding the psyche of his trainees, Millman also shed light on the question about the "killer instinct" that I had never seen in Anil, but do often see in other champion sportspeople. Before starting his training, Millman asked Anil a few questions aimed at getting a sense of his instincts and thinking, one of which intrigued me. The question was whether Anil's goal as a player was to annihilate his opponent or to survive. Anil's response was to survive. "Since time immemorial human beings have been trying to survive," Millman said. "And we have two perception systems that we've been using in that process. Primary focus, with which we concentrate on urgent immediate

Getting a reboot with coach Richard Millman at Scenic City Squash in Chattanooga, Tennessee, 2018.

circumstances at hand, and peripheral awareness, with which we inform ourselves of our surroundings. If I came out of my cave 20,000 years ago and I needed to get food, I'd go out and look for an antelope and I'm really focusing on the antelope. But if I have no peripheral awareness, the dry twig that I snap to announce that I'm present to the leopard that's hunting me is just as important as my primary focus. To be really successful in survival, including in the squash court, where the ball is your life, we need a marriage between primary focus and peripheral awareness."

With this explanation, I could easily see that primary focus, or the "killer instinct," is one part of the equation in the success of an athlete, but peripheral awareness, which is obviously part of Anil's arsenal of skills, is another. It also became clear to me that "the win at all costs" or "killer" quality exhibited by some top sportspeople isn't necessarily the only characteristic required to become a champion. Instead, as highlighted in director Gabe Polsky's recent film *In Search of Greatness*, which explores the careers of exceptional sportsmen, such as Pelé, Muhammad Ali, Tom Brady, Michael Jordan, and Wayne Gretzky, a more consistent common thread is non-conformity—certainly a quality more fitting to Anil, a gifted sportsman who brimmed with raw talent and always played the game with out-of-the-box creativity. For Anil, excelling as a sportsman was a form of self-expression, a passionate display of artistry, an act of love. The film also explores the ideas of authors David Epstein, who wrote *The Sports Gene*, and Sir Ken Robinson, who wrote *Genes, Brains, and Human Potential* and is known for his TED talk on the idea that standardized education kills creativity. Both warn against today's creativity crushing emphasis on structure and systems or early specialization as well as the effects of tiger parenting, the outlandish costs of training, travel, and equipment, and a fixation on measurements and data. Instead, it might be better to look back at the personalized approaches to coaching of Jack Barnaby and Yusuf Khan, who clearly had the right ideas in how to bring out the best in their wards.

With some fresh ideas and a recharge from Millman, Anil left the squash camp with hope for the possibility that he might have another championship title under his belt in the years ahead. What he wasn't expecting on his return from the journey, however, was a letter in the mail from Kevin Klipstein, the president and CEO of U.S. Squash. Upon opening the letter, he learned that its board of directors had chosen him to be inducted into the U.S. Squash Hall of Fame. The honor was just the boost he needed to follow through with his plans to start fresh with squash and participate in one more championship event.

"It was just so fine a way to cap off my career as a squash player—the best gift I could think of receiving at this time of my life, a crowning glory," said Anil, who, with typical humility was hesitant to share the news with others. As such, I made a point of letting all our friends and family know of the latest feather in the cap of his illustrious history in squash. Often comparing himself to the stellar pros who had preceded or followed him, such as Hashim or Jahangir Khan, and especially his coach Yusuf, Anil's view of himself as a squash player has always been quite modest. Yet, who really knows what he might have achieved if he'd dedicated himself full-time to professionally playing a sport he chose to continue to play on the amateur level for pleasure?

Other friends also urged him to share news of the accolade a little more freely. "My good friend Sundaram Tagore told me, 'Don't hold back. If you have good news to share, don't underplay it—enjoy it and make the best of it while you have it,'" said Anil. Tagore also saw the value of recognizing Anil's accomplishments on a broader intercultural level. "We have an enormous need for role models like Anil to make space for others to follow," Tagore said. "Anil is also truly a bridge builder. He left India at a young age and served a really significant purpose in the area of cultural diplomacy that allowed those of us who followed to move into that sphere more easily. He came and adapted and was sensitive to culture with constancy and the ability to communicate easily with people and he did it willingly at a time when there were not so many Indians in America. He was thrown into the caldron of culture and he savored it, and I can see that by the many friends he has and the way people talk about him with so much respect. He has used his ability in sport as a vehicle to reach out to a global group of people and build bridges, friendships, and very strong connecting points."

With a push from Tagore and me and other family and friends, Anil gradually shared the news of his honor with less reserve. "It was the 'Sundaram effect,'" Anil said. "The folks at A1A Crossfit

Anil after his induction into the U.S. Squash Hall of Fame in 2018 with Jean (left) and son Vivek and his wife, Jackie (right).

on Miami Beach, where I often work out, were amazed that a slight, low-muscle-content, older guy of Indian origin was inducted to a U.S. Hall of Fame! The owner actually Googled me to ascertain that I, an unlikely athlete, was a champion. Others—friends, my yoga mates, and my extended family—were delighted, too."

To enable him to really embrace the distinction, it helped him to remember his sense of sportsmanship and generosity as part of the elements that made him a worthy champion. "I had played since I was 10 or 11 years old," he said. "I loved to play so much that I played with everyone who wanted to play. I played with many C, D, or beginner players, set them up for shots, and got my exercise running for the ball. And, when I felt they were amenable to listen to my comments, I willingly helped them. I also made them feel motivated when I gave them the feeling of winning points or a game from me. I made some amazing, long-lasting friendships in return. This was one way to give back to the sport. And giving back was a continuous chord I had witnessed all through my life. I also saw 'giving back' as a duty due to my high socio-economic status in India. And by giving back in the ways I could and continue to do, and by being patient and respectful, I share the values I learned from squash, those of fairness, sportsmanship, camaraderie, and enjoyment. These are the qualities that make me feel like a true champion and a Hall of Fame inductee. I'd like to leave behind a memory of kindness and grace in competition as my permanent legacy."

Making the honor even more special was the fact that the induction ceremony was held on October 13, 2018, the day of his 72nd birthday at the U.S. nationals tournament at Drexel University in Philadelphia. Not only was the event a wonderful celebration of Anil's history in the sport, it provided us with the opportunity to see that new seeds for the future of squash were on the verge of being sown with the construction of the Arlen Specter Squash Center, a new 20-court complex aimed at making squash accessible to the vast middle of the population. Though situated in America, Anil believed the new center could also be the nucleus needed for recruitment and the development of the game and superlative play among international players from all walks of life.

The event also gave Anil an opportunity to reflect on his squash career and all the benefits the sport had brought him, including his very special relationship with Yusuf Khan, who passed away just two days before Anil's induction. It also allowed him to shine a light on the values he gained as a sportsman and express how they might be embraced by a future generation of squash players, which he summed up in the following excerpt of his acceptance speech:

When I first arrived in Cambridge in September 1965—it felt strange, very strange. I felt alone and anxious. The next day as a part of dorm crew, I teamed up with Tom Webber, a young blue-eyed blond boy from Spanish Harlem. Tom was a follower of Dr. King, I followed Mahatma Gandhi. We bonded and have been brothers ever since. Thank you, Tom, for our friendship of 53 years.

Soon after, I met my roommate Michel Scheinmann. He was warm and sensitive to foreign ways. He invited me to his family house in South Dartmouth. It felt like the informality and hospitality of my Indian home. I spent many Thanksgivings with him, his mother, Claire, and father, André. Thank you, Michel, for our brotherhood since 1965.

A few days later, I met Dinny Adams, the captain of the Harvard squash team. Our relationship grew and Dinny became my de facto guardian. Of the numerous examples of his support, one is especially appropriate. I was to play Sam Howe in the national finals in Rochester in 1969. That morning, as I stepped into the bathroom, I saw this simple message on the mirror written with shaving cream: "No tins." Dinny had figured out the match for me—the only thing between me and the championship was no tins, not more drop shots or nicks or pace, but no tins. The message stuck with me. I won. Thank you, Dinny, for being with me for 53 years.

Many of you may know of Stewart Brauns, but perhaps not this particularly endearing story about him. My parents made their first ever visit to the U.S. in 1968. Stewart, a very generous man, invited them and me and forty other guests to the Gaslight Club for dinner. The guests sat at their pre-assigned seats and each place had a flag of India and the U.S. twined together. My parents and I could not have felt more welcome. Thank you, Stewart, for your many kindnesses and friendship.

All of these are beautiful lifelong friendships where two cultures made bridges jointly to connect.

Later in 1969, it was 2-all and match point against me in the intercollegiate semi-finals at Yale. Spencer Burke, my opponent, hit a roll corner that looked like a sure winner. But only he could see it, and he called the ball out, enabling me to stay in the match. Thank you, Spencer, for allowing me to win my third intercollegiate championship. Your gold standard of fairness should be remembered long after names get blurry.

And thank you to the two coaches in my life. Yusuf Khan in Bombay taught me as a beginner. He taught me to stay calm, be patient, enjoy the process, and be fair. I was amongst the numerous national champions he had coached in India and the U.S. *Haardik shukriya*, my dear Pathan.

Jack Barnaby taught me the intricacies of hardball at Harvard. At one time he saw me practice reverse corners, a shot I had rarely seen in softball. He quickly came to me and told me, "You don't need the reverse corner, let your opponent hit it, and you run up there and counter with a Hashim Khan delicate feathery drop shot." Jack broke down the game to a level of simplicity that could be both understood and implemented. I was down 2-0 in national finals against Sam Howe again in 1970. During the break, Jack told me, "Hit the ball hard, put the pace on, don't give Sam time to play his deadly reverse corners." I followed his advice and I won in five games. That was Jack—he helped win championships. Thank you, Jack.

There is one omnipresent point in my thank you's: America embraced me and I embraced America. There is one central message, too: Global brotherhood is real. And for it to remain real and expand, I quote the Dalai Lama: "We need to make sure that global brotherhood and oneness are not abstract ideas that we profess, but personal commitments that we mindfully put in practice." Thank you, my dear friends, and God bless us all.

With these words, Anil made evident that he is not only grateful for the squash community's appreciation of what he brought to the sport, but also for what the sport gave to him. It's also clear that his mindset as sportsman is a reflection of his character, which serves as a refreshing counterpoint to the trends toward regressive nationalism, deadly hostilities, and partisanship now afflicting so many parts of the world. Anil also stands as living proof that a child born into a provincial context of hatred and division can become an international champion sportsman and ambassador for global brotherhood, even if on a modest scale in an under-appreciated context.

Considering the many adverse conditions that defined the context in which Anil emerged as a world-class player also goes to show that champions can come from the most unexpected of places. Amid the current era of global divisiveness, identity politics, and sports environments in which winning at all costs often trumps artistry, Anil's contrarian and sympathetic point of view, which in many ways shaped the game and the legacy of this surprising sportsman, begs a question: How many would-be champions of any sport might be simmering amid the masses of India or America or Africa or Brazil if given an eco-system that would support athletic excellence without killing creativity or marginalizing good sportsmanship?

For if one thing is clear in examining the squash career of Anil Nayar, the very finest qualities of a world-class sportsman have much less to do with winning or losing or fame or fortune and more to do with simply playing beautifully. And both India and America are fortunate to claim this unlikely sportsman as one of their own.

* * *

TIMELINE

1964—Wins both Junior and Men's National Champion titles in India

1965—First Indian to win the Drysdale Cup tournament in England, then considered the junior world championship event. Gets accepted into Harvard and rises to number one on freshman squash team after quickly learning the American hardball game.

1966—Wins second Men's National Champion title in India

1967—Wins first U.S. Intercollegiate National Champion title. Plays for Indian team in the first World Open Tournament in Australia.

1968—Wins second U.S. Intercollegiate National Champion title and first Canadian Men's National Champion title

1969—Plays as first Indian captain of the Harvard team, wins third U.S. Intercollegiate National Champion title and first U.S. Men's National Champion title. Receives Arjuna Award, India's highest honor for a sportsman, and Bingham Award, Harvard's honor for a graduating senior recognized as the year's best athlete in any sport.

1970—Wins second U.S. Men's National Champion title, second Canadian Men's National Champion title, as well as Men's National Champion title in Mexico and Bermuda

1971—Wins third Men's National Champion title in India

1972—Wins fourth Men's National Champion title in India

1973—Wins fifth Men's National Champion title in India

1974—Wins sixth Men's National Champion title in India

1975—Wins seventh Men's National Champion title in India

1976—Wins eighth Men's National Champion title in India

1979—Plays for Indian team in World Open in Australia

1982—Wins New York State Open Champion title

1987—Wins U.S. Masters National Champion title (40+ in hardball)

1988—Wins U.S. Masters National Champion title (40+ in hardball)

1989—Wins U.S. Masters National Champion title (40+ in hardball)

1990—Wins two U.S. National Masters Champion titles (40+ in hardball and 40+ in softball)

1992—Inducted into the Harvard Hall of Fame; wins U.S. National Masters Champion title (45+ softball)

1993—Wins U.S. National Masters Champion title (45+ softball)

1994—Wins U.S. National Masters Champion title (45+ softball)

1997—Wins U.S. National Masters Champion title (5.0 Skill Level)

1999—Wins U.S. National Masters Champion title (45+ softball)

2001—Cricket Club of India's courts are inaugurated in Anil Nayar's name

2010—Joins board of directors of Khelshala, an NGO founded by Satinder Bajwa to uplift the lives of underprivileged children in Chandigarh

2018—Inducted into U.S. Squash Hall of Fame

Acknowledgements

When we set off on the journey of writing a book together on Anil's brilliant squash career we had no road map, no timetable, and only a sketch of a plan. As such, we encountered lots of ups and downs, dead ends and detours—but also had a lot of fun—along the way until we reached our destination almost two years later. And we're grateful to each other for the love and effort each put in to making Anil's tale as authentic and upbeat as possible. We are also profoundly grateful for all the incredible support and camaraderie we enjoyed throughout the process and our sincere thanks go to the many people who went along for the ride and offered insight, direction, and ideas as we pressed forward.

We especially appreciate the help of Khalid Ansari, who was a constant, persistent rock of support from the moment he and Jean conceived the idea of putting Anil's story in print all the way to its conclusion. We're also indebted to Anil's sons, Sanjay and Vivek, for sharing their personal insights and early experiences with their father as well as several of the photographs that enrich this story. Our heartfelt thanks, too, go to the other members of Anil's extended family, including his sister, Asha Wollmann, and brother Vijay Nayar, who provided historical facts, dates, and photographs related to our family's experience, as well as his ex-wife, Linda, and his cousins Shobha Nayar and Ajay Nayar, who also provided information and photography on the Nayar family history.

As important as Anil's history in this tale are the legacies of other players—both in India and America—who played with or were influenced by Anil, and our thanks also go to every one of those who shared their thoughts and memories not only on Anil's game and character as a sportsman, but also on their own match play and the subtleties of the sport. Among them are Dinny Adams, the late Madhav Apte, Satinder Bajwa, Spencer Burke, Sunil Chainani, the late Soli Colah, Adrian Ezra, Ralph Howe, Sam Howe, Anil Kapur, Richard Millman, Geoff Mitchell, Ferez Nallaseth, Ananth Nayak, Chris Orriss, Palmer Page, Darius Pandole, Dinshaw Pandole, Naval Pandole, Tom Poor, Cyrus Poncha, Michel Scheinmann, Rick Sterne, and Larry Terrell.

Other seasoned aficionados of squash, culture, and/or the written word who helped us in the development of our story include Kishore Bhimani, who, despite various health issues, was willing and able to interview several Indian players, record their thoughts, and deliver some remarkable commentary on the politics, sports, and culture of India that add to some of the historical backdrops described in the book. We are incredibly grateful to him as well as his wife, Rita, for their assistance in contributing to our tale. We also profoundly appreciate the efforts of our friend Tom Webber, who wanted to make sure our written version of Anil's story would do him justice, volunteered to read drafts of the manuscript with an eagle eye, and offered valuable feedback. Sincere thanks are also due to our friend Sundaram Tagore for his encouragement, interest, and comments, which also made our memoir richer after reading an initial draft. And, of course, we thank our publisher, Sachin Bajaj.

We owe thanks, too, to James Zug, America's preeminent squash scribe and a seasoned authority on the sport, who also kindly read the manuscript and offered thoughts on fine tuning. His beautifully written book *Squash: A History of the Game* was also a trusted resource for information on some of the important players, dates, and turning points in the evolution of the sport referenced in our story. We very much appreciate, too, the thoughts of writers Rob

Dinerman, Doug Garr, Charles Salzberg, the late Raju Chainani, and Clayton Murzello, whose input and expertise also enriched the story.

Though we did our best to honestly and accurately record not only Anil's history, but also that of many of the people who participated in the sport throughout the course of his career, we hope that any readers who happen to come across a chronological or factual error or two—or who may differ with our interpretation of any events—will forgive us, as time often plays games with memories.—*Jean and Anil Nayar*

About the Author

Jean Nayar is a journalist and author who writes mostly about architecture, art, real estate, and travel. She contributes to various lifestyle magazines, including *Manhattan, Departures, Galerie, Milieu, Cottages & Gardens, Hamptons, Interior Design,* and *Ocean Drive* among others. A member of the Author's Guild and the American Society of Journalists and Authors, Nayar has also written more than a dozen books, including most recently *Living In Style Country* and *Living in Style New York*, both published by TeNeues. She divides her time with her husband, Anil Nayar, between their homes in New York and Miami Beach.

Credits

In addition to the friends, family, and colleagues we relied on for insight and images, we gratefully acknowledge numerous writers and photographers whose words and photographs appeared in various periodicals and books and also enrich the content of this book. These include Roy Blount Jr. and James Drake, whose words and photograph appeared in *Sports Illustrated* magazine and are reprinted with permission from Authentic Brands Group and Getty Images. Other references include John Hopkins's book *A Celebration of 100 Years of Squash at Pall Mall*; John Horry's observations in *British Lawn Tennis and Squash* magazine; Rob Dinerman's book *A History of Harvard Squash 1922-2010*; James Zug's book *Squash: A History of the Game*; Craig Lambert's story in *Harvard* magazine; Ike Shynook's articles in the *Democrat and Chronicle*; A.J Daly's pieces in *The Harvard Crimson*; Aziz Currimbhoy's article in *The Current*; Tim Wyant's story in *U.S. Jesters* magazine; and Raju Chainani's articles in *Simply Squash* magazine. Additional information from various articles in *The New York Times, The Times of India, The Sunday Standard, The Indian Express* news publications and *Squash* magazine and images and/or information from *The Gazette* in Montreal, the CCI's *From the Pavilion End* publication, *The Boston Globe*, director Gabe Polsky's film *In Search of Greatness*, author David Epstein's book *The Sports Gene*, Sir Ken Robinson's book *Genes, Brains, and Human Potential*, Harvard University and its Varsity Club publications, and the U.S. Squash, Professional Squash Association, World Squash Federation, and Jesters Club web sites also add to this story.

www.ingramcontent.com/pod-product-compliance
Lightning Source LLC
Chambersburg PA
CBHW020351080526
44584CB00014B/976